Fall

Fall

The Mysterious Life and Death
of Robert Maxwell, Britain's Most
Notorious Media Baron

John Preston

HARPER

An Imprint of HarperCollins*Publishers*

HarperCollins books may be purchased for educational, business, or sales promotional use. For information, please email the Special Markets Department at SPsales@harpercollins.com.

Originally published as *Fall: The Mystery of Robert Maxwell* in Great Britain in 2021 by Viking.

FIRST U.S. EDITION

Library of Congress Cataloging-in-Publication Data has been applied for.

ISBN 978-0-06-299749-4

21 22 23 24 25   LSC   10 9 8 7 6 5 4 3 2 1

To Cat Ledger
1958–2020

'Such a man rises above honesty,' said Mrs Hurtle.

Anthony Trollope, *The Way We Live Now*

He had come a long way to this blue lawn, and his dream must have seemed so close that he could hardly fail to grasp it. He did not know that it was already behind him, somewhere in that vast obscurity beyond the city, where the dark fields of the republic rolled on under the night.

F. Scott Fitzgerald, *The Great Gatsby*

Contents

Contents

List of Plates

Preface

The King of New York

Just as its owner had intended, the yacht that made its way slowly up Manhattan's East River and docked at the Water Club at East 30th Street in early March 1991 caused a considerable stir. For a start, it was far bigger than any of its neighbours – so big that it took up eight berths instead of the customary one. Four storeys high, gleaming white and topped with a mast bristling with satellite equipment, the yacht could clearly be seen from several blocks away.

The man's identity and the reason for his visit soon became the subject of much excited speculation. In several newspapers it even displaced reports of the end of the first Gulf War from the front pages. Who was this 'portly press baron with the bushy eyebrows, the square jaw and the sly smile,' people wondered.

What little was known about him piqued their curiosity even more. Born to a peasant family in Czechoslovakia, he had apparently fought for the British Army during the War and been awarded one of the country's highest medals for gallantry. Now he was understood to be the possessor of a vast mansion as well as a '40-button portable telephone'. He was also described as 'a symbol of an Age of Flash. Of big-time dreams and big-time deals.'

It seemed that his private life had been scarred by terrible tragedy and his business career by controversy. As for his personal fortune, this was estimated at between a billion and two billion dollars – a figure that was confidently predicted to increase by as much as $500,000 by the end of the year. Among the many publications he owned was the *Daily Mirror*, the biggest selling left-wing tabloid newspaper in the UK. This alone gave him enormous political influence. According to Bob Bagdikian, dean of the Berkeley

Graduate School of Journalism, 'Neither Caesar nor Franklin Roosevelt nor any Pope has commanded as much power to shape the information on which so many people depend.'

New Yorkers would have to wait several more days before they caught their first sight of the yacht's owner. But once seen, he was not easily forgotten. At nine in the morning on 13 March, a convoy of stretch limousines drew up beside a news-stand on 42nd Street. Out of the first limousine stepped an extremely large man dressed in a camel hair coat and a red bow-tie, with a green-and-white-striped cap perched on top of his head.

Showing unexpected nimbleness for someone of his size, he sprang up on to the sidewalk. A crowd of around 300 had gathered to witness his arrival, along with several TV crews. 'Good on you!' one of the onlookers shouted. Another one called for three cheers. As the hurrahs rang out, the man grinned in delight and took off his cap to reveal a head full of startlingly black hair. He twirled the cap in the air, before holding up his other hand for silence.

The cheers died away.

'This is a great day,' he announced in his booming treacly voice. 'A great day for me, but above all for New York. It's the first good thing that New Yorkers have seen happen in a long while. The city has lost confidence in itself. People are departing. I say enough! New York still has something to say. The fact that I have chosen New York is a vote of tremendous confidence in this city.'

Then, holding both arms above his head now, his fists clenched in triumph, he went even further.

'It is a miracle!' he said, 'A Miracle on 42nd Street!'

At this point he was approached by two policemen, who asked if he would mind moving on. The problem, they explained with uncharacteristic deference, was that so many people had come to see him they were spilling out into the road; as a result, lengthy tailbacks were stretching in both directions. Of course, said the man; the last thing he wanted was to cause any inconvenience. Rather than get back into his limousine, he strode away up 42nd Street, his camel hair coat trailing out behind. Far from dispersing, the crowd and the TV crews set off in pursuit, loath to let him out of their sight.

The man's name was Robert Maxwell, and this was the day that all his dreams had finally come true.

As he often liked to say later, Maxwell had come to New York in answer to a plea. A saviour was needed in the city's hour of need and Bob the Max, as he'd taken to styling himself, was not about to shirk his duty. This was not strictly true – indeed, it wasn't really true at all – but amid the excitement no one was in any mood to get too hung up on detail.

Eighteen months earlier, in the autumn of 1989, journalists on newspapers in Orlando, Newport, Rhode Island, and Fort Lauderdale were surprised to receive letters asking if they would like to come and work in New York for a while. Anyone who expressed interest was then sent – in strict confidence – a list of instructions on what not to do if they decided to take up the offer:

- Don't stop to talk to anyone who approaches you.
- Don't frequent restaurants in close proximity to the office.
- Don't make eye-contact with passers-by.

At the same time, Jim Hoge, publisher of the *New York Daily News*, launched the first salvo in what he strongly suspected would be a fight to the death. The *New York Daily News* was the oldest and most iconic tabloid newspaper in America. In its heyday, it had sold 2.4 million copies a day – more than a quarter of the city's population.

Brash, blue-collar and fiercely proud of the breadth and depth of its prejudices, the paper liked to style itself 'The Honest Voice of New York', a claim rather belied by the fact that it also ran a regular 'Gang Land' column – a kind of low-life social diary chronicling the ups and downs of the city's best known organized crime figures, such as Vincent 'Chin' Gigante and Anthony 'Gaspipe' Casso.

But the *News*'s heyday had long gone. For years, it had been hobbled by astounding levels of over-manning, widespread corruption, an exorbitant wage bill and machinery so antiquated that printers were reputed to have to blow black ink out of their nostrils for several hours after their shifts had ended. By 1989, it was losing $2,000,000 a month.

In a bid to break the unions' power, Hoge decided to take them on. He planned his campaign with meticulous precision. If they went on strike, as he was convinced they would, he intended to keep the *News* running with non-union labour – hence his appeal to out-of-town journalists to come to New York. In a former Sears warehouse in New Jersey, he even built a full-scale replica of the paper's newsroom so that people could be properly trained before-hand. The warehouse was surrounded by a chain-link fence topped with barbed wire and patrolled round the clock by security guards with German shepherd dogs.

The choice was stark, Hoge told the unions. Either they had to accept new machinery and a dramatically reduced workforce, or else the paper was doomed. To no one's surprise, negotiations swiftly broke down. On 20 October 1990, the *News* management dismissed most of its 2,400 unionized employees.

War had effectively been declared.

What followed was described as nothing less than a battle for the beating heart of New York. As well as using non-union journalists, Hoge also employed non-union delivery drivers. Their vans were regularly firebombed by enraged strikers and the drivers beaten up. Journalists who defied the strike were spat at as they passed through the picket line outside the newspaper's offices. Protest rallies were broken up by police in riot gear. Both the Mayor, David Dinkins, and the Archbishop of New York, Cardinal John O'Connor, appealed for calm.

No one took any notice.

Then came Hoge's most inflammatory move. Intimidated by the strikers, many of the city's news vendors had vanished from the streets. In place of the vanished vendors, Hoge recruited homeless people to sell the paper. Predictably enough, this sent the tempera-ture soaring still higher. 'Hoge is using the most desperate group of people in our city to do his dirty work for him,' said George

McDonald, leader of the biggest union, the Allied Printing Trades Council. 'The next thing you know he'll be using poor children to peddle his scab rag.'

Advertisers too had melted away. By 11 November 1990 the paper had shrunk to a third of its normal size and had just four full-page advertisements. By 12 December, less than two months into the strike, there had already been 888 'serious incidents', 144 arrests, 66 injuries, 11 people hospitalized and 147 trucks either destroyed or damaged.

Despite his efforts, Hoge had begun to suspect that this was a battle that no one could win. The paper's owners, the *Chicago Tribune*, indicated that they'd had enough, and wanted to put the *News* up for sale. Just about the only thing that Hoge and McDonald had in common was the hope that someone might appear out of the blue to buy the paper – someone with apparently bottomless pockets and a keen appetite for wielding influence and shaping opinions. As McDonald put it, 'Owning the *Daily News* is like a visiting card for sheikhs, kings and queens. It opens the door to people.'

By February 1991, the paper was down to just twenty pages and circulation had fallen to less than 300,000. Gloom was so deeply entrenched that scarcely anyone paid the least attention when Robert Maxwell announced that he was interested in buying a US paper valued in 'the mid-hundreds of millions of dollars'.

And then came another blow. The city's florists decided en masse not to use the paper to advertise their services in the week leading up to Valentine's Day – traditionally its most profitable week of the year. On 4 March Hoge issued a statement. 'The *New York Daily News* will cease publication on March 15th 1991 unless a binding agreement to sell the paper is reached by that date.'

Unbeknownst to all but a few, Maxwell had already sent a representative to New York to sniff the air and make discreet overtures to both Hoge and the unions. Ian Watson was a wiry Scot who edited one of Maxwell's papers, *The European*. He had his first taste of what might be involved when he took two union representatives out for dinner.

What no one had thought to tell Watson beforehand was that the paper's distribution had long been controlled by the Mafia. As well as taking a rake-off from sales, they also used its vans to deliver drugs to outlying areas. Over glasses of Chivas Regal, the three men had what Watson considered to be a perfectly amicable conversation about the necessity of accepting staff cuts.

'I said to them, "Look gentlemen, we're running out of time here. This paper will close in ten days' time unless we get a deal with you guys. We're the last hope you have."

'When I had finished, neither of them spoke for a while, and then one asked, "Have you ever been to New York before, Mr Watson?" '

Watson said that he had, but not very often.

'He said, "You've been extremely generous to us this evening, Mr Watson. Very generous indeed. And I want to return the favour. If you continue to put pressure like that on us, you and your fat boss will find yourself floating down the Hudson River with your fucking throats cut." '

They then stood up and left.

Two days later, undeterred by Watson's warnings, Maxwell made his carefully stage-managed entry into New York. The next morning Hoge had his first meeting with Maxwell in the headquarters of the publishers Macmillan on Fifth Avenue – Maxwell had bought the company at the end of 1988 for 2.6 billion dollars.

Whatever Hoge had been expecting, it was not this. "I remember at one point a butler came in with a silver tray with Maxwell's lunch on it. The butler put the tray down in front of him and went out. The next thing I know, I heard a loud crash. I looked up from whatever I was doing and Maxwell had picked up the tray and just dropped it on the floor. The butler came back in and said, "Yes sir?" And Maxwell said, "It's cold. Bring me something else." He then carried on working while the butler started picking everything off the floor. What struck me most was the fact that neither of them acted as if anything remotely unusual had happened.'

To help him in his negotiations, Maxwell summoned a number of people from London. Among them was Richard Stott, the Editor of the *Daily Mirror*. When their flight landed, they went straight to Maxwell's yacht, the *Lady Ghislaine* – named after his youngest daughter. There, Stott noticed something that made a big impression on him. Something that only lasted a fraction of a second, but which he found himself thinking about more and more in the months to come.

'As we arrived, Maxwell was showing a group of schoolchildren around. When he saw us a sense of relief and almost pleasure came across his face for an instant, and then the mask was back. I don't think it was because he was delighted to see us especially: it was because we were faces he knew. Just for a moment the loneliness of a man who delighted in meeting everyone and knowing no one showed through. It was the uncertainty and deep insecurity of the true outsider, a man who feels he has been precluded from the world of others and had therefore determined to build his own, with his own rules for his own game.'

The next morning, when negotiations began in earnest, Maxwell took over the top floor of Macmillan and gave each union leader his own office. For the next four days, he scarcely slept, moving constantly from one office to another, subjecting the occupants to a barrage of threats, promises and flattery. The *New York Times* noted nervously that Maxwell had brought 'a dash of British pomp and even a touch of Broadway showmanship' to negotiations. The union leaders seemed just as bemused as Hoge. 'He's certainly got charisma,' said one as he reeled out for a brief respite. 'He's like an English nobleman.'

While no one could doubt how far Maxwell had climbed, there was a good deal of mystery about how he had got there. How had someone from his background developed such a lordly manner and plummy voice? Perhaps inevitably, not all the descriptions were complimentary. Some said he was a terrible bully with the hide of a rhinoceros. There were even rumours that his empire might not be in such blooming good health as he liked to make out, but these too were swept aside in the furore.

At 4.22 p.m. on 14 March, with less than twenty-four hours to go before Hoge's deadline expired, Maxwell emerged from the Macmillan entrance to Macmillan in his shirtsleeves.

'We have a deal!' he announced.

The news galvanized the city. Outside the paper's offices on 42nd Street, people on the picket lines broke into spontaneous dancing. Cardinal O'Connor offered prayers of thanks, while the Republican Senator for New York, Alfonse D'Amato, chimed in with a biblical analogy of his own. Nothing quite like it had been seen since Lazarus had been raised from the dead, he claimed.

On the face of it, Maxwell had pulled off an amazing coup. But not everyone was convinced. Charlie Wilson, Editorial Director at Mirror Group Newspapers, who had conducted negotiations alongside Maxwell, felt the unions had been given far too many concessions. 'The nearer we came to the deadline, the more he gave them. That took me aback; it was as if his judgement had become clouded or something. I couldn't work out what was going on.'

Wilson wasn't the only one having doubts. Amid his relief that the 139-day strike was finally over, Jim Hoge couldn't suppress a feeling of disquiet, a feeling so strong it was almost a premonition of disaster. 'I could see that Maxwell was prepared to do anything to get it. The unions could see it too, and they'd run rings around him. He would say all this stuff about how he was going to get the circulation to over a million in less than a year, but there was no way he could ever make it work. Basically, he'd bought a death knell.'

Later it would emerge that the *Chicago Tribune* had been so desperate to get rid of the *New York Daily News* that they'd paid Maxwell $60,000,000 just to take it off their hands. Nothing, though, could dent his delight. This was the moment Maxwell had always longed for. The moment when he had become a true international media baron – a 'Lord of the Global Village'.

To seal his triumph there was one last thing he wanted Hoge to do. 'As soon as the ink was dry on the contract, he said, "I want you to call Rupert Murdoch and tell him that I've bought the *New York Daily News*." When I asked why, he said, "I just need you to tell me what his reaction is."

'I said, "Bob, I don't think that's very appropriate. Besides, why should the call come from me? Surely, it should come from you?"'

But Maxwell was insistent. '"Oh no," he said. "You've got to do it."' As it happened, Hoge had a number for Murdoch and managed to get him on the phone. 'I think he was in Australia so it may well have been the middle of the night. When he answered, I explained to him, "Mr Murdoch, Bob Maxwell would like you to know that he's just bought the *New York Daily News*."

'I remember there was a long silence and then Murdoch started laughing. He carried on laughing for quite a long time and when he'd finished, he said, "That is so courteous of Bob. Will you thank him from me."'

Then he hung up.

The first thing next morning Maxwell arrived at the *Daily News* offices to take possession of his new paper. Hoge and the paper's Editor, Jim Willse, were outside to greet him, standing beneath a huge Art Deco mural depicting a symbolic cross-section of New Yorkers under a lightning-forked sky. This time an even larger crowd had gathered.

'I love New York,' Maxwell told them. 'I *am* a New Yorker! Bob the Max will do his duty!'

Several members of staff were also there, some of them so relieved the strike was over that they were in tears. 'We're gonna build it up for you, Mr Maxwell,' one of them shouted. 'We're betting on you.' Although it was a cold morning and the sun hadn't yet risen above the skyscrapers, Maxwell was already sweating heavily. Off came the cap again, held aloft for longer this time, as if releasing pressure from a valve.

Photographers jostled to take his photograph. The motor-drives whirred as Maxwell continued to grin from ear to ear. But, for all his outward bonhomie, there was something not altogether convincing about it. 'I am a jungle man,' he often liked to say of himself, and the sense of a big beast on the prowl was never far from the surface.

'Will there be a change of Editor?' one of the journalists asked.

Putting his arm around Willse's shoulders, Maxwell declared, 'This man is my Editor for life!' Then, leaning in closer so that the microphones couldn't pick up what he was saying, he whispered, 'Just remind me of your name again.'

'What will happen to anyone who tries to cross you?' another of the journalists wanted to know.

Maxwell narrowed his eyes, causing his eyebrows – as black as his hair – to inch together. 'You'll get about as much pleasure out of chewing frozen concrete as you will fighting Captain Bob,' he told him.

A woman in the crowd called out that she had brought her baby specially to see him, even though she lived in Crown Heights, more than an hour's journey away on the subway. Greatly moved, Maxwell bent forward and kissed the baby's forehead. Then, doffing his cap one last time, he disappeared through the revolving doors.

The *New York Daily News* lobby is one of the wonders of 1930s design, reputed to be the inspiration for the *Daily Planet* offices in the original *Superman* comics. In the centre of the lobby stands what was once the world's largest indoor globe. Above it is a black-glass domed ceiling representing the infinity of space. Inset in the grey marble floor are brass lines giving the distances to the world's most important capitals: Jerusalem – 5696 miles, Paris – 3634, Mexico City – 2110.

No distances are given to anywhere in the Soviet Union, presumably because few if any Americans in the 1930s would have dreamed of going there. The whole effect is intended to give the impression of standing at the very centre of the Western world – at the same time as emphasizing just how insignificant humans are in the grand scheme of things. Beside the globe is a notice which reads, 'If the sun were the size of this globe and placed here then comparatively the Earth would be the size of a walnut and located at the main entrance to Grand Central Terminal.'

Walking past the front desk, Maxwell asked one of the security guards, a Miss Mackenzie, why she was smiling.

'I'm just happy, sir,' she told him. 'It's a happy day.'

It would not remain a happy day for Miss Mackenzie for long. Before he stepped into the elevator, Maxwell held up a copy of the *New York Daily News*'s front page for the photographers. As soon as they'd finished taking pictures, he dropped the paper on the floor.

Upstairs, Maxwell was shown into his new office. In preparation for his arrival, the bookshelves had been stacked with copies of his official biography, a richly sugared account of Maxwell's life written by his loyal amanuensis, Joe Haines.

His first act was to call in the paper's head of security, a man called Grover Howell.

'You are in charge of security?' he asked.

'Yes, sir,' Howell confirmed.

'Right,' Maxwell told him. 'I'm sacking the paper's entire security staff.'

Howell swallowed.

'Including me?'

'Oh yes,' said Maxwell. 'Including you.'

Just in case the penny hadn't dropped, he added, 'In fact, you are the first person I'm laying off.'

After a stunned Howell had been led away, Maxwell went to address the paper's advertising department. Before he spoke, he looked around the room. 'Why do we have only one coloured person in this department?' he demanded.

Several people stood up.

'Ah, it appears I am colour-blind,' said Maxwell. 'Are minorities well represented here? I will be looking at that.'

Before he went back into his office, one of the *News*'s executives told him quietly, 'That was great, Mr Maxwell. Absolutely great. But I thought you should know we call them black here. We don't really call them coloured.'

Maxwell tipped his head.

'Thank you for putting me right.'

In order to announce his purchase of the *New York Daily News* to a wider audience, he had decided to make a television commercial – to be aired the following evening. He was particularly keen this should be accompanied by suitably rousing music. As far as Maxwell was concerned, there was only one real candidate, the city's unofficial theme song: Kander and Ebb's 'New York, New York'.

Sadly, the rights were not available, one of the ad men informed him. Would he consider using something else, possibly Billy Joel's 'New York State of Mind'?

Maxwell looked at the man as if he was mad.

'Not is not a word that I accept,' he told him.

Picking up the phone, he asked to be put through to the head of Time Warner. 'You are speaking to Robert Maxwell. Have you ever heard of me? No? Well, does the *New York Daily News* ring a bell? I'm the new owner and I need to use "New York, New York" in our television commercials. What are your rules for licensing in an emergency? I don't have time to be pushed from pillar to post here. I want to pay a decent price; I'm not a schnorrer, but I'm not to be ripped off either . . . You can do that? Good, thank you. You've made my day.'

After banging the phone down, Maxwell did something that caused even more confusion. With no warning, he fell fast asleep. A good deal of whispered discussion followed about whether he should be woken or not. Before a decision could be taken Maxwell opened his eyes.

'The Prime Minister wants to speak with you,' another of his associates told him.

Maxwell looked around.

'Which one?' he asked.

That afternoon another incident occurred that made a big impression on Jim Hoge – and which he too would find himself reflecting on in the light of subsequent events. 'At one point my secretary ran into my office, white as a sheet. Apparently Mr Maxwell was very upset and wanted to see me straight away. When Maxwell came in, he said, "Look, you've got to help me out." He was pacing around and I could see he was embarrassed about something. Eventually, he said, 'Would you mind if I stood here with the door open and shouted at you for a while?"

'I told him to go ahead. Immediately, Maxwell started lacing into me, banging on my desk with his fist and saying how it was outrageous that I had an office that was larger than his. After about forty seconds of this, he said, "Thank you" in a much quieter voice and went out.'

Later, Hoge learned that this had all been staged for the benefit of Maxwell's youngest child, his 29-year-old daughter, Ghislaine, who had accompanied her father to New York and would shortly be appointed as his 'Emissary'. As soon as she saw her father's office, Ghislaine had complained that it wasn't big enough.

However absurd the incident may have been, it left Hoge turning over a question in his mind: how much of Maxwell's behaviour was for show and how much was real – and was Maxwell himself able to tell the difference?

Before he left for the day, Maxwell dictated an editorial that would appear in the next morning's paper. 'This evening in a dramatic blaze of glory . . .' he began.

He broke off saying it didn't strike quite the right note; possibly it might even be considered too self-serving. But anyone who feared that Maxwell's gift for hyperbole might have deserted him at this crucial hour need not have worried. After a few moments he began again:

'Today the *Daily News* is back on the streets where it belongs. It is as good as it was before and I promise you it will get better. You may ask why this Brit should want to save New York's hometown paper. My answer is simple: the *Daily News* is the greatest paper of the greatest city in the world. I want to put it back up there and then keep it there.'

The editorial, signed simply 'Maxwell', would appear beneath a headline, 'Roll 'Em', printed in a typeface so large it was only ever normally used to report moon landings and the deaths of presidents. As he walked back through the lobby, Maxwell passed Miss Mackenzie – now looking a lot glummer than she had done before.

That evening, Bob Pirie, Maxwell's investment banker and

President of Rothschild's Bank in New York, took him out to dinner at Fu's Chinese restaurant on 3rd Avenue, reputedly the best Chinese restaurant in town. It would be an evening Pirie would never forget. 'As we went up First Avenue, people would recognize him and open their car doors and come out and shake his hand,' Pirie recalled.

When they reached Fu's, something extraordinary happened. As soon as he saw Maxwell, the former Mayor of New York, John Lindsay, stood up and started applauding – whereupon the entire restaurant followed suit, the diners clapping away as he was led to his table. 'Maxwell was overwhelmed. I remember him saying, "In my entire life in London, no one's ever acted like this." '

All this flattery had clearly sharpened his appetite. Diners sitting nearby watched agog as course after course was brought to the table, each one dispatched with evident relish. Leaving the restaurant that evening, Maxwell was asked by a reporter waiting outside if he had any celebrations planned.

'I never celebrate,' he told her sternly.

Two days later a party was held on board the *Lady Ghislaine* to mark Maxwell's purchase of the *News*. Various grandees attended, including the Mayor, David Dinkins, and the former Senator for Texas, John Tower, whose hopes of becoming US Secretary for Defense had recently been derailed after accusations of womanizing – it was said that no woman under the age of ninety was safe with him in a lift.

When they arrived, each guest was asked to remove his or her shoes before being shown into the yacht's stateroom. There, they 'feasted on cold salmon, roast beef and Dom Pérignon champagne'. As the *Daily News*'s diarist noted, 'It was a very strange sight to see some of New York's most high and mighty standing around in their socks, or in blue bootees that had been specially provided to protect the cream deep-pile carpet.'

Among the invitees was the man Maxwell had just supplanted as the most talked-about businessman in New York: Donald Trump.

Like Maxwell, Trump had been obsessed with buying the *Daily News*. Three years earlier, he'd repeatedly phoned Jim Hoge to ask if it was for sale.

'Donald would never take no for an answer. He never asked whether the paper was making money, or anything like that: he just wanted it. I think about the fifth time he called, I said, Donald, let me put it to you in plain English: it's not for sale. At the time I had no idea why the hell he wanted to buy this struggling tabloid; it was only later that I realized he was looking for a base for his entry into politics.' But since then Trump's fortunes had tumbled and he no longer had enough money to buy – let alone run – a newspaper.

A year earlier, Trump had come to another party on board the *Lady Ghislaine*. Removing his shoes with obvious reluctance, he had handed them to Maxwell's valet, Simon Grigg, before donning his blue bootees. Trump then stood gazing at the yacht's décor – described by one visitor as '1970s Playboy Baroque'. As he did so, Grigg noticed a peculiar expression come over his face: 'It was almost like he was in awe, but didn't want to show it.'

This time, Trump chose not to share in Maxwell's triumph.

Jim Hoge spent much of the evening chatting to Liz Smith, doyenne of New York's gossip columnists. Known as 'The Grand Dame of Dish', and rumoured to be the highest-paid print journalist in America, Smith had left the *Daily News* at the start of the strike to join *Newsweek* magazine. The moment Maxwell saw the two of them talking, he padded over in his monogrammed slippers, hoping to persuade Smith to return to the paper. For some reason he had decided that the best way to woo someone whose career had been spent chronicling the marital squabbles of the rich and famous was by presenting himself as a devoted family man.

'He kept showing me all these pictures of his children and told me that he had been happily married to the same woman for forty-six years,' Smith recalled.

Hoge had also been on the receiving end of some syrupy homilies about the joys of family life. 'Maxwell was always telling us what a wonderful marriage he had – and by implication what lousy marriages we all had.'

As they drank their Dom Pérignon and ate their canapés, Hoge and Smith both had the same feeling – a sense that they were witnessing the end of an era. That the boom times were almost over and life would never be quite the same again.

'I remember Liz looking round and saying wryly, "Well, this may be the last hurrah, but it's certainly a blast." '

At the end of the party, after being reunited with their shoes, each guest was presented with a copy of Maxwell's biography. On the first page was a quote from Shakespeare's *Julius Caesar*: 'Ambition's debt is paid.' It's a quote generally taken to mean that an unquenchable thirst for power comes at a terrible price.

Less than eight months later, Maxwell's business empire would have imploded. His reputation would be for ever blackened, his name a byword for corruption and deceit. As for Maxwell himself, he would be dead in circumstances that were even more mysterious than anything in his life.

The Salt Mine

In the early 1920s, the Czechoslovak government, hoping to lure visitors to a remote province in the east of the country called Ruthenia, published a slim pamphlet listing the area's attractions. There wasn't a lot to see, the pamphlet admitted: 'The very best thing here is fresh air.' If you were very lucky, you might spot a wolf, or a wild boar, in the forest.

As for the people, there wasn't much to recommend them either. According to the pamphlet, they were not only unusually thick, but apt to be surly with it: 'The rather unintelligent Ruthenians, whose expression is almost blank-stare, sit in the market-place, side by side, gazing at the distance, seldom speaking a word or moving a muscle.' A far better bet was Ruthenia's large population of Jews, who were generally better-looking, more sophisticated and less grumpy.

In later life, Robert Maxwell seldom talked about his childhood, and what snippets of information he did provide tended to come richly coated in myth. Among the few things not in doubt are his date and place of birth: he was born on 10 June 1923 in a small town in Ruthenia called Solotvino, to a Jewish couple, Mehel and Chanca Hoch, and given – so he believed – the name Jan.

Just as Maxwell would go on to change his name four times by the age of twenty-three, so Solotvino too seemed unsure of its own identity. Originally on the southern edge of the Austro-Hungarian empire, the town became part of Czechoslovakia following the First World War. In the 1930s, it was reclaimed by Hungary before being absorbed into the Soviet Union at the end of the Second World War.

It wasn't so much that anyone particularly coveted Solotvino, simply that it stood on the border between two warring superpowers, right at the geographical centre of Europe. Then, as now, it was a bleak, isolated place, surrounded by thick pine forests and fields of sugar beet. In the winter, it was bitterly cold, in the summer swelteringly hot. The one thing that Solotvino did have was a salt mine. Unlike the rest of the town, this was a remarkable sight. An American visitor in 1938 wrote of standing on a little wooden catwalk watching the miners at work: 'Below us yawned a gulf so profound that workers loading salt blocks looked as small as mice . . . Crystalline walls reflected twinkling lights. Around us, like the roar of a far-off waterfall, rumbled the echoes of pneumatic chisels, cutting this titanic temple vaster still.'

The salt mine was by far the largest employer in the area. But, when Solotvino was part of the Austro-Hungarian empire, Jews were forbidden to work there. Although this rule was relaxed later, only six Jews ever found jobs in the mine. Even by Solotvino standards, the Hochs were desperately poor. Maxwell's father earned a living, of sorts, buying animal skins from local butchers and selling them on to leather merchants, travelling from town to town with a mule laden with pelts.

At six foot five, he was known as 'Mehel the Tall'. Unlike most of Solotvino's inhabitants, who seem to have been involved in smuggling of one kind or another, Mehel was considered to be doggedly law-abiding. The family lived in a two-room wooden shack with earth floors. In one room, there were a couple of beds, where the family slept. Once a year, as soon as the harvest was gathered in, all the mattress stuffing would be taken outside and burned. Then the mattresses would be restuffed with fresh straw.

The Hochs would eventually have nine children and, as the family grew, newborn babies and toddlers slept in cots suspended on ropes from the ceiling. At night, they must have looked like a flotilla of little boats sailing through the darkness. In the other room, the family cooked, ate and washed – water had to be drawn from a pump down the street. Around the back of the shack was a pit latrine, which would be emptied every few months by passing gypsies and the contents spread on the municipal flowerbeds.

When he was eight days old, Maxwell was circumcised. To cele-brate the event, his father decided the family should have a fish supper. Lacking a fishing rod, Mehel tossed a homemade Molotov cocktail into the river. Possibly he overdid the explosive; so many fish were killed in the ensuing blast that half of Solotvino reputedly gorged themselves as a result.

Maxwell was the Hochs' third child, and first-born son. Their oldest daughter had died in infancy, and their oldest surviving son aged two, of diphtheria. From the moment Maxwell was born, his mother doted on him. She fed him titbits from her plate at mealtimes and, when he was six, sold her only pillow to pay for a sleigh to take him to the near-est hospital after he'd been kicked in the head by a horse. As he grew older, she passed on her interest in politics to him – she was an enthu-siastic member of the Czechoslovakian Social Democratic Party.

Sometimes Maxwell would claim that he'd never really had a child-hood: 'I was never young. I never had that privilege.' But there were three things above all he recalled about life in Solotvino: 'I remember how cold I was, how hungry I was and how much I loved my mother.'

For her part, Chanca Hoch was convinced that her son had been blessed with extraordinary gifts and was destined to make an impact on the world: 'My boy will be famous one day,' she repeat-edly told a neighbour. 'I just feel it and know it.' This was such a ludicrous idea that it made even the normally dead-eyed Rutheni-ans fall about laughing.

If Maxwell adored his mother, he was terrified of his father. Mehel Hoch beat his son on a regular basis – often so hard that he broke his skin. On one occasion the young Maxwell threw up in the street. Grabbing him by the hair, his father rubbed his face in his vomit while passers-by looked on. The fear that his father engendered would never leave him, and nor would the shame he felt at being so frightened.

During the summer, the Hoch children ran around barefoot. In winter, two children would share one pair of shoes. Once a year a goose would be ceremonially slaughtered, but most of the time the family existed on a diet of maize, potatoes and watered-down milk. At home, the Hochs talked Yiddish, but, like most of the Jews in

Solotvino, they also spoke another three languages – Hungarian, Czech and Romanian.

The teenage Maxwell was remembered later as being able 'to take care of himself' – and, by implication, anyone foolish enough to cross him – and 'mischievous'. On the football pitch, he was described simply as 'aggressive'. Already, it seems, Maxwell was learning to throw his weight around. As he would tell a family friend years later, 'When in doubt, be brash like myself.'

Naturally left-handed, he was forced to write with his right hand at school as left-handedness was considered to be a sure sign of moral degeneracy. If Maxwell's writing was – and would always remain – a barely legible scrawl, he was a keen reader with a remarkably retentive memory.

At eleven, his mother sent him to a yeshiva – a Jewish Orthodox free school – where he studied rabbinical literature for a year before moving on to a larger yeshiva in Bratislava. But he seems to have lost his appetite for rabbinical literature pretty quickly and gravitated instead to selling trinkets – mainly bead necklaces.

On 15 March 1939 the Nazis invaded Czechoslovakia. The next day Hungary formally annexed Ruthenia. In Bratislava, the fifteen-year-old Maxwell cut off his long sidelocks – payot – to make himself look less Jewish, then caught the train back to Solotvino. His sister Sylvia, six years his junior, recalled meeting him off the train: 'We could barely recognize you. Instead of the shy yeshivabucher [Talmudic scholar] we expected, we saw in front of us a flashy young chap, the pre-war central European equivalent of a teddy boy.'

In Solotvino, the newly flash Maxwell found life suffocatingly dull. Just after his sixteenth birthday in June 1939 he decided to go to Budapest. The only time Maxwell ever talked about leaving his home town was in an interview he gave to *Playboy* magazine that appeared a month before his death: 'The Hungarians were taking over that part of Czechoslovakia and I said to my parents, "I'm leaving because I want to go and fight." They didn't want me to go, but I went anyway.'

He would never see his mother, his father, his grandfather, three of his sisters or his younger brother again.

According to Maxwell's account, he walked the 275 miles to Budapest, sleeping in haystacks and foraging food from hedgerows. Once there, he joined the Hungarian underground helping Czech exiles to escape to the West. In September, Hitler invaded Poland and war was declared.

Three months later, Maxwell was arrested at the Hungarian border and accused of spying – he'd been betrayed by the guide who was meant to be helping the Czechs escape. Brought back to Budapest, he spent the next four months manacled hand and foot in a windowless cell, being interrogated and beaten by the guards with rubber truncheons and bicycle chains. One blow across the face broke his nose.

Still Maxwell refused to talk. A few days later he was told that he'd been sentenced to death. At this point the French embassy took an interest – in the absence of a Czech embassy, the French had assumed responsibility for Czech citizens in Budapest. They protested that as Maxwell was still under eighteen he couldn't be executed without being found guilty of something. Unwilling to provoke a diplomatic incident, the Hungarians hurriedly arranged a trial.

In January 1940, he was loaded into the back of a van and driven off to the courthouse. Nearly fifty years later, Maxwell was a guest on the long-running BBC radio show *Desert Island Discs*. The presenter, Michael Parkinson, introduced him by saying, 'If our castaway needed the money, which he doesn't, he could sell his life story to Hollywood . . . It supports the theory that often truth is more exotic than fiction.'

Parkinson went on to ask Maxwell about being taken off to be tried back in 1940. 'Because I was a youngster, I was only sent to the court with one guard instead of two,' Maxwell told him. 'He had lost an arm in the First World War. I escaped relatively easily and made my way into Yugoslavia.'

He went into more detail when talking to his official biographer, Joe Haines. In this version, Maxwell brought down his manacles on the guard's head, knocking him unconscious, or possibly even killing him. Jumping out of the moving van, he hid under a bridge, where his handcuffs were removed by a 'gypsy lady'.

Free at last, Maxwell hitched a train ride to Belgrade and met up with another group of young Czechs determined to join the War. From Belgrade, they went overland to Beirut, where they were put up in a Foreign Legion camp before boarding a ship for Marseilles.

Intriguing though this story is, it does beg a number of questions. However stretched the Hungarian prison service may have been at the time, it seems odd that they couldn't rustle up a single two-armed guard to take him to court. In earlier versions of the story, Maxwell didn't say anything about hitting the guard with his manacles – he claimed to have used a stick.

Nor did he say anything about a mysterious gypsy lady. Why hadn't he thought her worth mentioning before? Had she simply slipped his mind? Then there's the question of what was she doing under the bridge in the first place? Did she live there, or just conveniently happen to be passing with a lock-pick? Or could there be another explanation? Had she crept onstage at a later date from some colourful corner of Maxwell's imagination?

Doubts have also been raised about other parts of his story. Two hundred and seventy-five miles is an awfully long way to walk, even for an energetic teenager. His cousin, Alex Pearl, insisted the two of them had gone together by train – with the tickets bought by their respective parents. Pearl remembered how excited they had both been by Budapest: 'We had never seen paved roads, street cars, big houses or anything like it.' The two of them had spent several days together before Maxwell, without warning or explanation, abruptly disappeared.

What does this prove? Only that Maxwell, for all his youthful heroism, had no qualms about embellishing the truth in order to paint himself in a more dashing light. There also seems something apt about such a keen self-mythologizer disappearing into the fog of war. Embracing the opportunities it offered for re-invention. By the time he emerged eighteen months later, he would have changed his religion, his age, his nationality and his name.

2.

Out of the Darkness

Before Robert Maxwell became Robert Maxwell, he was 'Lance-Corporal Leslie Smith'. Before he was Lance-Corporal Leslie Smith, he was 'Private Leslie Jones', and before that he was 'Ivan du Maurier'. He would also – for a brief period – be known as 'Captain Stone'. Then, far in the distance, as if seen through the wrong end of a telescope, comes Jan Hoch.

There were good reasons for Maxwell to hide behind so many aliases: the German High Command had declared that any Czechs captured while fighting for the Allies would be shot. As for any captured Czechs who were found to be Jewish, they would be handed over to the Gestapo. Even so, the frequency with which Maxwell chopped and changed his name suggests that he rather liked slipping from one identity to another.

In April 1940, Hoch arrived in Marseilles. Along with several other Czech exiles who had been on the same train, he went straight to the recruiting office and joined the French Foreign Legion. This involved having to lie about his age, claiming to be seventeen when he was still two months short of his birthday. In June, all the Czech forces in France – there were around 10,000 of them – were formed into the 1st Czech Division and incorporated into the French army.

But by now the French were crumbling under the German advance, and after a few weeks the 1st Czechoslovak Division was told to retreat to the port of Sète on the southern French coast. Winston Churchill had promised the leader of the Czech Government in exile that any of his countrymen who wanted to carry on fighting for the Allies would be evacuated.

Arriving in Sète, the remnants of the 1st Czech Division (only 4000 of them made it) saw four Royal Naval destroyers waiting off-shore. Anchored alongside them were three Egyptian transport ships. Two weeks later, in late July 1940, dressed in French army uniform, carrying a rifle in his hand and unable to speak a word of English, the yet-to-be Robert Maxwell stepped off the *Mohamed Ali el-Kebir* on to the dock at Liverpool.

Maxwell always claimed to have learned English in six weeks, from a woman who owned a tobacconist's shop in Sutton Coldfield. But this doesn't explain how he came to talk with such an extraordinar-ily plummy accent. It was only when he was uttering one of his characteristic Maxwellisms – somewhere between a proverb and a malapropism – that the mask would slip and it would become clear that English wasn't his first language.

'You can't change toads in midstream,' he would say gravely. Or, even more bafflingly, 'They have locked the stable horse after the door has bolted.'

By the time he arrived in Liverpool, Maxwell had already lis-tened to several of Winston Churchill's speeches on the radio. It was this, he maintained later, that first inspired him to become British – despite his not being able to understand a word of English: 'I could tell from the tone of his voice what he was saying.' As far as his own accent was concerned, Maxwell seems to have taken Church-ill's rumbling cadences, then added an extra helping of treacle.

Certainly he had no compunction about yoking himself and Churchill together – 'Like Winston, I wanted to fight on.' But the chances of this happening looked extremely remote. To begin with, Maxwell and his fellow Czech exiles were housed in some hur-riedly erected tents near Chester. He was then shunted around from one internment camp to another before ending up in Sutton Coldfield.

There, on 9 October 1940, fresh from his crash course in English at the tobacconist's, the seventeen-year-old Jan Hoch joined the Auxiliary Military Pioneer Corps. Far from being a crack fighting unit, the Pioneer Corps was a kind of officially sanctioned sump for misfits – full of people the army considered too incompetent, unstable or suspicious to fit in anywhere else. It was also the only unit of the British army open to foreigners. In 1940, there were more than 1000 Germans in the Pioneer Corps, many of them doctors who were reluctantly permitted to work as medical orderlies.

Sent off to south Wales to break rocks in a quarry, Maxwell spent what little free time he had reading books – on average, he would get through one Penguin or Pelican paperback a day. For the next three years, he broke rocks, washed dishes, peeled potatoes and wondered if he would ever get the chance to fight. A nurse, Benita de Roemer, who met Maxwell at the time, recalled him as being 'mercurial, mostly exuberant, but sometimes deeply melancholy'. Hoping to make himself appear more English, Maxwell changed his name to Ivan du Maurier – he smoked du Maurier cigarettes. But this simply led everyone to assume he was French, and give him an even wider berth than before.

Then, just when Maxwell's morale was at its lowest ebb, he got a lucky break. After an operation for appendicitis, he was sent to convalesce in Bedford. There he met a widow called Sylvia and they began an affair. 'Although she was much older than me, I was very much in love with her,' Maxwell recalled. Through Sylvia, he met a Brigadier Gary Carthew-Yorstoun, who arranged for him to be transferred from the Pioneer Corps to the 6th North Staffs.

In April 1944, Maxwell was promoted to corporal. A month later, he was promoted again – to sergeant – and put in charge of the battalion's sniper unit. Three weeks after D-Day, the North Staffs set sail for France.

Maxwell's first experience of battle was the battalion's assault on the village of La Bijude in Normandy. Despite being, by his own admission, 'scared all the time', he was recommended for yet another promotion – this time to an officer.

At the town of Villers-Bocage, Maxwell caused considerable alarm by turning up for reconnaissance duty dressed as a German major. By passing himself off as German, he explained, he would be able to get much closer to their lines. In case he was captured, he was given a new identity book in the name of 'Lance-Corporal Leslie Smith'.

During the fighting at the Orne river crossing, Maxwell's bravery made such an impression that a Canadian radio broadcaster mentioned him by name over the air. Although he was referred to as 'Leslie du Maurier', which was neither his real name nor the one he'd adopted six months earlier, his commanding officer insisted on giving him yet another identity.

By now even Maxwell must have been getting confused about his real identity, so it seems unlikely that if he was captured, the Germans would have either the patience or the ingenuity to work it out if he was captured. None the less, he was duly issued with a third identity book – this one in the name of 'Private Jones'.

It wasn't just Maxwell's name that kept changing – so did his appearance. In October 1944, worried about a possible communist uprising behind their lines, the Allied military authorities sent him to Paris. By now fluent in French –as well as German, English, Hungarian, Czech, Romanian and his native Yiddish – Maxwell's brief was to find out what was happening. In his wallet was a pass which read, 'The bearer of this pass, No 13051410, S/Sgt du Maurier LI is a British soldier and is authorized to be in Paris and to wear any uniform or civilian clothes.'

Although it's not clear what, if anything, he discovered there, the pass gave Maxwell a free rein to indulge his fondness for disguises. One day he would pretend to be a British officer, the next a French factory worker. It also confirmed what the British military authorities must already have suspected: Maxwell had a natural flair for subterfuge.

At the end of 1944, he learned that his commission had finally come through and he was now a second-lieutenant in the Queen's Royal Regiment. By way of celebration, he decided that yet another name change was in order. He appears to have picked 'Robert Maxwell' because it sounded distinguished and vaguely Scottish. Along with his old identity, he also shed his religion; for the next forty years he would never willingly admit to being Jewish.

While Maxwell was delighted with his new name, not everyone felt the same way. Fed up with all the paperwork involved, his bank manager told him that if he ever changed it again, he was closing his account immediately.

Late in the afternoon of 17 January 1945, 1/5th Battalion of the Queen's Royal Regiment crossed a frozen canal, the Vloed Beek, in south-eastern Holland. Conditions, as the official regimental history noted, 'were extremely bad'. For the last few days snow had fallen. In places it had melted and then frozen again, forming great sheets of ice that were as flat and grey as the sky above. To protect themselves from the cold – the night before, the temperature had fallen to minus 20 Fahrenheit – some of the soldiers stitched rabbit skins on to their battledress.

Having crossed the canal, the battalion headed to a nearby concrete works, where they spent a sleepless night huddled around campfires. The first thing next morning, they attacked the small town of Susteren. Within a few hours, the town had been taken, but at a heavy cost – thirty-nine Allied soldiers had been killed and twenty-nine were still missing.

The battalion then moved on towards the village of Paarlo on the banks of the River Roer. All around, the terrain was flat and featureless, broken only by dykes and belts of bare trees. By now, another thaw had set in. The sheets of ice had turned to mud, slowing progress to a crawl. To make matters worse, the retreating Germans had left behind large quantities of mines buried in the mud which had to be cleared before anyone could advance. Periodically, thick fog descended and everything ground to a halt.

Finally, on 29 January, the battalion succeeded in capturing Paarlo. But that night around fifty German troops crossed the Roer in rubber boats and attacked a row of houses in the village. Inside was a small group of Allied soldiers. Bursting in, the Germans rolled grenades along the corridors, then moved from room to room, spraying everyone inside with machine-gun fire.

Seeing 'fierce fighting in the dark', Maxwell's commanding officer,

Major D. J. Watson, led a counter-attack. Along with twenty other soldiers, Watson began to crawl towards the houses. The only light was a pale glow that came from distant searchlights bouncing off low cloud – 'Monty's Moonlight', as it was known.

Moving closer, Watson saw a wounded German lying in the street. 'The man started crying, "Please, friends, come and help me."

'I stood up, but the moment I did so another German a few yards away blazed at me with a Spandau. He missed me and hit a lance-corporal by my side.'

Withdrawing with his men, Watson witnessed a remarkable sight. As he wrote in his official account, 'Mr Maxwell, also a platoon commander, sallied out of the darkness . . .'

Maxwell had 'repeatedly asked to be allowed to lead another attempt on the houses'. At first, Watson had refused his entreaties; but when it became clear that the men inside were sure to be killed unless there was another rescue attempt, he changed his mind:

'The officer – Maxwell – then led two of his sections across bullet-swept ground with great dash and determination and succeeded in contacting the platoon who had been holding out in some buildings. Showing no regard for his own safety, he led his sections in the difficult job of clearing the enemy out of the buildings, inflicting many casualties on them, and causing the remainder to withdraw. By his magnificent example and offensive spirit, this officer was responsible for the relief of the platoon and the restoration of the situation.'

According to one of the soldiers there, Lance-Corporal Dennis, Maxwell's courage had nearly cost him his life. 'Thinking there were Germans upstairs, he ordered them to come down – in German.' In fact, there were several British soldiers there, one of whom shouted, ' "Yes, you fucker!", and let go with his rifle. He just missed.'

There may have been more to the incident than that. Maxwell's own account differs in one key respect from Watson's. 'My company commander [Major Watson] ordered me to retreat, saying the position was untenable with heavy German fire against us. I told Major Watson that I believed that some of his men in the other platoon may still be alive and was determined to lead a counter-attack . . . The major left me, saying that it was a stupid enterprise and I might have to face a court-martial if I came out alive. I organized my remaining forces and counter-attacked.'

In other words, Maxwell had effectively disregarded an order – and risked a court martial – to save the trapped soldiers. Was this also an exaggeration? Plainly it wouldn't have been out of character. Yet there is something about Maxwell's disregard for authority, his recklessness, his ability to inspire others and his sheer bravery that rings true.

Maxwell's men seem to have regarded him with a mixture of awe and suspicion. 'He had a smooth, silky way about him,' recalled one of them. 'A big fellow,' a former adjutant would tell the *Sunday Times* in 1969. 'Very dark. A bit of a mystery.' Understandably, they didn't much care for his habit of keeping all the banknotes from any Germans they captured, and giving them any loose change to share out.

At the beginning of March 1945, he was presented with his Military Cross by Field-Marshal Montgomery. A photographer was there to record the scene. In the photograph, a mustachioed Maxwell is standing to attention with his head slightly bowed and his eyes half closed. The day before, he had learned that his mother and one of his sisters had been murdered by the Nazis eight months earlier.

A week after he had been given his MC, Maxwell headed back to Paris on an army motorbike for seven days' leave. This time he had even more important business to attend to: he was getting married. Maxwell had first seen Elisabeth – Betty – Meynard across a crowded servicemen's club in Paris in the autumn of 1944:

'I stayed in the doorway, gazing at her,' he recalled. 'She was pretty, very vivacious, she was slim, well-built, above all I could not take my eyes off her face, on which shone and sparkled the most lovely pair of blue eyes I had seen. She had a lovely look of slight childish desperation as she was talked to by so many people at the same time. I loved her dearly then and there. From the minute I saw her, I wanted her for my wife.'

What Maxwell didn't mention was that Betty had been so struck by her first sight of him that she had nearly passed out. 'Bob had one of those mysterious and attractive faces,' she would recall in *A Mind of My Own*, the memoir she wrote fifty years later. 'A face of extraordinary mobility which captured your attention magnetically but could suddenly be transformed into a strange, steely mask, sending a chill right through you ... When he spoke, his swift-moving lips, thick and red like two ripe fruits, evoked luxury and youthfulness. Yet sometimes, thin as filaments of blood, they depicted death and carnage.'

Coming from a sophisticated – and prosperous – Protestant family, Betty had never come across anyone quite like Maxwell before. He was also unlike anyone her parents had ever come across before. Appalled by Maxwell's background, and by his boorish habits, the Meynards did everything they could to dissuade their daughter from seeing him.

Despite their efforts, the courtship quickly picked up speed. In December 1944, two months after the couple had met, they slept together for the first time. 'Although he was ablaze with desire, he did not rush me,' Betty recalled. 'I was ready for love, eager to be at one with him, and we made love. But despite my readiness, it was a painful first experience. He was in tears at the thought of having hurt me. Nothing was ever to move me more than my husband's tears, and by the time I next felt them mingle with mine, a full ten years of togetherness would have gone by.'

Maxwell's marriage proposal caused the Meynards to shed some tears of their own. Her father wrote to the Czech embassy asking for any information they could provide. The embassy replied that as far as they could tell, Maxwell had never been sentenced for any crime – which must have come as a comfort of sorts.

But after a visit from Brigadier Carthew-Yourston – still keeping a protective eye on Maxwell – the Meynards had a change of heart and gave the couple their blessing with as much grace as they could muster. The couple were married on 14 March 1945 at the town hall in the 16th *Arrondissement*. Betty wore a lace dress and a petticoat made out of parachute silk. Maxwell was in uniform, proudly sporting the ribbon of his Military Cross. 'Resplendent in his new service dress completed by my father's Sam Browne belt, he really looked like the hero of my dreams.'

The following day there was a religious service to solemnize the wedding at the Meynards' local Protestant church. Four days later, Maxwell rejoined his regiment. Shortly afterwards he wrote his new wife another letter. This one was rather more brisk and businesslike in tone. It began: 'Here are my six rules for the perfect partnership:

1. Don't nag.
2. Don't criticize unduly.
3. Give honest appreciation.
4. Pay little attentions.
5. Be courteous.
6. Have the utmost confidence in yourself and in your partner.'

But by then Maxwell was in no position to offer anyone handy tips on etiquette. Two weeks after his wedding, his platoon came to a village 'deep inside Germany'. He asked an elderly man where the German soldiers were. The man pointed out a group of sixteen houses. Maxwell told him to pass on a message to the soldiers inside – either come out carrying a white flag, or he would start shelling them.

Rather than obey his instructions, the soldiers ran out of the house. Maxwell opened fire. 'I got two of them,' he noted with satisfaction afterwards. A few minutes later, a white flag appeared above the church. As far as Maxwell was concerned, the tactic had worked so well that he decided to use it again when he came to the next town. A German prisoner was sent to tell the inhabitants to surrender immediately, or else the town would be destroyed. Shortly afterwards, another white flag appeared. But as Maxwell and his men entered the town a German tank opened fire. To teach the townsfolk a lesson, and ensure it didn't happen again, Maxwell took the mayor to the main square, where he shot him through the head.

According to one of his fellow soldiers, Victor Sassie, later to become a London restaurateur, he shot several other German civilians at the same time. This wasn't Maxwell's first experience of killing, of course. The 'death and carnage' that Betty had noticed in his lips hadn't got there by accident. Only the week before, he had been commended for his role in attacks on two more German villages: 'A Company led off successfully and by noon had cleared Sudweyne . . . [Lieutenant R. Maxwell] alone having killed fifteen SS men and taken fourteen prisoners.'

But this was the first time he'd executed an unarmed civilian in cold blood. It's also possible that some of the men he killed that day had already surrendered. Maxwell once told the journalist Mike Molloy that towards the end of the war he and his platoon had come across a heavily defended farmhouse: 'I got up close to the farm door and shouted in German, "Come out with your hands up. You are completely surrounded." They came out and I shot them all with my sub-machine-gun. I thought my boys would be pleased, but all they said was, "That's not fair, sir, those lads had surrendered."'

According to Molloy, an incredulous Maxwell had said, 'Can you understand such an attitude?'

At home, though, he told a different story. Maxwell's son Ian remembers his father coming into the kitchen at Headington Hill Hall one night while he and his brother Kevin were watching a documentary about the War. 'It showed some German lads with their arms in the air. Dad said, "I remember shooting boys that age. Just about the same age as you and Kevin. I always regret it."'

If in later life Maxwell would claim to be haunted by the incident, at the time he had no such qualms. Maxwell's letter to Betty describing the incident begins, 'I had a very amusing day yesterday. I will now give you a report of it . . .' The letter continues in similarly breezy tones. 'As soon as we marched off, a German tank opened fire on us. Luckily he missed, so I shot the Mayor and withdrew.'

A week later, Maxwell was given another spell of leave. He headed straight to London, where he had sent Betty to live – he felt she would be safer there than in Paris. 'Most of our time was spent in bed!' she would recall fifty years later. 'We just could not stop making love. Our need to feel close to each other was insatiable, and as I think of those days now, I remember so well Bob's incredible energy, well matched by my own. It was as if he needed to assuage all his pent-up desires and realize all his dreams, as if our carnal pleasure was the living proof that life had prevailed over death.'

On 2 May 1945, together with the 1/5th Battalion of the Queen's Royal Regiment, Maxwell marched into Hamburg. That night, Germany surrendered and the war was over. In July, he was posted to Berlin – part of an advance guard to pave the way for the take-over of the British section of the city from the Russian army.

Maxwell had a new wife, a new job, a newish name, and a blazing determination to make his way in the world. Thinking it might come in useful, he had also taught himself Russian. But before he could face his future, there were significant gaps to fill in from his past. Later that summer, he drove to Prague to find out what had happened to his family. He knew that his mother and one of his sisters had died, but next to nothing about the circumstances of their deaths.

In Prague, Maxwell learned that throughout the war conditions had deteriorated in Solotvino. Men of working age had been taken away to labour camps, while the women were forced to watch a number of the town's inhabitants being shot, including most of the rabbis. Then, in April 1944, on the orders of Adolf Eichmann, the centre of Solotvino was turned into a ghetto. Five thousand Jews were confined there, with fifteen to twenty people crammed into each room of the town's houses. There was a strict 5 p.m. curfew; after that, no one was allowed to step outside.

Four weeks later, everybody in the ghetto was loaded into cattle trucks – seventy to a truck – and taken by train to Auschwitz, 350 miles away. The journey took three days. Each truck was given two buckets – one full of water, the other for use as a toilet – and two loaves of bread.

Most of the people who survived the journey were gassed the

same day they arrived. Along with Maxwell's mother, two of his sisters, his brother and his grandfather also died in the camp's gas chambers. His nineteen-year-old sister, Shenya, was arrested in Budapest in the winter of 1944 and never seen again. She probably suffered the same fate as other Jews who were arrested at the time: forced to strip naked, roped together, then thrown off a bridge into the Danube.

Despite being incarcerated in two concentration camps, Mauthausen and Buchenwald, Maxwell's older sister Brana had managed to survive the War, So too had his younger sister Sylvia, who narrowly missed being put on a train to Auschwitz. She had been rescued from Budapest station by the Swedish businessman Raoul Wallenberg, who issued all Jewish children under the age of fifteen with Swedish identity papers.

Just like Maxwell's mother, his grandfather and three of his siblings, his father, Mehel, had also died in Auschwitz. Instead of being gassed, he is believed to have been shot – either as soon as he arrived or shortly afterwards.

3

An Adventurer of Great Style

A few months after arriving in Berlin, Maxwell decided to get himself a dog. He had noticed that a number of British officers kept dogs, and felt it might make him look more distinguished. The trouble was that by then there were hardly any dogs, or pets of any kind, left in Berlin: food was so scarce that most of them had been eaten.

One day, suffering from toothache, Maxwell visited a dentist called Dr Eibisch. During the War, Eibisch had been one of a host of dentists who had treated Hitler's rotting teeth. He mentioned to Maxwell that he knew of a kennel where he might find a dog. It was the same kennel that had bred Hitler's German shepherd, Blondi – a gift from Martin Bormann, head of the Nazi Party Chancellery.

Maxwell went straight there and found that the breeder had just one dog left, improbably named Barry. He bought him on the spot. Distraught to have lost Barry – and with him his chances of keeping the kennel open – the breeder committed suicide a few days later. A photograph taken at the time shows a grinning Maxwell, wearing an immaculately tailored tunic instead of his old battle-dress, standing in the back of a Mercedes and holding Barry up for the camera.

But while Maxwell was delighted with his new dog, his fellow officers were aghast when they learned where he had come from – and what had happened to the man who had bred him. 'Do you know, the other officers all felt sorry for him?' Maxwell would tell Mike Molloy years later, his hands spread in disbelief. 'Can you believe it? Sorry for the man who'd bred dogs for Hitler?'

Berlin, as Maxwell wrote to Betty, was 'a shambles. You can ride in a car for an hour without being able to see one house intact. The people are on starvation rations and no doubt before the year is out thousands of them will perish of hunger.' The stench of decomposing bodies permeated people's clothes and stuck in their nostrils. Splintered trunks of trees were covered in notices appealing for news of loved ones. Desperately hunting for tobacco, Germans fought for the privilege of emptying ashtrays in Allied messes.

What struck another British soldier, George Clare, most of all was the strange silence everywhere. 'This absence of the constant roar of city life was more unsettling than the sight of bombed and shelled buildings, of jagged outlines of broken masonry framing bits of blue sky. I had been prepared for that, but not for a city hushed to a whisper.

'Yet Berlin was not a lifeless moon-scape. It lived – albeit in something of a zombie trance – mirrored in the dazed looks of many of the people I passed, more often noticeable in men than women. But then the men were mostly old or elderly, bowed and bitter-faced. The few youngish ones who were about – emaciated shadows of the soldiers who had almost conquered an entire continent – looked pathetic and downtrodden in the tattered remnants of their Wehrmacht uniforms.'

Maxwell's first job in Germany was at the Intelligence Corps headquarters at Iserlohn, 250 miles from Berlin. Along with the other British officers working there, he was given a pseudonym to protect his identity. For the next six months, he became 'Captain Stone', part of a team interrogating German prisoners and others who had worked for the Nazi regime.

He only narrowly missed getting hold of what was then the most sought-after document in the world. Among the people Maxwell interviewed was Major Willi Johannmeir, Hitler's former adjutant. Johannmeir had been in the bunker in Berlin with Hitler on the day he'd committed suicide. Not only had he witnessed and signed Hitler's will, but he was also believed to be in possession of a copy of it.

There had been three copies in all. Hitler had intended that two should be passed on to his successor, Admiral Dönitz, while the third – Johannmeir's – was to go to Field-Marshal Ferdinand Schörner, Commander-in-Chief of the German army. Arrested before he could reach Schörner, Johannmeir refused to say where his copy was hidden unless he was promised his freedom. As Maxwell had neither the authority nor the inclination to do a deal, a senior officer, Hugh Trevor-Roper – later Lord Dacre – was sent out from London to take over the interrogation.

It's not clear what promises Trevor-Roper gave, but Johannmeir swiftly had a change of heart. Together, they drove to his house late one night, where Johannmeir fetched an axe and with some difficulty – the ground was frozen solid – dug up a bottle from his back garden. Inside was a rolled-up copy of Hitler's will.

In February 1946, Maxwell was promoted to captain and transferred to Berlin. In June he became a British citizen. By then he had also been reunited with his two surviving sisters. Having arranged for them both to come to England, he paid for Sylvia, then sixteen, to attend a boarding school in Somerset, and Brana to move to America, where she had several cousins. Along with his new passport, Maxwell was rapidly acquiring some new airs and graces. On leave in London, he went to a dinner dance at the Regent Palace Hotel off Piccadilly Circus. There he bumped into a man called Lou Rosenbluth, who had served with him in the 1st Czech Division – before the War, Rosenbluth had been goalkeeper for the Slovak national team.

The two men had last seen one another six years earlier on the beach at Sète waiting to be evacuated from France. 'I looked around and there was this captain with a swagger stick in his hand,' Rosenbluth recalled. 'I jumped up. I was so pleased to see him just like I had been when I saw he was going to get on the ship at Sète.'

But the Maxwell that Rosenbluth remembered was not the same Maxwell who now peered down his nose at him. 'In a posh accent, he said, "Don't I know you from somewhere?" I got so annoyed. I was so pleased to see him, and he says that to me. I said to him, "If you don't remember – don't bother", and I sat down. I often think about it. Maybe I was sensitive because of the young lady I was with, but he must have known who I was.'

On 11 March 1946, Betty gave birth to a son, Michael Paul Andre Maxwell. As soon as he heard the news, Maxwell wrote her a letter whose tone suggests his new starchy manner wasn't confined to Lou Rosenbluth: 'First, let me congratulate you from the bottom of my heart. And secondly, let me tell you that I love and worship you beyond anything that you might imagine.'

Berlin had now been divided into four zones: the French, the British, the Russian and the American. Fluent in Russian, English and French, Maxwell could easily pass from zone to zone without attracting attention. As he'd proved before, he also had a natural bent for subterfuge. All this made him a highly prized asset as far as British Intelligence was concerned.

Rumours that Maxwell had spied for the British, the Russians or later the Israelis – and possibly some combination of the three – would dog him for the rest of his life. Always, he swatted them aside. Yet it's plain that Maxwell was involved in espionage work for the British while he was in Berlin. He even boasted about it to another old Berlin hand, Geoffrey Goodman, later to become a *Daily Mirror* journalist.

'One of my secret jobs was to find out what the Russians were up to, stripping East German industries,' Maxwell told Goodman. 'We knew there were plans in Zhukov's office. [Marshal Georgy Zhukov was the Commander of the Soviet Occupation Zone in Berlin.] My job was to get hold of them. I had a close friendship with a Red Army colonel who knew the set-up and the combination of the safe.' One night the two of them broke into Zhukov's office and photographed the documents, before replacing them.

Maxwell also went on a number of undercover trips to Czechoslovakia, then teetering on the brink of a communist takeover – it would become part of the Eastern Bloc in February 1948. According to documents in the Secret Service archive in Prague, Maxwell's presence in the country soon attracted the suspicions of the Czech Ministry of the Interior:

File VII/s-2219/2347-4/12-46   *In Prague, 18 December 1946*

Ministry of the Interior received the following confidential notice:

*Maxwell R., intelligence major, former name unknown, formerly a
citizen of Czechoslovakia, honoured by the English King, has already
been in Czechoslovakia three times as a reporter, covering editorial
stories, and KEITH, major, former name Karel Klinger, comes from
around Kolín.*

*The Ministry of the Interior is requesting an immediate search for
the above-listed personnel. If any of them are found in Czechoslovakian
territory, they should be monitored. It is mandatory to report to the
Ministry of the Interior in the event of their being positively identified.*

Although they made a mistake with his rank, there's no doubt that
this was Maxwell, flying beneath the radar in his former homeland.
Nor was it an isolated incident: throughout the 1940s and 1950s, Maxwell carried on making regular undercover trips to Czechoslovakia.

In October 1947, the Czech embassy in London wrote a secret letter to the Ministry of the Interior: 'From a totally credible source I
learned that Mr Maxwell, director of the European Periodical Publicity and Advertising Co., is a spy agent for the British authorities . . .
Mr Maxwell is originally from Ruthenia and his native name is Ludvik Hoch. He is an adventurer of great style and an enemy of
Czechoslovakia and the new Slavic democracies in Europe.'

Another file describes him as 'very closely linked to the Intelligence Service.' The file goes on to give a physical description of
Maxwell, presumably for the benefit of anyone assigned to follow
him. 'He is a very handsome man,' the writer noted. 'Almost a double
of the American actor, Clark Gable.'

For the time being, Maxwell had a new job to keep him busy. In July
1946, he was put in charge of the Public Relations and Information
Services Control's press section at a salary of £620 a year – untold
riches in post-war Berlin. Any German who wanted to put on a play,
show a film or publish a book had to get permission from PRISC.

As the organization's censor, Maxwell was also responsible for weeding out any diehard Nazis still trying to keep the swastika flying.

At the same time, PRISC had a wider brief: to reintroduce Germans to the virtues of democracy. One way to do this was to set up a free – or free-ish – press. *Der Telegraaf* was the first licensed newspaper in the British sector of Berlin. Broadly Social Democrat in tone, it quickly became a big success: within months of its launch it was selling half a million copies.

Maxwell not only censored the paper's articles but singlehandedly kept it on the road, making sure it never ran short of newsprint, or printing ink. No one was quite sure how he did this, but they soon learned not to pry too deeply. What was clear was that Maxwell, still only twenty-three, had a genius for bartering, browbeating and generally getting what he wanted.

Later on in life, he could never pass a spotlight without stepping into it. But at this stage, just like Harry Lime in Graham Greene's *The Third Man*, Maxwell seemed to belong in the shadows, slipping quietly from occupied zone to occupied zone.

Der Telegraaf was owned by a company called Springer-Verlag. Before the war, Springer-Verlag had been the world's leading publisher of scientific books. Now, along with everyone else in Berlin, the company had fallen on hard times. Soon after Maxwell started work at PRISC, Julius Springer, a cousin of Springer-Verlag's owner, Ferdinand Springer, paid him a visit. He'd come to complain about how little paper was available for printing books. Maxwell listened impatiently for a few minutes, then kicked him out. Incensed, Julius Springer wrote to the Foreign Office, who sent Maxwell a sternly worded letter telling him to be more respectful.

He chucked this in the bin.

A few days later Maxwell had another visitor: Ferdinand Springer himself. Distinguished, erudite and urbane – he was known as 'The Kaiser' – Springer was everything Maxwell was not. But, much to their surprise, the two men hit it off. Idly at first, then with increasing fascination, Maxwell listened as Ferdinand Springer explained how the company had prospered in its heyday.

Founded more than a century earlier by Ferdinand's father, Springer-Verlag had published books by most of the world's leading scientists, including Albert Einstein and Max Born, the father of quantum mechanics. They also published a large range of scientific journals. The beauty of the business was that the books and journals they produced had a captive readership: every library, every university, every scientific institute, wanted a copy. What's more, the scientists who wrote these books and journals were so thrilled to see their work in print that they scarcely expected to be paid anything in return.

Ever since he'd been a boy in Solotvino, Maxwell had dreamed of making his fortune. Breaking rocks in South Wales, he'd passed the time by thinking up money-making schemes. His dream was to find a commodity which would be in huge demand after the war, and which he could obtain for next to nothing. Out of nowhere the answer had just landed in his lap: the commodity was knowledge. It was cheap, it was plentiful, and if he chose to set up a similar company to Springer-Verlag in Britain, he would have the field to himself – unlike Germany, Britain had next to no tradition of academic publishing.

Best of all, there was a ready-made stockpile on his doorstep. No new academic research had been published during the war, and as a result, Springer had a colossal backlog of material. Sixty-three thousand books, along with tens of thousands of journals, had been removed from Berlin and stored in an enormous warehouse a hundred miles away to escape the Allied bombing. There was also a huge amount of scientific research conducted during the war that had never even been printed due to lack of paper.

It turned out that Springer too had a dream. What he hoped to find, he told Maxwell wistfully, was someone who would transport this backlog of material out of Germany and distribute it abroad – at the time German nationals were forbidden from making large shipments to other countries. Springer was convinced the demand was there. All over the world academics were dying to read about the latest research on the pulmonary system of the flea, or new developments in Metallurgical Thermochemistry. It was simply a matter of sorting out the supply. But so far his efforts had proved fruitless.

Did he by any chance know of anyone who might be able to help?

As it just happened, said Maxwell, he might.

In November 1947, 369 'large packets' were sent from Germany to London. By then, Maxwell had been demobbed from the army and had gone back to England to be with Betty and their baby son. He had also secured worldwide distribution rights to all of Springer-Verlag's publications. Four months later, 150 tons of books and another 150 tons of journals were loaded on to a goods train and taken to Bielefeld in western Germany. From there, a convoy of trucks brought them to London. These were followed by another enormous consignment of manuscripts – so large that seven railway carriages were needed to transport it from Berlin to Southwark, where the carriages sat in a siding for several weeks beside a pickle factory.

Among the people Maxwell met around this time was a man called Peter Croxford, who, like him, had recently been demobbed. 'He was bloody arrogant,' Croxford recalls. 'A bit of a mad hatter. That's what made the most impression on me. I remember we were in a taxi once and he kept barking instructions at the driver. "Go right here!" and so on. I thought, bloody hell, who is this man?'

When he wasn't in the back of a taxi shouting at the driver, Maxwell drove around London in an enormous grey Dodge with Barry the German shepherd in the back – he'd had the car shipped out from Germany along with Springer's books and journals. As Maxwell had already learned in Berlin, it was important to make an impression.

After six months, he moved premises, to a larger office in Percy Street off Tottenham Court Road. One day he called Peter Croxford with an odd request: 'Maxwell said could I rig him up with a dummy telephone? He wanted to be able to press a button and his phone would ring. Halfway through a meeting he would press the button. The phone would ring, he'd pick it up and start speaking some foreign language. It was purely for show – so that everyone would think he was much busier and more important than he really was.'

Where did Maxwell get the money from to set up in business? Certainly not from Ferdinand Springer, who was in no position to fund anything at the time. It's possible that Maxwell may have saved some of his salary in Berlin, but it could never have been enough to hire special trains and convoys of lorries. And while Betty's parents were not short of cash, they had no intention of throwing it at Maxwell.

The money, it transpired, came from an unexpected source. Shortly before his death in 2000, Desmond Bristow, a former Intelligence Officer, spoke about MI6's relations with Maxwell: 'It was obvious that Maxwell had been doing odd things for MI6 in Germany, and he suggested we should subsidize him to buy a book business. He effectively became our agent.' As far as Bristow was concerned, nothing like this had ever happened before, so MI6 must have thought Maxwell was worth investing in. 'I was certainly not aware of any other case of MI6 buying a business for anyone.'

However murky Maxwell's past may have been, the way ahead seemed clear. Imbued with his mother's sense that destiny had some very big plans for him, he had often discussed them with his fellow soldiers, oblivious to the incredulous guffaws they prompted.

'I am going to go to England,' he would tell them. 'To become a gentleman, and a squire.'

4.

Difficulties With Pork

In the early 1950s, Robert Maxwell went into business with a German organic chemist and refugee called Kurt Wallersteiner. Like Maxwell, Wallersteiner had a genius for making deals – and, like him, he wasn't one to shirk a challenge. A few years earlier, Wallersteiner had been asked by the communist government in China to supply them with a hundred tons of indigo blue dye. But a Chinese official mistakenly added an extra zero to the order, turning it into a thousand tons – almost the world's entire output of indigo blue dye at the time.

Undeterred, Wallersteiner bought up every scrap of indigo blue dye he could find and against all odds succeeded in fulfilling the order. This was to have unexpected consequences. When the Chinese army invaded South Korea in June 1950, the British and American troops stationed there found to their astonishment that the Chinese infantrymen were all wearing bright blue uniforms. As a result, they were much easier to spot and shoot. Wallersteiner's coup was also responsible for the fact that for the next twenty-five years almost everyone in China wore blue.

Together, Maxwell and Wallersteiner became involved in another deal: they arranged for a large consignment of chemicals to be shipped to Germany in exchange for an assortment of glass, china and textiles. However, the two men calculated they would make more money if they sent everything they received straight on to Argentina. In return, the Argentines would send them 2000 tons of pork bellies.

Then came a snag. When the meat arrived in England, the Ministry of Food condemned it as inedible; anyone who ate it risked contracting botulism. Maxwell and Wallersteiner managed to ship some of the condemned pork to Holland, where it was immediately sealed in cans, but the rest sat in a warehouse growing mouldier by the day.

In desperation, they turned to a former Austrian diplomat called Sir George Franckenstein. Before the war, Franckenstein had been the Austrian ambassador in London. A staunch opponent of Hitler, he had taken British citizenship and been knighted by King George VI. Franckenstein was also a noted after-dinner speaker, renowned for his ability to talk off the cuff on a variety of subjects, from early Alpinists to the maternal habits of chimpanzees.

Although he had since fallen on hard times, Franckenstein had kept in close touch with his former homeland. Maxwell and Wallersteiner persuaded him to approach the Austrian government with what they conceded was a risky plan: Franckenstein was to tell the Austrians that Wallersteiner was an official representative of a country called Oceania.

The only problem with this was that Oceania didn't exist – Maxwell and Wallersteiner had made it up. Using all his diplomatic skills, Franckenstein managed to convince the Austrian government to sign a trade agreement with Oceania and take the condemned pork. In return, they received a consignment of prefabricated wooden houses. When these arrived, a show home was erected in High Wycombe, fitted out with electricity as well as plumbing, and unveiled with a great fanfare in the local press.

It failed to attract a single buyer.

Fortunately, they had better luck elsewhere. Facing an influx of post-war immigrants, Canada agreed to take all the prefabricated houses they could provide. Meanwhile, the pork that had gone to Holland for canning had been sent on to Germany, where food standards were considerably lower. In exchange, Maxwell and Wallersteiner received several thousand tons of German cement.

At this point they hit another snag: the British denied them a licence to import the cement. By now even the normally indomitable Wallersteiner was becoming disheartened. But just when all seemed hopeless, they succeeded in selling the cement on to the Canadians, who needed it to make foundations for all their new prefabricated houses. However fraught the deal may have been, everything, it seemed, had worked out in the end.

And then, on its way to Canada, the freighter carrying the concrete sprang a leak. Seawater flooded the hold, the cement set rock-hard, the freighter barely made it into harbour and the entire consignment was lost.

Maxwell's business career had begun modestly enough. Four years earlier, he had bought ninety shares in a company called Low-Bell, set up the previous year by another Czech émigré, called Arnos Lobl. Low-Bell traded in an extensive range of goods, including caustic soda, Turkish carpets, deer skins, eucalyptus oil and dried sardines.

Lobl left soon afterwards and the company became Low-Bell & Maxwell.

It may have had a grand address at 133 Grand Buildings, Trafalgar Square, but the office consisted of a single room, whose only window was obscured by a large billboard for Ivor Novello's new musical, *Perchance to Dream*. It was also the headquarters of EPPAC – the European Periodicals Publicity and Advertising Company Ltd – which was both the British agent for Springer-Verlag and the supplier of German newspapers to the few German prisoners of war left in the country.

In order to distribute the scientific journals he'd imported from Germany, Maxwell realized that he needed to join forces with an established publisher. He approached a company called Butterworth & Co., publishers of medical and legal textbooks, whose Managing Director – a man called Major John Whitlock – had also been an Intelligence Officer. Whitlock suggested that Maxwell should go and see their financial advisers, Hambros Bank.

Sir Charles Hambro, the Chairman of Hambros Bank, had been an original member of the Special Operations Executive, SOE, forerunners of the modern SAS. He too had close links to British Intelligence. Hambro took an immediate shine to Maxwell. After just twenty minutes of listening to him outline his plans, he took the remarkable decision to issue him with a chequebook, telling him he could draw up to £25,000 with it – more than £350,000 today.

Would Hambro have been so eager to help someone who didn't share his and Whitlock's Intelligence background? It seems unlikely.

In April 1949, Maxwell became the Managing Director of Butterworth's new subsidiary, Butterworth–Springer Ltd. Six months later he set up another new company, Lange, Maxwell & Springer, to be the sole UK distributor for Butterworth–Springer. In 1950, LM&S had a turnover of £250,000. By 1951, it had gone up to £600,000. The same year, Maxwell changed the name of Butterworth–Springer to Pergamon, the town in Asia Minor whose legendary altar is believed to have served as the model for 'the seat of Satan' in the Book of Revelations.

It's hard to exaggerate the impact that Maxwell had on the tweedy, genteel, hopelessly antiquated world of British publishers. While there were a number of Jewish émigrés who would transform British publishing after the war, none of them were like Maxwell. With his blustery manner, his electric ties, his newly grown pencil moustache and what one employee called his 'sledgehammer personality', he made an unforgettable impression.

At the same time, darkness – and the whiff of chicanery – was never far away. According to Desmond Bristow, Maxwell continued working for British Intelligence throughout the 1950s, collecting useful information from the scientific conferences he went to, as well as passing on misinformation that MI6 had provided him with. 'He started supplying, from our point of view, pretty spurious stuff to the Russians.'

Meanwhile Sir Charles Hambro continued to take a close interest in Maxwell's activities. One of his associates at Hambros Bank was yet another former spy, called Count Vanden Heuvel. Popularly known as 'Fanny the Fixer', Heuvel had been MI6's wartime Station Chief in Berne.

In early 1951, Maxwell, Fanny the Fixer and Arthur Coleridge, the Managing Director of a once-prosperous book wholesaler called Simpkin Marshall, met up for a drink in the Savoy Hotel.

Although Simpkin Marshall had 125,000 books in print and an annual turnover of a million pounds, its glory days were long gone.

Now it was slipping towards bankruptcy and frantically casting around for a buyer. By the end of the evening, Maxwell had agreed to pay £50,000 of the company's debts, with another £110,000 to come over the next nine years. In return, he took over as Managing Director.

For Maxwell, it was an astonishingly good deal. For Simpkin Marshall, it would quickly turn into a disaster. Just like Butterworth's, they had no idea what had hit them. Immediately, Maxwell moved the company's stock to 242–244 Marylebone Road and rechristened the building Maxwell House. No one knew what to make of this. Was it a joke? If so, it was a very un-English sort of joke, being both absurdly self-aggrandizing and calculated to annoy the manufacturers of Maxwell House coffee – then the biggest selling brand of instant coffee in America.

Where had the money to buy Simpkin Marshall come from? Not from MI6 this time, but almost entirely from Kurt Wallersteiner, who agreed to lend Maxwell £50,000. A year later, in 1952, Maxwell asked him for another loan – this time for £100,000. Wallersteiner, whose willingness to do business with Maxwell doesn't appear to have been adversely affected by their difficulties with the condemned pork, was happy to oblige.

In return, he received a block of shares in Simpkin Marshall – shares which, Maxwell assured him, would soon be yielding a healthy dividend. Business appeared to be booming. By now Maxwell had become a major figure in British publishing. Everywhere, he was founding companies and doing deals – deals to sell books, deals to buy books, deals to open up new markets. One of his great coups was persuading the Russians to take large quantities of medical and scientific periodicals; hitherto the Russians had been staunchly resistant to doing business with the West.

Amid this whirl of activity, it would be easy to imagine that Maxwell didn't care much, if at all, about what he was publishing, that he would have been equally at home selling Turkish carpets, or dried sardines. But the truth was more complicated. Although Maxwell always had one eye fixed on his profit margins, every so often the other would give off an unexpectedly idealistic gleam. Later in life, he would tell his official biographer, Joe Haines, that it was the bombing of Hiroshima and Nagasaki that made him aware of the role science was going to play in the modern age. As a result, he came to see that, properly harnessed, science could benefit the world instead of bringing it to the edge of destruction.

Although this may sound suspiciously like something dreamed up for a corporate brochure, it's quite possible that Maxwell was being sincere. Even his swelling band of detractors would have to admit that he effectively invented modern scientific publishing in Britain. By giving scientists a far bigger platform to disseminate their research than they'd ever had before, Maxwell completely changed the way in which science was conducted, both in Britain and around the world. This in turn would pave the way for a number of key breakthroughs in physics and medicine.

But while idealism was one thing, business was quite another. In October 1953, Wallersteiner had what proved to be a nasty shock. When he asked for his £100,000 back, Maxwell offered him more shares in Simpkin Marshall. These shares, Maxwell told him, would give Wallersteiner 20 per cent of Simpkin's profits. Another few months would go by before it dawned on Wallersteiner that there never were going to be any profits. Far from thriving, the company was on the verge of bankruptcy.

Wallersteiner had another shock when he announced that he intended to call a creditors' meeting to get to the bottom of the matter: Maxwell slapped an injunction on him. Under the terms of the injunction, Wallersteiner was forbidden from contacting any other Simpkin Marshall creditors. However, Maxwell could do nothing to stop him from engaging a firm of City accountants – Peat Marwick – to examine Simpkin Marshall's books.

Peat Marwick's report made grim reading. It concluded that the company was even more deeply in debt than Wallersteiner had suspected. What's more, it turned out Maxwell had used money borrowed on behalf of Simpkin Marshall to shore up his other concerns – essentially, he'd been asset-stripping the main business while switching the loans about from one company to another to make them appear more successful. This may have been the first time that Maxwell had used such a ploy, but it wouldn't be the last.

The news soon leaked out. In June 1955, 200 creditors voted to bring in the Official Receiver to wind up Simpkin Marshall. 'It appears doubtful whether the company was at any time solvent,' the Receiver declared.

An unabashed Maxwell took it on the chin. 'I've come down flat on my arse,' he said. 'But I'm going back up again. And I'll stay up.'

The affair not only sharpened his determination to prove himself; it left him with a deep-seated loathing of the British Establishment. With their snobbery and their petty-mindedness, their ways were never going to be his ways. In part, this was because they tended to abide by the rules while he ignored them, but, typically, Maxwell didn't see it like that. 'If a gentleman of the Establishment offers you his word or his bond,' he was fond of saying, 'always go for his bond.'

Never slow to nurse a grievance, he became convinced that the Establishment was out to thwart him. In one sense, of course, he was right. However much he longed to be an English gentleman, it must have dawned on Maxwell by now that he would never be allowed to join the club. He could change his name, his accent and his religion, but ultimately it made no difference. Always, he would be on the outside, both hammering on the glass trying to get in, and determined to make mincemeat of everyone behind it.

As for Kurt Wallersteiner – possibly wiser and certainly poorer than before – he returned to what he knew best. The next year he attracted the attention of the US Justice Department for trying to organize the importation into the USA of 'a quantity' of gallnuts from communist China, something that put him in violation of the Trading With the Enemy Act. Gallnuts are swellings on the bark of trees caused by particular types of parasite. They are mainly used in the manufacture of clothing dyes.

5.

Mortality

By the time Kurt Wallersteiner came to the notice of the US Justice Department, Robert Maxwell had learned he was dying. One day in September 1955, Betty had found him sitting at his desk in the house they had recently bought in Esher, racked by pains in his chest. X-rays revealed malignant tumours in both lungs. The specialist told him that he had no more than four weeks to live.

As he faced the prospect of imminent death, Maxwell cast around for any crumbs of comfort that religion could provide. He talked to a Christian Scientist, the Chief Rabbi, a Roman Catholic priest and a Church of England vicar, but none of them were able to convince him that God existed, still less that there might be an afterlife. Instead, he spent hours lying in his hospital bed gazing at a Chinese picture of a prancing horse which Betty had hung on the wall.

'That picture now came to signify life itself and Bob would look at it with tears in his eyes.'

Maxwell was now the father of six children: Michael, Anne, Philip, twin girls Christine and Isabel, and Karine. As he told Betty, he hoped to have the same number of children as his parents – nine – thereby re-creating the family he had lost. But it looked as if this ambition, along with all his others, was about to be thwarted. Allowed out of hospital for a final weekend, Maxwell spent it making plans for the childrens' education and organizing the future of Pergamon. Among the visitors that weekend was Pat Savage, a master at Summer Fields school where Maxwell's older son, Michael, then nine years old, had recently started. Before lunch Maxwell took Savage for a walk round the grounds of their house.

'He then confided to me the shattering news that he had cancer in both his lungs. As we walked around the house, Bob pointed to the tennis courts. "It is quite incredible," he said, "that a month or so ago I was playing on that court – and in another month I shall be dead."'

When Maxwell returned to hospital, his children were brought to his bedside to say their farewells. 'We had decided to tell the children only that daddy needed an operation and had to go back to hospital,' Betty recalled. 'But I saw the agony in Bob's eyes as he said goodbye to all the little ones for what he really thought might be the last time.' His daughter Isabel, then aged four, remembers being taken to the hospital. 'I had no idea I was supposed to say goodbye – my mother hadn't said anything about his being ill beforehand. I can remember him being in bed and my saying "Hello, Daddy", but that's all.'

At first neither Maxwell nor Betty thought to question the specialist's diagnosis. It was only a week after Pat Savage's visit that Betty decided to seek a second opinion: she asked the radiologist who had treated George VI, Peter Kerley, to take new X-rays. While these revealed a tumour in one lung, the other turned out to be a false alarm – nothing more than 'the shadow of an excrescence' on his rib. Kerley recommended that the tumour be removed for a biopsy, along with the tissue surrounding it. In all, Maxwell lost half a lung. The operation was followed by a nine-day wait for the results: 'Bob, now mentally alert and in dreadful pain, became despondent and just did not seem to recover the will to live.'

When the results eventually came through, the tumour turned out to be benign.

Maxwell's brush with mortality left him with an enduring sense of living on borrowed time, and prompted him to bang his own drum even more forcefully than before. He also gave up smoking cigarettes – previously he'd been a sixty-a-day man.

In 1956, hoping to announce himself to the world as a cultural grandee, Maxwell put up the money for a filmed production of *Giselle* by the Bolshoi Ballet starring the world's leading ballerina,

Galina Ulanova. It was filmed over two nights at the Royal Opera House in Covent Garden, but as Maxwell didn't have enough money to pay for an orchestra, the dancers had to dance to taped music while the conductor was filmed waving his arms about in an empty orchestra pit. In the event, filming overran by several hours – mainly because Maxwell kept clambering up on stage and telling an increasingly infuriated Ulanova what to do.

Then came an even more devastating blow. In January 1957, Maxwell and Betty were on holiday in Barbados when they received a telegram telling them that their three-year-old daughter, Karine, had developed a high temperature and been taken to hospital. Immediately they caught a plane back to London. When they arrived, they learned that Karine had been diagnosed with leukaemia.

In the hope of finding a cure, Maxwell wrote letters to all the world's leading leukaemia specialists, including one to a Swedish doctor: 'Quite recently my little daughter has been stricken with leukaemia. I am sending you a copy of the report of her case, as well as some slides, and ask you to let me know whether you, or anyone else whom you know, have anything "in the works" of an experimental nature which could be tried to save or to prolong her life. In the hope that you or your colleagues may soon come up with an answer to this terrible scourge, I, as her father, thank you in advance on her behalf, as well as mine, for whatever you might be able to do.'

Maxwell must have thought there was a chance that such a direct approach might work; after all, it had done before. When Isabel and Christine had been born in Paris in 1950, both of them contracted infantile cholera. Neither was expected to survive. Maxwell, who was in Berlin at the time, managed to obtain supplies of an experimental drug which had never been used on humans before. Driving through the night, he headed for Paris. When he arrived, he drove his car straight through the security barrier at the hospital. The girls were then given injections of the drug directly into their heads. Within a few days they had recovered. Subsequently all the children at the hospital who were suffering from cholera were given the drug and it later became the standard treatment.

But this time there was to be no last-minute reprieve. Before Karine could be moved to a hospital in Boston for treatment, she died in her father's arms. Isabel Maxwell remembers her and her twin sister, Christine, being told of her death: 'There seemed to be a great commotion in the house. We went to our parents' bedroom door, but it was closed. My mother opened it and her eyes were red with tears. Somebody said, or she said, that Karine had died. Although I can remember hearing the words, we didn't really understand anything – we were only six years old. We couldn't cry or anything like that. Instead we just went back upstairs and carried on playing with some dolls. But I do remember feeling very strange as we sat there playing.'

Karine's death shattered Bob and Betty Maxwell. 'My heart was torn apart,' Betty wrote later. But while she was prostrate with grief, Maxwell, she noticed, kept his feelings carefully stoppered up. 'Bob did not express his sadness openly; he seemed to contain it within himself.'

Fiercely resistant to any glimmer of introspection, Maxwell's response to misfortune was to immerse himself in activity. Over the next year he travelled so much that he became the British airline BOAC's first passenger to fly one million miles. Karine's death changed him in other ways too. Now there was an emotional distance to him too, Betty noticed. 'In the normal course of events, we barely saw each other at all.'

It's possible that Maxwell had other reasons for his emotional reserve. Not long before Karine fell ill, Betty had begun to suspect he was having an affair with his PA, Anne Dove. Just like Sir Charles Hambro, Dove had been in SOE during the war. Whether or not Hambro had a hand in her appointment, he was certainly happy about it: 'Charles told me that he was pleased I was with Maxwell looking after things,' Dove recalled.

When interviewed for the job, Dove had been greatly taken by Maxwell's 'tremendous life-force'. Since then, Betty realized that 'relations had certainly gone beyond those of employer and personal assistant – much to my dismay'. Meeting them both off a plane from Moscow, 'I sensed with the unerring instinct of a wife in love, that I had to fight back to oust an intruder from my patch.'

Betty decided to write her husband a letter in which she 'poured out all my pent-up sorrow at the way he had shattered my blind faith in him'. Maxwell's reply managed to combine contrition, self-pity and denial to a masterly degree: 'I have been suffering terribly and have tortured myself into a stupor because of the terrible pain and unhappiness that I have caused you. I do not say this because I want you to lavish any sympathy on me, but so as to show you how deeply sensitive and affected I am whenever anything seriously happens to cause you misery or harm . . . I swear I love you and only you. I have not betrayed you. I love you, believe me, please.'

At Betty's instigation, the two of them took another holiday – to the south of France. Their days soon fell into a pattern. In the evenings they would go to Monte Carlo, where Maxwell would play roulette. 'Although he did lose sometimes, on the whole he won enormous sums, and we would go back to the hotel around three in the morning, padded with wads of money. We would then order a light dinner accompanied by champagne and make love till we finally fell asleep until lunchtime, the next day!'

Just to make sure he shouldn't face any further temptation, Betty insisted that Anne Dove be moved. First, she went to live in New York, where she worked in Maxwell's office. However, New York appears not to have been far enough away for Betty's liking. A few months later Dove moved again 'for health reasons'.

This time she went to Tibet.

Throughout the 1950s, Maxwell's fortunes steadily rose. In 1955, the first international conference on atomic energy was held in Geneva. Maxwell rented a large villa on the shores of Lake Geneva to which he invited every scientist of note attending the conference. His knowledge of atomic energy may have been skimpy – according to one colleague he knew what a mushroom cloud looked like, but that was about it. However, he had a remarkable ability to make a little go a long way. He always made sure he learned the jargon; he was able to absorb information at a phenomenal rate and he gave every impression of knowing what he was talking about. What's more, Maxwell genuinely enjoyed the company of scientists. He respected them – they were the only people he regularly deferred to – and on the whole they respected him.

Perhaps most important of all, he had an unerring ability to home in on people's weakest points. According to another colleague, 'He was smart because he knew just what to offer to buy a person – fame or money.' Unused to being made a fuss of, still less lionized, the scientists eagerly rolled over before Maxwell's flattery. By the end of the conference he had signed up all the key players in the field. In future, their research would be published by Pergamon.

The next year, Maxwell was in Moscow interviewing leading Soviet scientists. The Russians thought sufficiently highly of him to allow him to talk to the scientists in the Vice-President's room at the Soviet Academy of Sciences. The year after – 1957 – he was back to attend the British Trade Fair, the only British publisher to do so. The same year the Russians launched Sputnik, the first satellite. Caught in a panic that their technology was lagging behind, the American State Department decided they needed to translate as many Russian scientific papers as they could lay their hands on. Maxwell landed the contract – worth around $10,000,000 over the next three years.

At home Betty moved, almost continually, from one pregnancy to another. 'Every time Bob looked at me I seemed to become pregnant,' she would say later. Her role in life, she had decided, was to keep her husband as contented as possible. If Maxwell was happy, she would be too – or so she hoped. But, as she increasingly came to see, this involved sacrificing her own ambitions as well as her own individuality.

On one of their trips to Moscow she found herself saying to the head of the Soviet Academy of Sciences, 'Academician Topchiev, I will let you into a secret: Bob gets up at six every day of his life, he works nonstop until nine at night, he travels for Pergamon, he eats

Pergamon, he drinks Pergamon, he makes love to Pergamon and the money just pours in! That is the truth.'

Betty had also begun to suspect that Maxwell might possess even more hidden sides than she'd realized. On the same trip, she was in their hotel room one morning with Babs Whipple, wife of the American astronomer Fred Whipple, when Maxwell burst in carrying a large parcel wrapped in brown paper. The parcel, he told them, contained lists of book titles that he'd obtained for publication in the West. He had to return the parcel before lunch – without fail – but before then he wondered if they could photograph the contents for him.

Fred Whipple lent them his 16mm movie camera and together Betty and Babbie Whipple began photographing the documents, one shot at a time. As they were doing so, Betty saw that they were not in Russian as Maxwell had claimed. Instead, they were in German, which she happened to have some knowledge of. Nor were they book titles, but lists of 'German firms whose equipment is to be dismantled and transported to the Soviet Union'.

'I remember feeling cold all over when I realized they were not lists of books,' Betty recalled. Clearly, Maxwell was still passing on information to his old masters at British Intelligence – some of which he must have picked up at the numerous Soviet conferences on atomic power that he attended during the 1950s.

Betty wasn't the only one frustrated by Maxwell's secrecy. In December 1958, Springer-Verlag decided to sever all contact with him. They'd become increasingly fed up with his lack of transparency, his fondness for keeping people in the dark. None the less, in late 1959 Maxwell was able to write to Sir Charles Hambro giving a breezily upbeat account of his circumstances: 'My various businesses are flourishing. I have paid all my debts and borrowings, including income tax, and our cash at the bank since the beginning of the year has fluctuated between £70,000 and £100,000. I feel sure you will be pleased to know that the business you helped me start is doing so well.'

A few months earlier, Maxwell and Betty had gone on another

business trip – to Poland. To begin with, he had been in good spirits, but the longer the trip went on, the darker his mood became. 'I tried, as sensitively as possible, to get inside the black hole of his mind, but he simply refused to let me in, resenting my every initiative in that direction. Everything to do with his past was still an open wound and the slightest intrusion caused him untold pain.'

Despite this, Maxwell insisted they went to Auschwitz. It turned out they were almost the only visitors. 'Endless grey clouds seemed to hang over the remaining wooden huts where prisoners were once herded, or over the vestiges of their foundations. It was as if the smoke from all those millions of calcinated corpses still hovered between heaven and earth, refusing to disappear lest the world forgot.

'We walked from one crematorium to another, then followed overgrown tracks leading to a marshy woodland pond. A dilapidated metal structure still stood there, above the level of the water. A rusty wheelbarrow had long since tipped its last cargo of ash into the murky depths. We kneeled beside the dull grey waters and Bob plunged his hands into the mire, pulling out handfuls of greyish mud full of calcified, pulverised bones. He took a white handkerchief from his pocket, carefully placed those macabre relics in it, then burst into tears. I could not say a word. Only silence was appropriate in the face of such anguish.'

Soon after their return, Maxwell decided the family should move into a new house – a house more befitting their new circumstances. Headington Hill Hall was an Italianate mansion set on top of a hill overlooking the eastern fringes of Oxford. But it had been unoccupied for the last fifteen years and was in state of advanced decay. In some rooms the ceilings had collapsed, in others the floors had gone. The house was owned by Oxford City Council, who had neither the funds nor the will to do it up. When Maxwell offered to pay for the repairs in return for being allowed to rent it, the council was so delighted they practically threw the keys at him.

Why didn't Maxwell buy a house of his own? Clearly, he could have afforded one, yet for the rest of his life he was happy to remain a tenant in what he always liked to describe as 'the best council house in the country'. Possibly it was because possessions never meant much to him. But maybe he instinctively shied away from putting down any permanent roots in case these too might be torn up.

In February 1960, while Maxwell was away, Betty moved into Headington Hill Hall's only habitable bedroom. Woken in the middle of the night by a mysterious creaking noise, she went to investigate, and found that it was coming from an ancient weather vane on the roof. On her way back to her bedroom, she had another shock. 'As I walked upstairs, something attracted my attention to a door on the landing . . . I distinctly saw the door handle move up and down. I stayed glued to the top of the stairs, scared out of my wits . . . I was absolutely certain I was alone in the Hall, and this time I knew for certain that I had a ghost for a companion.'

Although no one else ever saw the ghost, Betty remained convinced that Headington Hill Hall was haunted. Meanwhile Maxwell was fleeing his own demons in the only way he knew how: more work, more hobnobbing, more travelling . . . The first words his son Philip ever spoke were, 'Goodbye, Daddy.' But however hard Maxwell worked, or how far he travelled, tragedy was never far behind.

When she came to write her memoir, Betty was hardly able to describe what happened next. She prefaced it with a quote from Edgar Allan Poe's short story 'Manuscript Found in a Bottle': 'We are plunging madly within the grasp of the whirlpool – and amid a roaring and bellowing, and shrieking of ocean and of tempest, the ship is quivering – Oh God! – and going down.'

6.

Down on the Bottom

On 28 December 1961, three days after Betty Maxwell gave birth to their ninth child, a daughter, Ghislaine, her oldest son, Michael, then aged fifteen, was being driven back to Oxford from a party a few miles away in Thame. The car he was travelling in smashed into the back of an unlit lorry, full of onions, that had broken down by the side of the road.

Although the chauffeur, Samuel Swadling, was not badly hurt, Michael sustained serious head injuries. The next day, another of Maxwell's chauffeurs, Brian Moss, was sent to look at the car: 'It was a Rover three-litre, a big machine, and the roof was completely ripped off. I remember seeing that the driver's mirror had also been torn off and was lying on the floor behind the back seat.'

Betty, who had given birth in her sister's maternity clinic in France, rushed back to England. She found Michael in a coma. The prognosis was bleak. The doctors couldn't tell if Michael would ever emerge from his coma, and even if he did there was a strong possibility he would be brain-damaged. 'I cried so much then that I seemed to have exhausted the source of tears within me and have not been really able to cry since.' Meanwhile, Maxwell was 'shaken to the very core of his being; he could not believe that fate had dealt him such a cruel blow after all he had already endured'.

The effect on the rest of the Maxwell family was equally devastating. Philip, the second son, 'worshipped his brother, suffered deeply, and began a prolonged struggle to accept his loss'. It was to be a struggle from which he never fully recovered. His sister Anne, aged thirteen, 'lost her natural companion and a brother she adored. It would take her years to come to terms with her grief.'

The twins, Isabel and Christine, 'clung to each other and allowed no one to penetrate their world'. Ian – then five – filled notebooks with blood-spattered drawings and played endlessly with toy ambulances and model figures in white coats. Meanwhile Ghislaine, 'who should have been the centre of our love and attention, was hardly given a glance and became anorexic while still a toddler'.

To begin with, the family clung to what few shreds of hope there were. Betty spent every spare moment by Michael's bed. 'I would do anything to stay beside him. I did the work of a hospital orderly, talked to other patients and their parents. I saw people with horrific injuries, parents driven mad by their heart-rending sorrow.'

Then, at the beginning of December 1962, twelve months after the crash, they received a letter from the Consultant Neurosurgeon at the John Radcliffe Hospital: 'It is now five months since my last report on this boy in which I said I could see no prospect of any recovery from his state of total disability . . . I examined him again on the 29th of November . . . I should say at the outset that I could see no sign of significant improvement . . . this means that his condition has been static for approximately eight months now.

'He shows no appropriate emotional expression, no signs of recognition of what is going on around him, and he has made no attempt to talk . . . He does not blink in response to a loud noise beside him . . . My previous impression has been confirmed and I see no further prospect of any further improvement here. As I said in my last report, his expectation of life is enormously reduced as a result of this injury, but it is not possible to say how long he is likely to live in this state; it might well be for many more months yet.'

Christine Maxwell, then aged twelve, remembers going to see Michael in hospital. 'I went sometimes, but after a while I couldn't do it any more because it was so upsetting. It was just a nightmare because here was this person who was there, but not there. When you moved around the room, his eyes would follow you, and yet there was absolutely nothing there.'

Her twin sister, Isabel, found it just as upsetting. 'I only went to see him three times. I just couldn't do it any more – I was so traumatized. And then I felt guilty for a long, long time that I hadn't been. It was an absolute disaster. A disaster which tore the fabric of our family for ever.'

Betty continued to visit Michael every day. 'I took it upon myself to be Michael's only regular visitor, so that everyone else could return to a normal life, knowing that I was watching over him.' Later, she would tell Joe Haines that Maxwell never once went to see him, that he had effectively shut him out of his life. Yet this turns out not to have been the case. Brian Moss remembers how he would often drive Maxwell back to Headington Hill Hall from London. 'It would always be late at night, around midnight. We'd get near Oxford and he's say, "Are you in a hurry, Brian?"'

'When I told him I wasn't, he'd say, "We'll go to the hospital." This happened a number of times. We'd sit by Michael's bed and Maxwell would talk to him. Then, after a bit, he would say, "You try, Brian. You used to take him to school – he might recognize your voice." So I would try to talk to him, but there was never any response. Despite that, I know Maxwell always thought there was a chance Michael might come through. To begin with, he would talk about sending him to America for treatment. But after a while I think he must have realized that it was pointless. There was nothing anyone could do.'

Throughout it all, Maxwell never told Betty about these late-night visits. The only plausible explanation for this was that he found it too painful; he couldn't face her seeing him at his most vulnerable. As Betty had realized when she and Maxwell first began going out together, behind his brash exterior lay a vast lake of insecurities. 'He was incredibly sensitive . . . Bob's desperate need to be loved was so great that he tortured himself . . . At first he almost persecuted me to arouse my love, and when I reached the point of being in love with him, he simply would not believe it and carried on with his perpetual doubts.'

Perhaps Maxwell also found it easier to visit at night, when he would be less exposed, when there were fewer people around to witness his anguish. But it also offers a telling glimpse of how he and Betty were slowly drifting apart – each in their increasingly separate worlds.

At times, Maxwell would refer to Betty as 'Mummy', and expect her to provide the comfort and uncritical devotion his own mother had once given him. But at others he would plunge into extended sulks, blaming her for whatever problems he was going through at the time. However great Maxwell's desire to be loved may have been, somewhere inside him the suspicion seems to have taken root that his emotional ties to Betty – above all the neediness they prompted – risked distracting him from his chosen course. If left unchecked, they might destroy his dream.

It wasn't just Betty who was being pushed away; all emotional ties were kept to a minimum. Maxwell had no real confidants, only glorified acquaintances, and while he continued to see his two sisters, Brana and Sylvia, both of whom were now living in London, they were never particularly close.

There were other effects of Michael's accident too. While Maxwell didn't blame Samuel Swadling for what had happened – he kept him on the payroll for many years afterwards – his attitude towards his children changed. 'The most obvious thing was that we were effectively confined to barracks,' his son Ian remembers. 'He obviously had this horror of something happening to another of us. But then the whole tribe was in a state of shock. I think it must have been especially hard for my sister, Ghislaine, because she was basically ignored.'

This took such an extreme form that one day when she was just three years old, Ghislaine stood in front of her mother and said simply, 'Mummy, I exist.' In an attempt to compensate for the fact that she had been neglected, her parents began showering Ghislaine with attention. Pretty, coquettish and indulged, she soon became her father's clear favourite. Perhaps Maxwell saw something of his younger self in Ghislaine's wilfulness, her refusal to compromise and her apparently cast-iron belief in her own allure. The result of all this attention, as Betty noted ruefully, was all too predictable: 'She became spoiled, the only one of my children I can truly say that about.'

Isabel Maxwell remembers that for years after Michael's accident 'the whole family seemed to drift about in this grey fog. Every time we wanted to go anywhere, my father would ask, "Where are you going? How are you going? Do you have to go in a car?"' On one occasion, several of the children went out to the local cinema in Headington. Halfway through the film, a notice appeared on screen telling them to come home immediately.

However isolated an existence they may have led, as they grew older the Maxwell children began to realize they were different – or at least that people saw them as being different. When Isabel was eleven, she and Christine invited some children they'd met at school to come and play in the garden at Headington Hill Hall.

'At the end of the afternoon we said, "Thank you very much. We hope you had a nice time."

'The children said, "Yes, yes, but we're very disappointed."

'Christine and I looked at each other. "Oh dear, what happened?" we asked.

'"You're not wearing tiaras."

'We were completely nonplussed. At first we couldn't work out what they were talking about. Then we realized that must be how people thought we lived.'

At around the same time, a mother came to the house to pick up her daughter, who was playing with Christine. 'The doorbell rang and I opened the door. There was this woman and with her she had another daughter – a little girl of about six. What made the most impression on me was the expression on this little girl's face as she stared through the door. It was literally as if she was green with envy. I've never forgotten it.'

The little girl might have been less envious if she'd known what life inside Headington Hill Hall was like. Always a draconian father, Maxwell became an even harsher disciplinarian after Michael's crash – as if setting more rigid boundaries might minimize the danger of any other tragedies befalling them.

'He did have a very warm playful side to him,' Ian Maxwell recalls. 'Whenever he would go abroad he would bring us back wonderful presents. I remember when we were little, he would turn all the lights out, get down on all fours and pretend to be a wolf chasing us around. At the same time he was also a very emotionally remote, rather disapproving man. I always felt I had to court his approval. You could never do small talk with the old man. Either something was of consequence or it wasn't. On the whole my mother protected us from him; she shielded us from his displeasure or his disappointment. But I think all of us were scared of his anger – of the way he could turn at any moment.'

Mealtimes were a particular trial. As they sat around the dining room table, each child in turn would be assigned a topic and expected to talk on it for several minutes. At the end Maxwell would offer his verdict on their performance. 'We'd have to talk on things like "What are the most important things that have happened this year, and what are our predictions for next year on both the global and the personal level?" He always expected us to make speeches. If there was a birthday, everyone had to make a speech. If a professor came to lunch, the same thing would happen.'

As far as Isabel Maxwell was concerned, watching the direction of her father's gaze as it passed around the table was like following a lighthouse beam. 'I used to dread it stopping at me. Then he would ask some question and I'd go, stutter, stutter, stutter, and try to give him the answer I thought he needed. It would be terrifying. I remember once Ian brought a friend of his home from school and Dad asked him some question. The boy went, "Well, um . . ." And Dad says, "Um? That's mental laziness. Start again." The boy tried to speak, but he just couldn't. It was excruciating; he probably became a damaged person for the rest of his life.'

One thing that roused Maxwell to an even greater pitch of fury was any suggestion of slacking at school. 'We lived in mortal fear if we got a bad mark. Then he would say in front of everyone else, "What the hell happened to you? You're so obviously lazy and careless. Where did it all go wrong?" '

Nor were these the only consequences. 'Dad always beat us if we'd been lazy or inattentive,' remembers Ian. 'Or if we'd lied – that was another beating offence. He would beat us with a belt – girls as well as boys – and then afterwards you would have to write him a letter saying how you were going to be different in future.'

Constantly, Maxwell drove his children towards self-improvement. If they ever wanted an example to aspire to, he would hold up his mother as a beacon of industriousness, self-sacrifice and almost everything else. Before they sat exams, they were always given a mnemonic to commit to memory – WWHW. It stood for What? Why? How? Where? Armed with this formula, Maxwell believed, they would be able to answer any question they were set.

Like the self-made Jay Gatsby, the central character in F. Scott Fitzgerald's novel *The Great Gatsby*, he had a mania for compiling 'to do' lists. These, he insisted, would lend both structure and meaning to their lives. All of them – including Betty – had to pay special attention to what he referred to as 'The Three Cs': Consideration, Concentration, Conciseness. It made no difference that Maxwell's own powers of consideration were shaky in the extreme – as was his grasp of conciseness. Whenever he felt Betty was being long-winded, he would bellow, 'Next!' Later, she pointedly added a fourth C to the list: Courtesy.

Before Philip, then aged sixteen, went on a trip to the States, Maxwell wrote him what even by his standards was an unusually formal letter: 'You may find it helpful for me to set out the aim and purpose of your visit.' Five single-spaced, closely typed pages followed. Under the section headed 'Gaining Experience And Having A Good Time', they included the advice: 'You must plan meticulously your days and your entire programme. This is not only because good planning means good discipline but so that you can get the most out of the time available . . .'

This was followed by another section titled 'How To Make Friends Amongst Young And Old' – something that was best accomplished 'By being genuinely interested in people, their problems and experiences; by avoiding selfish and provocative acts and postures; by being considerate and helpful as well as being interested in one's conversation; by being clean and well turned out.'

But there was one subject that was scarcely ever discussed around the dinner table, or anywhere else. All the time Michael was lying unconscious in his hospital bed just half a mile away. 'Sometimes Philip would try to bring it up, but I think it was just too painful for my father to go there,' Ian remembers. 'He was haunted by it. Haunted that he couldn't do anything about it. Haunted that he couldn't bring his son back.'

Then, on 27 January 1968, almost exactly seven years after his car crash, Michael Maxwell died of meningitis. He was twenty-one. 'For seven long years I had sat at his bedside,' Betty wrote. 'Hoping and praying at first that he would recover consciousness, and then gradually accepting that his brain had been damaged beyond any reasonable recovery. I would sit there beside my sleeping prince, remembering the bright, exceptionally gifted and considerate child who had now grown into manhood without knowing it.'

As she sat by Michael's bed, Betty had often wondered whether any part of him still existed – and might continue to exist. 'Since Michael's brain was no longer with him or with us, where was it? In limbo? It was the greatest challenge yet to my faith and I had no one to help me.'

Michael's funeral was held at the local Anglican church, St Andrew's in Headington. Afterwards the family gathered in Maxwell's and Betty's bedroom at Headington Hill Hall. 'I think he wanted us all to share our memories of Michael,' Ian recalls. 'But he couldn't; he just burst into tears. We were all overcome, both by the funeral and by the sight of this big alpha male being so distressed. I'd never seen him like that before and it made a huge impression on me.'

Somewhere in the back of Maxwell's mind must have been the thought that history was repeating itself in the cruellest possible way. He had set out to re-create the family he had lost by having nine children, just as his parents had done. Two of his siblings had died in childhood, leaving him with six brothers and sisters. Now the Maxwells were also left with seven children.

Betty organized both Michael's funeral and the erection of his gravestone in the churchyard, on which she had inscribed his name and dates, and, in a veiled reference to Maxwell's Judaism, a quote from St John's Gospel: 'In my father's house are many mansions.'

7.

The Man Who Gets Things Done

One evening, shortly before he left their house in Esher to move into Headington Hill Hall, Maxwell went to supper with their neighbours, a family called Davie. Their son, Jonathan, then a boy, remembers how his father and Maxwell used to play tennis together, something they continued to do despite his father being convinced that Maxwell cheated on a regular basis.

'After we'd finished eating, Bob stood in front of the fireplace with a glass of wine in one hand and a cigar in the other. He had an important announcement to make, he told us.'

The Davies waited expectantly.

Maxwell turned to Jonathan's father. And then, in the same solemn tones as before, he said, 'Dick, I want you to be the first person to know that I've decided to become Prime Minister.'

On 3 November 1964, Robert Maxwell, the newly elected Labour Member of Parliament for Buckingham, stood up to make his maiden speech in the House of Commons. Like all venerable institutions, the Commons has its own particular way of doing things. Traditionally, newly elected MPs are expected to wait several weeks, even months, before making their maiden speech. They are also advised to keep it short and stick to a single subject.

This, however, was not one of those occasions. To general astonishment, Maxwell gave his maiden speech on the first day of the new parliament – something that had never been done before. 'It is with a great sense of humility that I rise to speak here for the first time,' he began. But humility didn't stop him from talking at length on a wide variety of topics, including working conditions in the brick industry – very poor – and provisions for sewage disposal in his constituency – even worse.

A month later, the Prime Minister, Harold Wilson, was due to give an important speech on foreign policy in which he planned to announce that the new Soviet Premier, Alexei Kosygin, would be visiting the UK early in the new year. Before Wilson had a chance to speak, Maxwell once again rose to his feet. MPs from both sides of the House shouted at him to shut up. Maxwell ignored them. He spent the next nineteen minutes giving an exhaustive analysis of the shortcomings of the Foreign Office: 'I am extremely disturbed that it is not implementing speedily or energetically enough, recommendations relating to the need for our diplomats to do a great deal more to promote British exports,' he declared.

In a desperate attempt to make Maxwell sit down, his fellow Labour MPs began tugging at his jacket, but to no avail. Meanwhile, Wilson sat there glowering. By the time Maxwell wound up, it was too late for either of the London evening papers to carry details of the Prime Minister's speech. That evening Richard Crossman, Labour's Minister of Housing and Local Government, described what had happened in his diary: 'It was absolutely disastrous,' he began.

Maxwell would always claim that he became a Labour MP purely through conviction, that the combination of his mother's influence and his loathing for the British Establishment made him a natural socialist. When he was interviewed by the selection committee of the Buckingham Labour Party, he told them, 'I come from a very humble farm-labouring family and would rather cut off my arm than betray my class.'

But once again there was rather more to it than that. After the Davie family had recovered from their shock at being told that Maxwell intended becoming Prime Minister, Jonathan's father, Dick, asked him a question. 'My father said, "I'm very flattered to be the first person to know that, Bob, but do you mind my asking which party you are going to be supporting?"

'Bob said, "Well, of course I'm Conservative, but I'm not a member of the Establishment, so I've got to become Labour."'

In the 1959 General Election, 'Captain Robert Maxwell' as he was called on the ballot paper – unlike other enlisted soldiers he'd clung doggedly on to his wartime rank – was narrowly beaten by the Conservative candidate, Sir Frank Markham. Throughout the campaign, Markham never missed an opportunity to remind people about Maxwell's origins, telling them the Labour Party hadn't been able to find a candidate in the whole country, let alone Buckingham: 'They had to go all the way to Czechoslovakia!' After conceding defeat, Maxwell refused to shake Markham's hand. Instead, he loosed off a final message to his supporters: 'Long live socialism and victory!'

Five years later, in October 1964, he tried again. This time he dropped the 'Captain' in case it smacked of elitism. There were other changes too. Normally he was driven around in a maroon Rolls-Royce by his chauffeur, Brian Moss. But after giving the matter some thought, Maxwell decided this too sent out the wrong message; perhaps a less flashy form of transport might be more fitting.

'I used to drive him down in the Rolls from London,' Moss recalls. 'And then another driver would meet us on the Buckinghamshire border in an old Rover.'

Midway though the campaign, Maxwell swopped the Rover for an equally ancient Land Rover. In a largely rural constituency this seemed sure to boost his man-of-the-people credentials – even if Maxwell's Land Rover had been fitted out with a desk and specially cushioned seats, as well as a shag-pile carpet. Occasionally, he would drive himself, but this brought hazards of its own. Just before election day, Maxwell was arrested by the police after another driver – a man called Edward Cole – spotted his Rolls-Royce weaving back and forth across the road.

At the time, Maxwell was on his way to Buckinghamshire, where his Land Rover and chauffeur were waiting at the county line. 'He swerved and then bent over to his left,' testified Cole when the case came to court. 'For a few seconds I didn't see him at all, then he got up again and put his left hand to his face.' In his hand was what appeared to be a small black box.

'Maxwell,' Cole told the magistrate in an appalled voice, 'had been shaving while he was driving.' At the time he was estimated to have been travelling at around 90 mph.

However, it wasn't so much Maxwell's car, or his driving habits, that concerned people so much as his background. Whenever he gave a speech, hecklers would bellow out the same old refrain: 'You're a bloody foreigner!' Maxwell's reply never varied either: 'If I am a foreigner, so is the Duke of Edinburgh,' he told them. 'He too was born abroad, but from what I can tell he seems to be quite popular.' Then, in a voice tremulous with indignation, would come the knockout blow: 'I chose this country. *Did you?*'

By the time Maxwell been found guilty of dangerous driving and fined £25, he had become the new MP for Buckingham – winning the seat by a margin of 1481 votes, a swing of 3.3 per cent. Among the first to offer their congratulations when he arrived at the House of Commons was the *Jewish Chronicle*. They called to let him know how delighted they were to have another Jewish MP.

'I'm not Jewish,' Maxwell told them, and put the phone down.

As he soon proved, his maiden speech was just the beginning; there was a lot more where that had come from. All this was too much for the Conservative MP Edward Du Cann. Infuriated by the new MP's bombast, he complained, 'I have never heard anybody make so many speeches as he has in the last two days.'

Nor was Du Cann the only one feeling the strain. Trying to find an explanation for Maxwell's behaviour, Richard Crossman put it down to the thickness of his skin. 'I don't suppose there's anybody who is less aware of the impression he creates,' he wrote, 'and it's no good trying to warn him. He wants to shine.' Perhaps the sharpest observation of all came from a member of the Buckingham Labour Party: 'What you have to understand is that Captain Maxwell needs to be needed.'

Having become an MP, Maxwell had reclaimed his rank: from

now on, he would always be 'Captain Maxwell MC'. Yet it would take more than a Military Cross to save Maxwell from ridicule. 'Who is the biggest gasbag in the Commons?' asked the *Sunday Express*'s 'Crossbencher' columnist. 'Who else but handsome, debonair, 41-year-old publisher Robert Maxwell. Seldom a speech is made by anyone else without Captain Maxwell popping in to interrupt. After only four weeks in Parliament already he is becoming one of its biggest bores.'

But still: Maxwell ploughed on, heedless of convention, politesse or people tugging at his jacket. Over 700 years Parliament had witnessed blowhards of every persuasion, yet no one quite like him had ever been seen, or heard, before. As Harold Wilson sat waiting for a chance to deliver a speech of his own, he whiled away the time by keeping a tally of how often Maxwell stood up to speak. In the course of less than ten months, it came to more than 200.

Others, though, were very taken with the new arrival. The Conservative MP Sir Gerald Nabarro, an exuberantly mustachioed hanger-and-flogger, thought Maxwell set an admirable example. What impressed him most of all was the size of his family. Writing in his *News of the World* column, Nabarro prophesied that Edward Heath, recently elected leader of the Conservative Party, would be the first unmarried occupant of 10 Downing Street since Arthur Balfour sixty years earlier.

While Heath's sexual orientation has long been a source of speculation, few bachelors have ever been quite as confirmed as he was. None the less, Nabarro was hopeful that even now he might find a suitable match: 'Personally, to make the man and image complete, I would like him to carry a beautiful bride over the threshold to share his occupancy with him. Many well-known politicians are notably philoprogenitive. For example Mr Robert Maxwell (Labour Buckingham) has four sons and four daughters. Of course, any connection between the size of family and party political activities is entirely circumstantial. But no politician is complete without vigorous progeny and a happy home life.'

Helped by Betty, Maxwell proved to be a hard-working and

conscientious MP. In the 1966 General Election, he was re-elected with an increased majority – his election slogan was 'The Man Who Gets Things Done'. Taking him at his word, his fellow MPs decided to hand him a notoriously poisoned chalice.

Shortly after the General Election, Maxwell was appointed chairman of the House of Commons Catering Committee. At the time the catering arrangements in the House of Commons were a shambles. Whatever their political leanings, MPs all felt able to agree on one thing: the food was disgusting. There was also remarkably little of it. As much as a third of the catering supplies, it was estimated, were being stolen by the staff.

But while employees were occasionally caught trying to leave the Palace of Westminster with joints of beef, even legs of lamb, hidden under their coats, the vast majority of thefts went unnoticed. Despite being heavily subsidized by the Treasury, the 'Refreshment Department', as it was known, had lost £33,000 in the previous tax year – more than £400,000 in today's money. It also had a £61,000 overdraft. 'No one was exactly queuing for the job,' Richard Marsh, the Minister of Power, admitted.

Maxwell, however, leaped at the offer. Immediately after being appointed, he announced that the department would make a £20,000 profit in 1968. As soon as they heard this, MPs gleefully predicted his downfall. But within weeks Maxwell had sacked large numbers of staff, slashed the number of items on the menu and banished tablecloths as a pointless expense. More drastically still, he proposed introducing vending machines into the most historic building in England.

Shell-shocked MPs struggled to adjust to this blizzard of changes. No one was more incensed than Sir William van Straubenzee, a rotund, red-faced man with tufted sideburns who represented the impregnably safe Conservative seat of Wokingham. He was so annoyed that he took the unusual step of raising the subject during a Commons debate:

Van Straubenzee: 'Why have avocado pears disappeared from the menu?'

Maxwell: 'Avocado pears have been available at the buffet in the Members' Dining Room for the last three weeks.'

Van Straubenzee: 'What about cold lamb cutlets?'

Maxwell: 'Cold lamb cutlets can be provided if the kitchens are given twenty-four hours' notice.'

But van Straubenzee hadn't finished yet; there was something else he was even more incensed about: 'Why is *oeuf en gelée* not available in the Members' Dining Room?' he demanded.

Patiently, Maxwell explained that it was no longer practical. 'The average daily consumption of *oeufs en gelée* during the summer was approximately twelve a day,' he said, most of which, he suspected privately, had been eaten by van Straubenzee himself.

Others found the upheavals almost as unsettling. In his diary, Richard Crossman described how that afternoon he'd gone to buy a cup of tea in the tea room. Instead of his usual little jug of milk, he had been handed a paper sachet. 'I discovered that instructions have been given by the fellow who runs the Catering Department to serve powdered milk in tea. We'd already had foreign cheese forbidden in our own restaurant, but powdered milk was going a long way. I asked Bob [Maxwell] how he could allow this to happen and he explained, "I've given a chap a commission of £200 a year for any savings he got, and he made a saving of £100 a week on powdered milk." "Well, you can't make that saving," I said. "Off with it this afternoon", and I'm glad to say it went.'

Despite his misgivings, Crossman found his attitude slowly changing. 'What a miraculous man that fellow is,' he wrote of Maxwell. 'However much people hate him, laugh at him, boo him and call him a vulgarian, he really does get things done.' In his diary entry for Tuesday, 12 December 1967, Crossman confined himself to a single sentence: 'The Catering Sub-Committee under Bob Maxwell is making a profit.'

Against all the odds, Maxwell had triumphed. Even so, this was hardly what he had in mind when he became an MP. More than ever, he yearned to make an impact. To be noticed. The opportunity finally came when five female typists in Surbiton, trying to do their bit for the economy, decided to work an extra half-hour a day for no money. Harold Wilson was so impressed that he invited the women to lunch at the Commons. This was the beginning of what became known as the 'I'm Backing Britain' campaign.

As soon as he heard about it, Maxwell decided to start something similar: a 'Buy British' campaign. Although various bigwigs were roped in to lend their support, the campaign quickly ran into trouble. There were accusations that it was jingoistic and would jeopardize Britain's plans to join the European Common Market. It didn't help that the 'Buy British' T-shirts turned out to have been made in Portugal.

On 7 February 1968, Maxwell arranged for full-page announcements to appear in *The Times* and the *Daily Telegraph* headed '100 Uncranky Suggestions of Ways to Help Your Country – and Yourself'. Far from being uncranky, several of these suggestions struck people as actively deranged, especially one calling on children to give up their free school milk.

Two days later an editorial in the *Telegraph* offered its own suggestion: 'Mr Maxwell's campaign should be laughed into the oblivion it deserves before it does real harm.' The *Observer* was even harsher, writing, 'The mysterious Captain Robert Maxwell has at last achieved his ambition . . . with his totally misguided campaign and his string of TV appearances. Looking like an impossibly successful stall holder in Petticoat Lane, he has contrived to emerge as a National Figure.'

Within a few days, 'Backing Britain' was quietly dropped. At the same time, people began to wonder if Maxwell really had pulled off such a miracle with the Refreshment Department. An article in the *Sunday Times* claimed that it wasn't just food that had been cooked in the Palace of Westminster's kitchens – so had the books. Apparently Maxwell had used an unusual and possibly unique form of bookkeeping. As well as including the Treasury subsidy within the profits, he had omitted to mention several significant expenditures. When the accounts were submitted to the Exchequer, the £20,000 profit was revised downwards – to just £1,787. After they had been audited, this figure was revised again – to a £3,400 loss.

Furious that his business methods had been questioned, Maxwell threatened to sue the paper and complained to Parliament's Committee of Privileges – the body which investigates allegations of misconduct against MPs. The Editor of the *Sunday Times*, Harold Evans, was summoned to appear before the Committee to repeat the paper's claims.

'When I came out of the Committee of Privileges, Maxwell was sitting on a bench waiting,' Evans remembers. 'I expected him to start shouting at me, but instead he couldn't have been more jolly. He even said, "Well done!" as if I'd just done something he approved of. It was very strange.'

Harold Evans wouldn't be the only one to be wrong-footed by Maxwell's unpredictability. 'He seemed to have two modes: either he would thump the table and bellow at you, or else he would turn seductive and pretend to be your friend. As I think he intended it to be, this was extremely disconcerting. You never knew which Maxwell you were going to get. But it also left me wondering what lay behind all that bustling belligerence.'

When the Committee of Privileges delivered their verdict, they sat squarely on the fence: the *Sunday Times* article, they decided, was not unfair to Maxwell, nor did it prove he had been guilty of any misconduct. This was a long way from being a full exoneration, but as far as Maxwell was concerned it left him without a stain on his character. 'I note that this senior committee of the House of Commons has unanimously decided that my conduct was entirely proper,' he told *The Times*. At the same time he decided not to pursue his lawsuit.

None the less, questions about Maxwell's conduct rumbled on. It wasn't just the way he had blatantly massaged the figures and assumed he could get away with it. There was also his sensitivity to criticism – unexpected in someone with such a thick hide. Then there were the rumours about the wine cellar. According to House of Commons gossip, Maxwell had secretly balanced the Refreshment

Department books by selling off much of the Palace of Westminster's wine cellar – reputed to be one of the best in Europe – to an anonymous buyer for a fraction of its market value.

As the buyer was never identified, the mystery remained unsolved. Within months, it had slipped everyone's minds. But, in years to come, few guests who dined at Headington Hill Hall went away without remarking on the outstandingly good wines that had been served with their meal.

8.

Roast Beef and Yorkshire Pudding

One morning in early 1963, Rupert Murdoch was sitting in his office in Sydney when the telephone rang. 'I got this strange phone call from an investment banker I knew,' Murdoch recalls. 'He said, "I'm calling from Sydney airport. I'm here with Captain Robert Maxwell and he would love to see you." '

The name meant nothing to Murdoch, so he looked him up and found that he was a Labour MP, as well as the Chairman of Pergamon Press. 'Maxwell arrived and started telling me about his business. He'd just bought some little book company in Australia that was marketing encyclopedias. He said, "I've really got to get a partner." ' It soon became clear that Maxwell had grand ideas about his new venture. 'At one point I asked him, "Are we talking about South East Asia as well as Australia?" He said, "Oh yes, we'll do that too." '

Unbeknownst to Murdoch, Maxwell had just been in India, where he had attracted the attention of the Commonwealth Relations Office. They subsequently wrote a letter to the Director of British Information Services in New Delhi: 'Thank you very much for keeping us in the picture about the activities of Maxwell of the Pergamon Press during his visit to India . . . There is little we can do about him, except to drop the odd word of warning in places where our confidence is respected. He is a very enterprising fellow. It is a pity that the quality of his publications is so poor.'

Intrigued by Maxwell's proposition, Murdoch invited him to dinner that night. By his own admission Murdoch was 'a bit spellbound' by Maxwell – so much so that he agreed to take his encyclopedias for a million Australian dollars. In return, the two of them would become equal partners in Pergamon Australia. At the end of the evening, Murdoch told him, 'I'll come to London to see you and we can work it out.'

A couple of months later – before he'd had a chance to go to London – Murdoch met up with an old friend of his who had worked on the *Adelaide News* and was now the head of advertising at IPC. Over lunch Murdoch told him about this great deal he had done with Maxwell to sell his encyclopedias. His friend's reaction was not what he had been expecting. 'Immediately, he started laughing and said whatever you do, don't touch that.'

It turned out that IPC had originally owned the encyclopedias. Having tried and failed to sell them, they had decided they were worthless and had offloaded them – for free – on to Maxwell. 'He was trying to con me. I must say I thought it was quite funny, but the man was obviously a crook. The next time I saw him I said, "Look, I don't think we were made to be partners, so let's forget it." Maxwell said OK and that was that.'

As far as Murdoch was concerned, he never expected to see Maxwell again, still less have anything more to do with him. But here he turned out to be wrong. This wasn't the end of their acquaintance; it was only the start.

Five years later, in October 1968, Professor Derek Jackson, about to embark on his sixth marriage at the age of sixty-two and running a little short of cash, decided to sell his 25 per cent stake in the *News of the World*. While Jackson was hopeful that his latest marriage might last longer than its predecessors, his friends were not so optimistic: his track record did not inspire confidence. On the same day that his third wife gave birth to his only child, Jackson had abandoned her in the maternity ward and run off with her half-sister.

A keen amateur jockey, Jackson was bisexual: among his many male lovers was the artist Francis Bacon. 'I ride under both rules,' he declared proudly. Jackson had had a distinguished war. As an expert on spectroscopy – the study of the absorption and emission of light – he'd been instrumental in developing the strips of tinfoil known as 'chaff' that were dropped over Germany to cripple their radar.

Despite this, he had a love of everything German – and an equally broad streak of anti-Semitism. Whenever he met Oswald Mosley, whom he idolized, he would greet him by giving him a peck on the cheek and a pinch on the bottom.

Jackson had inherited his stake in the *News of the World* from his father, Sir Charles Jackson, who combined running the paper with building up one of the world's largest collections of silver spoons. When Sir Charles took over the *News of the World* in 1902, the circulation was 40,000. By 1948, it had gone up to 4.4 million.

After the war, Derek Jackson became a tax exile in Ireland. Soon after his arrival, the Irish government decided the *News of the World*'s obsession with sexually rapacious vicars represented such a threat to the moral fabric of the country that they banned it. Every week, Jackson's copy would arrive at his house in a plain brown envelope.

But this didn't stop him from keeping a keen eye on the paper's fortunes, or the state of his shares. He was, he anticipated, in for a big payday as soon as the sale went through – so big that Jackson would be able to keep his new wife, and any subsequent ones, in the style to which he had become accustomed.

Jackson's decision to sell his shares prompted panic in the *News of the World* boardroom. No one was more shocked than his cousin, Sir William Carr. Popularly known as 'Pissing Billy' on account of his alcohol intake – reckoned to be Herculean even by Fleet Street standards – Sir William had taken over from Derek Jackson's father as Chairman of the paper. Anyone wanting a meeting with him was strongly advised to arrange it before noon; afterwards, he tended to be incoherent.

Not surprisingly, the *News of the World*'s fortunes had slumped under Carr's chairmanship. Even so, it was still a hugely profitable concern. In October 1968, the paper's shares were valued at 28 shillings each. As by far the largest-selling Sunday newspaper in the country, it also wielded enormous influence.

Jackson gave Sir William first refusal on his shares, but Carr's offer was only a fraction above the market value, so he decided to sell to the highest bidder – thus precipitating a takeover battle. This was the moment Maxwell had been waiting for, the moment when he would finally move from the wings on to centre stage. Having secured Derek Jackson's pledge to sell him his 25 per cent stake, his opening bid for the paper was £26,000,000 – 37 shillings and 6 pence a share. But while Maxwell may have been hell-bent on buying the *News of the World*, Betty was a lot less keen: 'I had heard it was a scandal sheet with nude pictures and I like serious reading,' she told a journalist. 'Personally, it is not a newspaper I would like in the house with young children and young girls.'

The news of Maxwell's bid was relayed to Sir William, who was laid up in bed with flu. Immediately he called for an extra-strong drink and issued a statement. The bid, he said starkly, was 'impudent'. The Editor of the *News of the World*, Stafford Somerfield, was equally appalled. Described as 'bow-tied in manner and with a big round face', Somerfield had a reputation for pursuing 'salacious puritanism with missionary zeal'.

By an odd coincidence, he too had been in bed when he heard the news, being treated for high blood pressure in a nursing home. The nurse had told him it was imperative he should remain lying down, or he was at grave risk of having a heart attack. Idly, Somerfield glanced at a copy of the *Evening Standard* she had just given him to read.

'That did it,' he recalled.'

Immediately, Somerfield jumped out of bed and began to get dressed. 'Why are you putting your trousers on?' the nurse demanded. 'Something I've just remembered,' he told her. Within twenty minutes, Somerfield was back in his office. There, he wrote an editorial for Sunday's paper: 'We are having a little local difficulty at the *News of the World*,' he began. 'It concerns the ownership of the paper. Mr Robert Maxwell, a Socialist MP, is trying to take it over . . . I think it would not be a good thing for Mr Maxwell, formerly Jan Ludwig Hoch, to gain control of this newspaper which I know has your respect, loyalty and affection – a newspaper which I know is as British as roast beef and Yorkshire pudding.'

Somerfield went on in similar vein for some time before frothing up to a rousing finale: 'This is a British newspaper, run by British people. Let's keep it that way.'

The editorial caused a storm. The *Times* wrote that, judging by the contents of the *News of the World*, 'indecent assault, incest, buggery and the disarrangement of young ladies' underclothing in darkened railway carriages' were a lot closer to Somerfield's heart than roast beef and Yorkshire pudding. As far as the Liberal MP David Steel was concerned, the editorial was 'a revolting piece of chauvinism. Mr Maxwell is not everybody's cup of tea, but he is as disgustingly British as anyone I know. He even has a Rolls-Royce with a telephone in it.'

Amid all the excitement, the paper's share price soared to 48 shillings and 6 pence. On 22 October, Maxwell increased his bid to £34,000,000: 50 shillings a share. Privately, Somerfield conceded that things were looking bleak. Then, two days later, his telephone rang at midnight as he was about to go to bed. It was a friend of his on the night desk of the *Daily Express* who had just heard some news he thought would interest him. Suspecting he might be overheard by his colleagues, the man chose not to be too specific, or to mention any names.

He said simply, 'Your saviour is here.'

Every October, as he had done since he was a teenager, Rupert Murdoch flew from Sydney to Melbourne for the Caulfield Cup – one of the biggest events in the Australian flat-racing calendar. But this year it was a race he would never see. 'I was in bed in a hotel in Melbourne at about seven o'clock in the morning when the phone rang.' This time the caller was Lord Catto, Chairman of the merchant bankers Morgan Grenfell. Catto told a bleary-eyed Murdoch that he'd just had a meeting with representatives of the Carr family. Two weeks earlier, when Murdoch had heard of Maxwell's bid for the *News of the World*, he had been politely rebuffed. But now everything had changed. 'Apparently Carr's representatives had told him, "You better get your young man over here fast."'

Murdoch was galvanized. 'My first thought was "Oh God!" My second thought was that I'd better catch the first plane to London. So I called my wife in Sydney and said get to the airport with a bunch of clothes and my passport.' While he flew to Sydney to pick up his belongings, Murdoch's office persuaded Lufthansa to delay their London flight until he arrived.

Four hours after he'd first heard the news, Murdoch ran across the tarmac at Sydney airport clutching an overnight bag. Just like Maxwell, this was the moment he had been waiting for. Murdoch's father, Sir Keith, had been the most successful newspaper executive in Australia. But when he died in 1952 most of his assets disappeared in death duties. All that was left was a small afternoon tabloid in Adelaide – the *News*.

Rupert Murdoch turned the *News* into a huge success and used it as the cornerstone of what soon became a sizeable newspaper empire. But he was still virtually unknown outside Australia. Now aged thirty-seven, Murdoch too dreamed of owning a British paper, of setting up base camp in Fleet Street. The problem was that Maxwell's offer of £34,000,000 was way out of his league.

Despite this, Clive Carr – Sir William's nephew – thought Murdoch should meet his uncle as soon as possible. A meeting was arranged for the following morning. Having heard about Sir William's habits – 'I knew he was a big drinker and a big gambler' – Murdoch realized he needed to act before the Stock Exchange opened at ten. He suggested breakfast at eight. Reluctantly, Sir William agreed to eight-thirty.

When Murdoch arrived at Carr's flat in Belgravia, he found a large reception committee ready to greet him, including representatives from Carr's bank, Hambros – Maxwell's champion, Sir Charles Hambro, had died five years earlier. Unused to getting up so early, Sir William's mood was not improved by the scrambled eggs his housekeeper had served him for breakfast. 'She must have put milk in them,' he told Stafford Somerfield, 'They were awful.'

'Old man Carr was very patronizing,' Murdoch recalls. 'There was a lot of "I love Australians", and all the rest of it. He told me that Maxwell had put in an offer of fifty shillings a share and asked what I was going to do about it.

'I said, "Well, I'm prepared to put in some assets and buy some shares, and in return I'll get thirty per cent of the company."'

Ripples of disbelief ran round the table. But that wasn't all: Murdoch had one more condition. 'I told them, "I've got to be Chief Executive."'

Carr was flabbergasted. 'Immediately he said, "Oh, that's not possible." Then he gave me some more patronizing stuff about if you come here, I can see you'll do very well, young man. I've known so many nice Australians . . . '" Deciding that he'd heard enough, Murdoch thanked Carr for breakfast and said he was heading straight back to Australia with no hard feelings.

'Maxwell's an evil man, you know,' Carr told him.

'Well, I'm not an evil man,' Murdoch said. 'I'm here to help you if you want, but I don't like to waste your time on dither.'

Standing up, he headed for the door.

'I was about to go when this senior guy from Hambros Bank said, "No, no, Rupert. Could you just go into this room for a moment?"'

Murdoch sat and waited. By the time he was asked to come back, Carr had caved in and agreed to almost all of his demands. Three days later, Murdoch quietly bought up 3.5 per cent of the *News of the World* shares. Maxwell had been openly scornful when he heard that Murdoch was interested in the *News of the World*; if this was his only rival, plainly he had nothing to be worried about. At this stage the Carr family had 25 per cent of the shares, Maxwell 25 per cent and Murdoch a mere 3.5 per cent.

But on 24 October 1968, Maxwell had a rude shock. Murdoch called a press conference, where he announced that he planned to increase his own stock holding to 9 per cent and secure another 30 per cent of *News of the World* shares in return for a diverse array of his Australian titles.

Battle had been joined. For once in his life, Maxwell was lost for words. It seemed that the Carrs were so desperate to stop him that they were prepared to sell to someone who currently owned just 3.5 per cent of their shares. To make matters even worse, Murdoch was also a foreigner, an outsider. But Murdoch had already realized something that was only just starting to dawn on his rival. However suspicious the City of London were of him, this was nothing compared to their attitude to Maxwell:

'I could *smell* that the Establishment would not let him in.'

And while Murdoch may have been Australian, he was at least 'a quiet Australian', as the *Times* noted approvingly. Over the next few weeks Maxwell did everything he could think of to discredit Murdoch, paying people in Australia to dig up any dirt they could find. He even tried – unsuccessfully – to buy the Adelaide *News*.

For his part, Murdoch retaliated by recalling how Maxwell had tried to rip him off over the encyclopedias deal. Maxwell promptly sued for libel. And so it went on. Amid what was now open warfare, the Carrs began to wobble. Like them, Stafford Somerfield was equally unimpressed by Murdoch's raw colonial ways, writing in his diary, 'His Australian accent was ghastly.'

Fortunes swung one way, then the other. An Extraordinary General Meeting was arranged for 2 January 1969 at which shareholders would decide which of the two offers to accept. By now the Carrs and Murdoch together had 40 per cent of the shares, Maxwell had 25 per cent, while around 30 per cent of the shareholders had yet to make up their minds which way to go.

At this point, Maxwell scored a significant victory: he demanded that any shares acquired since the takeover battle began should be excluded from voting. To Murdoch's fury, the Takeover Panel, which oversaw important takeovers and mergers, agreed with him. What had started to look like a foregone conclusion had now become too tight to call.

In the meantime, Murdoch had gone back to Australia to be with his wife, Anna, and their baby daughter, Elisabeth. In December, the Murdochs returned and were photographed arriving at Heathrow with Elisabeth in a basket. Despite himself, Stafford Somerfield was impressed: 'Here comes Murdoch, back from Australia, smiling and fatter; beautiful blond wife on one arm and baby on the other. The boy doesn't miss a trick. Everyone will fall for the baby.'

Even so, Murdoch was not feeling optimistic: 'The financial press had come out 100 per cent for Maxwell – including friends of mine from college who were now working as financial journalists.'

At 10.30 on the morning of 2 January 1969, Maxwell's Rolls-Royce pulled up outside the Connaught Rooms in Covent Garden. He was dressed in an electric-blue suit and an astrakhan hat, and reported to be looking 'swarthy and grim'. Shortly before, the Carrs had arrived in their Rolls Royce, accompanied by a fleet of cars containing 'a large number of women in fur coats'.

By the time Maxwell made his entrance, the hall was already packed with more than 500 people. As well as the women in fur coats, there was a sizeable contingent of what were described as 'small men in mackintoshes' – traditional *News of the World* readers who had come to show their support for Carr. Later it would emerge that many of these men in mackintoshes were in fact *News of the World* employees who had been lent single shares for the day so they could vote for him. All of them had had to sign contracts promising to return their share certificates as soon as the vote was over.

This was Anna Murdoch's first sight of Maxwell. Twenty years later she wrote a novel, *Family Business*, which included a lightly fictionalized version of the *News of the World* takeover battle. Maxwell appeared as 'Socialist millionaire Piers Molinski', and was referred to simply as a 'dreadful man'.

Looking thinner and more sickly than ever, Sir William Carr spoke first. He was greeted with a lengthy burst of applause – timed by Stafford Somerfield at forty-eight seconds: 'Hundreds of pink, upturned faces gazed at him through the haze of tobacco smoke.'

His voice seldom rising above a whisper, Carr began by striking an unexpectedly philosophical note for a shareholders' meeting: 'What is money when you can get so much more out of life?' he wondered. Taking frequent sips of water and peering at prompt cards that were held up to jog his memory, he went on to say that

'Mr Murdoch has enjoyed great success in Australia and he will bring new blood and energy to our organizations.'

Murdoch spoke next. As he watched, Stafford Somerfield found that his feelings were even more mixed than before: 'He rises from the centre of the hall in the front row. His dark clothes, tie and white shirt are discreet. He has an engaging smile. He looks fresh – boyish almost.' But not everything had changed: 'Once again I think how excruciating his Australian accent is.'

Then it was Maxwell's turn. Before he could begin, a member of the audience shouted out, 'What is your name and what are your qualifications to speak?'

Maxwell rode this easily enough. 'My name is Robert Maxwell and I represent twenty-five per cent of the shares,' he said.

But he'd hardly finished speaking when boos started to ring out – boos that appeared to come both from the women in fur coats and the men in mackintoshes. Maxwell ignored them. He tried to carry on, but still the boos rang out. Even Murdoch was surprised. 'Every time Maxwell tried to say anything everyone started booing; it was a pantomime.'

'May I make a statement in reply to your opening remarks?' Maxwell asked Sir William in a brief lull between boos.

'Yes,' Carr told him, 'but you must not speak for longer than Mr Murdoch. That was three minutes and ten seconds.' The boos turned to laughter. Standing on the dais in his electric-blue suit, Maxwell appeared stunned. Whatever he had been expecting, it was not this.

Pointing a finger at Carr, he said, 'Are you going to give me a fair hearing, or not?'

'Just get on with it,' Sir William told him in a much firmer voice than before.

What nobody there knew was that two weeks earlier Maxwell and Carr had had a secret meeting to try to find some common ground. This too had not gone well. At the meeting Carr had asked Maxwell if he would be able to stay on at the *News of the World* – as Chairman – if his bid was successful.

No, said Maxwell.

Why not, Carr wanted to know.

It was often said of Maxwell that whenever he saw a belt, he could not resist hitting below it. On this occasion, he had swung especially hard. 'Because every time I have a haircut in the Savoy at four o'clock in the afternoon, I see you and your cronies still drinking Martinis,' he told Sir William, 'and I don't think that is suitable training for any Chairman of mine.'

Now as Maxwell struggled to make himself heard above the boos and catcalls, a thin smile could be seen flickering across Carr's haggard features.

'Go home!' someone cried.

'Get back to the Old Vic!'

'Get lost!'

'What about the pensioners?' one man wanted to know.

Again Maxwell took no notice. When he launched into a lengthy denouncement of the *News of the World*'s board, the smile disappeared from Carr's face. Standing up with some difficulty, he said, 'I don't think the shareholders care a twopenny-cuss what you think about their board. Does the meeting wish to hear any more from Mr Maxwell?'

Impassioned cries of 'No! No! No!'

'In which case I will now put the resolution to the meeting,' Carr went on. 'Do the shareholders approve of the link-up between the *News of the World* Organisation and News Ltd of Australia which increases the company's capital to £6,573,000 by making a further 5,100,000 ordinary shares of five shillings each to be allotted as fully paid to News Ltd?'

So many hands went up that it took several minutes to count them. The final result was 299 in favour and only 20 against. To widespread astonishment, Rupert Murdoch had become the new owner of the *News of the World*.

Outside, Maxwell gave a terse statement: 'The law of the jungle has prevailed.' A few days later, Murdoch was asked what he thought of Maxwell. 'He called me a moth-eaten kangaroo,' he said in an affronted voice. By then Derek Jackson had been told what had happened. He'd gone riding in the Swiss Alps accompanied by his latest fiancée and it took a while to track them down. 'I am the most disappointed man in the whole world,' Jackson declared. 'I regard the *News of the World* board as raving mad.'

For Maxwell, the whole episode left him badly bruised. Far worse than the financial cost – around £200,000 – was the humiliation, the way he'd been jeered at, condescended to and cold-shouldered. But what hurt most of all was how he had been out-foxed by someone he hadn't taken seriously until it was too late. As baffled as he was angry, Maxwell retreated to Headington Hill Hall. 'He came limping home and I put him to bed,' Betty recalled. 'He was terribly disappointed, but the next day he decided to shrug the whole thing off . . . Nothing gets him down for long.'

The truth of this was about to be put to the test in ways that neither of them could have imagined.

9

Robert Maxwell's Code of Conduct

Once again, encyclopaedias would prove to be Maxwell's downfall – the same encyclopaedias he had tried to sell Rupert Murdoch in 1965. The next year Maxwell paid £1,000,000 for the company that published *Chambers Encyclopædia*. Later that year he brought out a new fifteen-volume edition of the *Encyclopædia*. To publicize his new project, Maxwell took out newspaper advertisements which brimmed with missionary zeal: 'I'd like to give every child in this country the freedom to learn from the world's greatest storehouse of knowledge.' Hoping to convince people that the venture had the royal seal of approval, he also put a prominent dedication to the Queen on the front page of each volume.

On 22 February 1967 Maxwell called a press conference at the Dorchester Hotel in London. There, to general amazement, he announced that in the last year he had personally sold 7000 sets of *Chambers Encyclopædia* worth £1,000,000. What's more, he claimed to have orders for another £1,500,000. As a feat of salesmanship, this was unprecedented. Lists were handed out to the journalists at the press conference giving details of how many sets of encyclopedias he had sold and where: 1500 sets in America, another 1500 in Japan, 500 in India and so on.

By now Maxwell was so taken with encyclopedias that he added the eighteen-volume *New Caxton Encyclopedia* to his collection, and set up a new company, the International Learning Systems Corporation – ILSC – to run them all. He even published *Robert Maxwell's Code of Conduct for Direct Sellers*, a kind of etiquette handbook for door-to-door encyclopedia salesmen.

What lay behind Maxwell's obsession? As a keen autodidact, the idea of a storehouse of knowledge that anyone could dip into at will had an obvious appeal. But naturally there were commercial motives too. The beauty of encyclopedias was that anyone who bought a subscription was effectively locked into a contract for as long as it took to publish the entire edition. Usually this took several years, but in some cases it could go on for decades. Not everyone, though, was convinced by Maxwell's success story. When the Standard Literature Company of Calcutta was asked to confirm that they had bought 500 sets of *Chambers Encyclopædia*, the company replied the real figure was considerably less.

It was in fact zero.

Nor were these the only figures that had been heavily massaged. Far from selling 7000 sets of *Chambers Encyclopædia*, Maxwell appeared to have sold around 700. Undeterred, he kept on repeating his claims that he was the most successful encyclopedia salesman the world had ever known. While some may have had their doubts, others were only too happy to cling to his coat-tails hoping to share in the spoils.

Saul Steinberg was an American businessman who had made a fortune out of leasing IBM computers. Aged twenty-nine, he owned a twenty-nine-room house on Long Island and was reputed to have made more money more quickly than anyone else in America. Steinberg had heard a lot about Maxwell, and liked the sound of him. He may have been a brute, but he appeared to be a very successful brute.

In the spring of 1969, Steinberg approached Maxwell with an offer. His company, Leasco, would buy Pergamon Press and all its subsidiaries, including ILSC, for £25,000,000, of which Maxwell would get £8.500,000 – £135,000,000 today. While Steinberg would remain Chairman of Leasco, Maxwell would become Deputy Chairman, with 2.5 per cent of the shares.

Maxwell also liked the sound of Steinberg. Not only would he gain a huge amount of money from the sale; he would also have access to Steinberg's American markets. But before buying Pergamon, Steinberg's accountants naturally wanted to go through the books. While the rest of Maxwell's empire appeared to be in good shape, ILSC was a shambles – mainly because no one could work out how many sets of encyclopedias Maxwell had really sold.

Maxwell always liked to claim that accountancy was not a science but an art, and now he came up with a suitably creative solution. He told Steinberg that, much to his regret, the Pergamon accounts had been unavoidably delayed. Apparently, he was doing business in so many countries – more than forty in all – that it would take longer than usual to put the figures together. As a result, the final version wouldn't be ready until September.

Just in case Steinberg became suspicious, Maxwell produced a glossy annual report claiming that ILSC had made sales worth £7,500,000 in its first eighteen months of business and was looking forward to a 'bright and profitable future'. For good measure, he asked his solicitor to give an 'unprejudiced' view of the company. Unswayed by the fact that Maxwell was paying him to give his opinion, the solicitor wrote that 'Mr Maxwell is a man of undoubted integrity.'

Everything seemed back on track – but not for long. In Maxwell's 1967 annual report, he had confidently predicted that Pergamon would make around £2,000,000 profit in 1968. Now, with the sale to Leasco in the offing, he did everything he could to maximize the company's profits so they hit his £2,000,000 forecast.

In order to do this, Maxwell gave full rein to his artistic leanings. Pergamon's warehouse at Olney in Buckinghamshire was full of unsold back issues of their journals. Previously, these back issues had been declared worthless. But now, it seemed, two buyers had emerged who were prepared to pay a total of £974,000 for them. And who might these buyers be? By a remarkable coincidence, they turned out to be Maxwell's own subsidiaries. Once again, he was using one part of his empire to prop up another.

Before the 1968 accounts could be sent to Steinberg, they had to be approved by Pergamon's board. At two o'clock on 2 April 1969 a board meeting was held in Pergamon's headquarters in Fitzroy Square. Maxwell had barely entered the room when he announced he couldn't hang around as he had an important appointment – he had to take the President of Nigeria round the House of Commons.

The accounts were quickly signed off. Although ILSC was listed as having behaved 'disappointingly', the £2,000,000 target for the entire Pergamon group had been met. The following morning the Stock Exchange announced that Pergamon had made 'record profits' in the last tax year.

With everything apparently sorted out, Maxwell invited Saul Steinberg to Headington Hill Hall so they could get to know one another better. There, he introduced him to the Prime Minister, Harold Wilson, the philosopher Isaiah Berlin and his near-neighbour, the Duke of Bedford. As Maxwell anticipated, Steinberg was bowled over. 'His scope of relations was amazing to me,' he would say later. Steinberg was also introduced to Maxwell's children. 'He had an incredibly limp handshake,' Isabel recalls.

Betty Maxwell was equally unimpressed. 'Saul accompanied by his wife came for lunch: she had nothing to say and spent her time before and after lunch working furiously on a small tapestry which in the circumstances was extremely impolite. Saul, on the other hand, kept on admiring the house, saying how nice it would be to live there, which made me uneasy to say the least.'

But while Steinberg was eyeing up the Headington Hill Hall curtains, another storm was brewing. Having tussled with him over the running of the House of Commons Catering Committee, the Editor of the *Sunday Times*, Harold Evans, had been left with a lingering suspicion there was something dodgy about Maxwell. He decided that the paper should investigate further. As he looked through Pergamon's interim accounts, Evans had a peculiar sense of *déjà vu*. 'I'm not an accountant, but even I could tell that something was odd. I remember saying, "Where are the profit figures?" There just didn't seem to be any. Even so, I didn't have that much confidence in my own judgement and I thought there was a risk I might have got it wrong.'

In the interests of fairness, Evans invited Maxwell to come to the *Sunday Times* so he could put his side of the story. The meeting soon descended into a shouting match. Maxwell was already convinced that their investigation was part of a Rupert Murdoch-led attempt to smear him. 'First of all, he told me he'd been to see the proprietor of the *Sunday Times*, Lord Thomson. The message was quite clear. I remember thinking, "Harry, watch out for yourself." '

Things went from bad to worse when Evans told him that, as far as he could see, Maxwell had been falsely inflating his profits. 'He kept thumping the table and saying I didn't understand what I was talking about. He may even have stormed out. I know I didn't enjoy it much. But then two or three days later I'd see him at some party and he'd be all cheerful and jolly, just as he'd been when I came out of the House of Commons Committee of Privileges. Again, I found it very strange.'

On 17 June 1969, Steinberg gave Maxwell a personal guarantee that the deal was on; it was just a matter of drawing up a formal offer document. News of the proposed takeover made the front pages of all the broadsheet newspapers: Maxwell, Britain's most flamboyant publisher, was about to join forces with America's youngest self-made multimillionaire.

But by now Jack Anderson, Leasco's Chief Accountant, was starting to have his doubts. Like Harold Evans, he felt there was something dodgy about Maxwell, even if he couldn't put his finger on quite what it was. Anderson threatened to pull out of the deal unless he was given access to Pergamon's files in Headington Hill Hall.

Again Maxwell reluctantly complied.

When Anderson looked through Pergamon's invoices, one of them stood out. It was for 100 complete editions of the *Journal of Inorganic Nuclear Chemistry*. This came in twenty-nine volumes and sold in America for $133,000 – almost a million dollars today. Anderson may not have known much about inorganic chemistry, but he knew a rat when he smelled one. Could there really be a hundred academic institutions in America prepared to stump up $133,000 for a full set of an extremely obscure journal?

The next day – 11 August – Anderson went to see the Pergamon warehouse in Olney. He was not reassured. All of their old journals were jumbled together with no indication of which of Maxwell's various companies owned which. It didn't help that the warehouseman, a Pole named Tadeusz Kamienski, could barely speak English.

Five days later, Saul Steinberg was lying by the pool of his twenty-nine-room house in Long Island. He'd just celebrated his thirtieth birthday and was on the verge of pulling off a deal that would make him a major international player. All in all, things could hardly have been any better.

'I had the feeling that everything was right with the world,' Steinberg recalled. 'I was rich and my family was wonderful when Robert, my valet, came with a vodka martini and said George Bello, my Finance Director, was on the phone from London.'

Robert brought the phone. Steinberg put it to his ear.

'Saul,' Bello told him. 'We've discovered a major problem.'

Instantly, Steinberg's good humour vanished.

'I shouted for another vodka martini, drank it in one and screamed, *"Whaaat?"'*

On 21 August, Maxwell was summoned to appear before the Takeover Panel to explain the discrepancies in his figures. That afternoon Steinberg pulled out of the deal. The news stunned the City. Dealing in Pergamon shares was immediately suspended on the Stock Exchange. However much Maxwell blustered and frothed, he was powerless to do anything. Then, from the other side of the Atlantic, came what looked at first like a lifeline, but which soon turned into a noose. Steinberg announced that he was prepared to go through with the deal under one condition – Maxwell's influence had to be severely curtailed.

To make matters worse, the *Sunday Times* finally published their profile of Maxwell. After all the months of investigation, the profile turned out to be pretty thin stuff. The worst they could come up with was that he was popularly known as 'The Bouncing Czech'. Even so, that didn't stop Maxwell from denouncing the journalists who had written it as 'the forces of evil'.

Nor did it do anything to set Pergamon shareholders' minds at rest. On 10 October 1969, five days after the *Sunday Times* piece was published, Maxwell was removed from Pergamon's board at an Extraordinary General Meeting of shareholders, along with eight other directors. In their place, seven Leasco nominees, including Saul Steinberg, were appointed. Although Maxwell kept the proceeds from the sale of his shares – over £1,000,000 – the company he had founded almost twenty years earlier no longer belonged to him.

As a final twist, the meeting took place at the Connaught Rooms in Covent Garden, where nine months earlier Maxwell had been humiliated in his bid to buy the *News of the World*. After the meeting was over, he was asked how he felt. For once, all Maxwell's brashness, all his booming self-assurance, had disappeared.

'You can't expect me to be anything other than very, very sad.'

Three weeks later Betty Maxwell was awakened by the sound of banging. Looking out of her bedroom window, she saw a wooden fence topped by rolls of barbed wire being erected between Headington Hill Hall and the headquarters of Pergamon – housed in what had once been the Victorian servants' quarters next door.

The same day a firm of locksmiths arrived. On the orders of Pergamon's new directors, the locks were changed on their offices to prevent Maxwell or any members of his family from coming in. The two buildings were so close to one another that a single basement ran beneath both properties. At the same time as the locks were changed, an iron gate was erected in the basement of Headington Hill Hall to make sure no one could gain access to the Pergamon end of the cellars.

Nothing could illustrate quite so starkly how far and how quickly Maxwell had fallen. Not only had he lost control of his company; he had also been physically barred from setting foot inside it.

10

The Lights Go Out

Throughout all this Maxwell had continued being a Member of Parliament. But his career had proved to be rather less dazzling than he had anticipated. Although he had transformed the fortunes of the catering department and played a key role in piloting through the Clean Air Act of 1968 – intended to tighten controls on pollution – that was about it. Despite all his speeches, all his interventions, his hopes of climbing any further up the ladder, far less of becoming Prime Minister, had come to nothing.

In June 1969, Maxwell was interviewed on the television show *Today*. Clearly in a peppery mood, he was asked by the interviewer, Sandra Harris: 'Mr Maxwell, while you're surrounded by tremendous wealth, do you still think about poverty?'

Maxwell: 'I can never be separated from my origins. I came from a working class and I'm part of them and will continue to support them.'

Harris: 'Did you ever consider being a member of any other party?'

Maxwell: 'That is a scurrilous suggestion and quite untrue. Just because I've made a couple of shillings, I'm not about to change sides.'

Harris: 'Does property mean a lot to you?'

Maxwell: 'Quite unimportant. I merely have property as a means of getting things done that need to be done. I'm completely unattached.'

Harris: 'You've also been described as a tremendously ruthless man. A man who is very, very difficult to cross. Does what other people say about you bother you at all?'

Maxwell: 'No.'

In May 1970, confidently expecting victory, the Prime Minister, Harold Wilson, announced that a General Election would be held on 18 June. Maxwell's campaign slogan – 'Harold and Bob Will Finish the Job' – gave an indication of the company he felt he belonged in. This time round he was driven around his constituency in another Land Rover – painted bright red. A hole had been cut in the roof through which Maxwell's head would appear from time to time topped by a cloth cap, further underlining his socialist credentials.

As before, his family, principally Betty, were on hand to lend support. So too was a woman called Eleanor Berry, the youngest daughter of Lord Hartwell, the former proprietor of the *Daily Telegraph*. Berry had had a troubled history, having been diagnosed with a number of mental conditions – including schizophrenia, obsessive-compulsive disorder and manic depression. At the time she was at university and in the middle of writing her thesis – on the Marquis de Sade.

Berry and Maxwell had first met when her brother, Nicholas Berry, the financial correspondent of the *Daily Telegraph*, had taken her to one of the Maxwells' parties in the late 1960s: 'Nicky introduced me to RM who was standing in a marquee wearing a towelling dressing-gown . . . He was very nice and friendly and it suddenly dawned on me that he generated a livid, brutal, astonishing and overwhelming sexuality.'

As far as Berry was concerned, it would be the start of a life-long obsession: in her eyes Maxwell would be a father figure and fantasy lover all rolled into one. Both flattered and amused by Berry's eccentricities, Maxwell quickly developed a soft spot for her. A few months later, Berry was sectioned after attacking a man in a jeweller's shop in Paddington Station – he had misspelled the word 'steppe' on a gold pillbox she had asked him to engrave. Confined to a mental hospital in north London, she was prescribed anti-psychotic drugs and a course of electro-shock treatment.

On the day the treatment was due to start, Berry had been wheeled into the operating theatre and was about to be given an anaesthetic. But before the anaesthetic could be administered, the door burst open. With the electrodes already attached to her head, Berry looked up to see Maxwell standing in the doorway, dressed in a white flannel suit.

If anything, the doctors were even more astonished than she was.

'Who are you?' one them asked.

'I am Robert Maxwell,' Maxwell announced. 'Member of Parliament for Buckingham.'

'How dare you come in here when you're not scrubbed up!'

Maxwell took no notice.

'I order you to turn that fucking machine off.'

Removing the electrodes from Berry's head, Maxwell then carried her outside to where his Rolls-Royce was waiting. Behind the wheel was another of his chauffeurs – a man called Hoppit.

'Floor it, Hoppit!' Maxwell told him. 'Head for Oxford.'

Not surprisingly, the incident made Berry even more slavish in her adoration. During the election campaign, she helped hand out leaflets and distribute Maxwell's daily bulletins, known as 'Maxwellgrams'. When they were out canvassing together, Betty and Berry would sometimes discuss their shared interest in de Sade. Betty, it seems, was fascinated by de Sade's belief that every pleasure contained an element of pain. 'I wondered if she had been referring to the sex act,' Berry recalled, 'but I thought it would have been more than inappropriate to ask her.'

The polls continued to put Labour well in front – by as much as 12 per cent. Victory seemed assured. Then on the evening before the election came an incident which Berry was tempted to regard as an omen. She'd previously noticed that whenever Maxwell gave a speech at the local Labour headquarters an elderly man would be sitting in the back row with his eyes closed. No one else liked to go near him because they complained that he smelled. However, Maxwell would always ruffle the old man's hair as he went past and ask, 'How you doing, Grandpa?' Shortly before he was about to give his Eve of Polls speech, all efforts to rouse the old man in the back row failed. It turned out he had died some time earlier.

Nor was this the only unusual event to have taken place. On election day, Berry helped drive Labour supporters to the polling stations. Still feeling apprehensive about the result, she took 60 mg of Diazepam before getting into her car. 'Doctors say that 60 mg is a colossal dose, but I have always been able to tolerate it.'

After polling had closed and the votes were being counted, it became increasingly clear that the result was going to be much closer than anyone had anticipated. Early the next morning, the Maxwell family and Berry went to Buckingham Town Hall to hear the result. Outside was a crowd of Labour supporters, angry and dejected at the way the pendulum appeared to be swinging against them. One man was brandishing a red flag with a hammer and sickle sewn on to it.

Somehow he persuaded Eleanor Berry to climb on to the roof of the Town Hall, take down the Union Jack and replace it with the Red Flag. She managed to find a fire escape which led up to the roof. There, she lowered the Union Jack and – amid cheers from below – hurled it to the ground, where it was promptly doused in lighter fuel and set alight. But raising the Red Flag defeated her. Instead she waved it above her head – to more cheers from below.

At this point the police intervened, telling her through a loud-hailer that she had to come down immediately. Suffering from a sudden attack of vertigo, Berry found her legs had turned to jelly. When the police finally managed to coax her down, they asked her why she had done it.

'Because I wanted to please Mr Maxwell,' she told them. 'I am in love with him and I'd be prepared to die for him if necessary!'

It soon became clear that the voters of Buckingham did not share her devotion. In keeping with a nationwide swing to the Tories, the Conservative candidate won the seat by a majority of more than 2500 votes.

Maxwell's parliamentary dream was over.

After the result had been declared, he drove Eleanor Berry back to Headington Hill Hall in his campaign Land Rover. On the way they discussed a novel she had recently read, *The Man Who was*

Afraid, by Maxim Gorky. The novel's main character is a man called Foma Gordyev who starts off by being fixated on becoming rich: 'He could never have enough of the jingle and sound of money'. Increasingly, though, he feels hamstrung by society's conventions. Despising his fellow merchants, he tells them they deserve to be 'scorched in sizzling dung for centuries on end'. In the end, bankrupt, friendless and ridiculed, Gordyev becomes a down-and-out on the streets of his hometown.

When Berry had finished describing the plot, Maxwell remained silent for a while. Then he said quietly, 'I know what loneliness is like.'

On 13 July 1971, the Department of Trade and Industry published its report into the sale of Pergamon to Leasco. Maxwell had done everything he could to delay publication, but when the blow finally came it was as devastating as he had feared.

The report concluded: 'He [Maxwell] is a man of great energy, drive and imagination, but an apparent fixation as to his own abilities causes him to ignore the views of others if these are not compatible . . . Notwithstanding Mr Maxwell's acknowledged abilities and energy, he is not in our opinion a person who can be relied on to exercise proper stewardship of a publicly quoted company.'

Within the space of three and a half years, Maxwell had lost his eldest son, his company, his parliamentary seat and now his reputation. At a press conference, he denounced the report as a 'witch-hunt' and claimed to have been victimized by the 'so-called City Establishment'. But the damage had been done. As Betty recalled, it was as if the family had suddenly become pariahs: 'Almost overnight, the invitations vanished from our mantelpiece.'

From Courchevel in France, where she had gone skiing with her sister, she wrote her husband a letter: 'I have thought quite a lot, going up the sunny or snowy or blizzard slopes about what I could say to you to give you some courage, as you sounded so sad on the phone the other night. The essence of what I wish to tell you is that I love you, irrespective of your worth in terms of cash or otherwise . . . I love you for the exceptional life you have already given me and the privilege I have had to share your life for twenty-five years and be loved by you for all that length of time . . .

'If you feel that we must give up Headington Hill Hall and live elsewhere or emigrate to China or live underground or in a tree-top, I am game. No waves are static and I would much rather swim and have swum with you than vegetated with small, unintelligent and uninteresting beings.'

Meanwhile Maxwell and Leasco continued to exist awkwardly side by side. The arrangement was further complicated by the fact that the basement of Pergamon contained the generators and boilers for both properties. Every so often Maxwell would be spotted after dark in the Pergamon offices, stalking the corridors. Although the locks had been changed and guards employed to patrol the building, none of them had the nerve to tell him to leave.

After one of Maxwell's nocturnal visits, during a particularly cold snap, it transpired that the boiler had been mysteriously extinguished. As a result, Pergamon's central heating no longer worked. Leasco retaliated by turning off Headington Hill Hall's power supplies, leaving the building without light, heat or a telephone line.

Cut off from the outside world, alone in the darkness, Maxwell brooded on his misfortune and plotted his revenge.

The Grasshopper Returns

On the morning of 12 February 1974, an announcement came over the PA system at Pergamon Press. All employees were immediately to stop what they were doing and go straight to the canteen, where they would receive some important news. Around 100 people gathered, chattering apprehensively to one another, wondering what was going on. After they'd been waiting for several minutes, Robert Maxwell walked in. The room fell silent. People stood aside to let him go by.

Climbing on to a chair, Maxwell looked down at the upturned faces.

'I'm back,' he said.

Then he got down and walked out.

Four and a half years earlier, when Saul Steinberg had ousted Maxwell from the Pergamon board, he'd assumed that in doing so he had taken full control of the company and its subsidiaries. But it wasn't long before Steinberg realized he had made a terrible mistake – a mistake so basic that it's remarkable no one spotted it before. What he and his directors had failed to notice was that Maxwell still controlled 70 per cent of an American company called Pergamon Press Inc. (PPI).

On the face of it, PPI might have seemed pretty unimportant, just another of Maxwell's bewildering network of subsidiaries. In fact, it was the engine room of the entire business: the company had exclusive rights to sell Pergamon's journals in America. Effectively, Leasco had paid £25,000,000 for an empty shell.

Bob Miranda was one of PPI's key directors in America. 'I think Leasco were too dumb to realize what had happened. They had bought a company which was essentially devoid of cash flow. All the profit was coming to us. Even though they were producing the material, we kept the money.'

The moment Steinberg discovered what had happened, he launched a flurry of lawsuits trying to wrest back Pergamon Press Inc. from Maxwell's control. No stranger to issuing writs himself, Maxwell ignored them. 'I remember our lawyers thought we didn't have a leg to stand on,' recounted Miranda, 'but Maxwell said, "Do exactly what I tell you and everything will be OK."'

His plan could hardly have been more simple. In the past, PPI had handed the money that had been earned in the US back to Pergamon in Britain. But not any more. 'We basically sat on the money and refused to give it back. At the same time we weren't paying any of our bills. In effect, we were starving out the parent company.'

It didn't take long for this to drive the normally urbane Steinberg to the point of apoplexy. The angrier he became, the more delight Maxwell took in goading him. 'It was like a game with him,' Miranda recalls, 'but it was a game he was determined to win.'

Steinberg demanded Maxwell's immediate resignation from PPI. Maxwell refused. Claiming – quite rightly – that PPI were refusing to pay their rent, Steinberg tried to force them out of their offices in Elmsford, New York. Maxwell promptly counter-sued, alleging harassment. In the end the police intervened; every morning Miranda had to go and pick up his office key from the local sheriff.

And so it went on, back and forth. All the time Pergamon, increasingly starved of funds, was sinking fast. In Chicago, a group of its American editors and authors confronted the new Chairman, Sir Walter Coutts, threatening to withdraw their services unless Maxwell was reinstated. 'They absolutely hammered me,' Coutts complained later. His wife was even more incensed. Lady Coutts told a friend that she had 'never imagined a crowd of men could be so unpleasant'.

The next morning, Sir Walter called Maxwell and told him, 'I have enough contacts in the City of London to sink you as far as you'll ever go, and you'll never come up again.' By way of a peace offering, Maxwell sent the couple an enormous bouquet of flowers. Sir Walter was briefly placated – until he discovered that the flowers had been bought on Pergamon's account.

Meanwhile, behind the barbed-wire fence at Headington Hill Hall, life had undergone another upheaval. 'As children, the biggest difference for us was that we couldn't go and play in the Pergamon offices any more,' Ian Maxwell recalls. 'It was as if there was a kind of apartheid going on between us and them.' But there were other, less tangible differences. 'Generally, they were dark times. There seemed to be a fear in the air; a fear that we would be ostracized, or that something else terrible would happen.'

There were material changes too; for the first time in years, the Maxwells were having to be careful with money. The previous summer they had spent their holiday cruising around the Mediterranean on a 210-foot-long motor yacht called the *Shemara* – the yacht was so big that it had been requisitioned by the Royal Navy during the Second World War for use as a training vessel. In the summer of 1969, Betty took the children camping in Wales.

Maxwell didn't come with them; he was far too busy to take a holiday. 'Basically, my father was hardly ever at home, and when he was he always seemed to be in a hurry. A lot of people abandoned him when he lost Pergamon, people he'd been able to rely on in the past. I think he felt very lonely and under attack, and it left him with a renewed sense that he had to do everything on his own.'

Much of Maxwell's time was spent in America, trying to accumulate enough money to buy back Pergamon. Together, he and Bob Miranda would drive across the country, visiting potential clients. 'He was a nightmare to travel with,' Miranda remembers. 'When he had finished reading a newspaper, he would just throw it out of the car window. It used to drive me crazy.'

The two of them stayed in cheap motels beside the freeway. 'We used to share a bedroom to save money. I spent a lot of sleepless nights with him – he could never sleep for more than a couple of hours at a time. Then he would wake me up in the middle of the night for someone to talk to.' But in all the time they spent together,

Miranda noticed that Maxwell never spoke about anything personal. 'He was very secretive about that sort of stuff. Instead, he was like an actor; he could be one person one minute, and then another person entirely fifteen minutes later. I guess that was why I could never really consider him as a friend.'

As Pergamon's fortunes continued to plummet – by now they had debts of nearly £5,000,000 – the City started to lose faith in Steinberg and to look more favourably on Maxwell. Even Sir Walter Coutts began to think the unthinkable. Through gritted teeth, he conceded there were things Maxwell could do that no one else could: 'He has a computer brain in that he can read things, particularly in the scientific magazines, which he will store away. At the right moment of time it will come out of the computer and he will be able to talk to those people in the same language that they talk among themselves.'

By early 1973, Coutts admitted privately that Pergamon was close to bankruptcy. On 20 November, Maxwell offered him a deal – he would give Pergamon back some of the money from PPI, but only if he was allowed on to the board.

The offer was eagerly accepted.

Two months later, on 20 January 1974, Saul Steinberg agreed to sell Maxwell his personal 38 per cent holding in Pergamon for just 12 pence a share. In all, this brought him around £600,000. Barely four years earlier, he'd paid £9,000,000 for the same shares. Then they had been valued at 185 pence each.

At the beginning of February, Sir Walter Coutts was chairing a board meeting at Pergamon's headquarters next to Headington Hill Hall when the door burst open.

'Right,' said Maxwell. 'We're taking over now. You can all go.'

That afternoon the barbed-wire fence was taken down and the iron gate in the basement removed. Shortly afterwards, Coutts resigned as Chairman. Later on, he reflected on the whole affair, and on Maxwell's character in particular: 'He has an ability to sublimate anything that stops him getting what he wants. He's so flexible he is like a grasshopper. There's no question of any morality or conscience. Maxwell is Number One and what Maxwell wants is the most important thing and to hell with anything else.'

In an attempt to show there were no hard feelings, Maxwell held a dinner at Headington Hill Hall for members of the Pergamon board, including Sir Walter and his wife. At the end of the evening, he stood in the porch making a great show of wishing each guest goodbye in a different language.

To his surprise, Lady Coutts replied in a language that Maxwell didn't recognize: 'Kwaheri ashante sana sitaki kukuona tena.'

In Swahili, this means: 'Goodbye. Thank you very much. I don't wish to see you again.'

12.

Strife

Maxwell may have triumphed, but it had come at a cost – a much greater cost than anyone realized at the time. Betty, though, had long had intimations of what was to come. Fifteen years earlier, shortly after they had moved into Headington Hill Hall, she had written Maxwell a letter – one that was in stark contrast to the letters she had written him in the past:

'I find it a sorry state of affairs that on one of the finest Sundays of the year you decided to show a detestable facet of your character; you behaved in a completely callous and self-centred way and were totally oblivious of other people around you. I have also had a tough two years in which – just to remind you – I have given birth to a baby, lost my mother, and had a consequently difficult summer sorting out our family affairs in Paris. I had two miscarriages, no doubt brought on by rushing about and my complete exhaustion. I am at the end of my tether and so are you.'

By December 1965, things were even worse: 'I am so intensely miserable that I have decided to confide my thoughts to paper in order to concentrate and force myself to think what I can do to remedy the situation, and also to draw your attention, if you will bear with me, to your attitude toward your family and me . . . We are both mentally and physically exhausted. We have not been able to unwind for years . . . It affects us in different ways: you have become exceedingly short-tempered, snappy, nagging, despotic. Your weight has gone up, you sleep badly. Your use of uncouth language does you no credit, nor does your complete lack of respect for what I represent, notwithstanding all my failings.

'You must curb your intemperate, short-lived but wounding

judgements of my every move and utterance, control your excessive swollen-headedness and show some appreciation for my great devotion to you alone, throughout our lives. I note that you are unstinting in your compliments when you need me and yet so stingy with your rewards when the battle is won.

'I am prepared to do without friends, entertainment, joy of any kind in my own pursuits. The only thing I am not prepared to give up in life is you. I love you. You wanted me for what I am, you have got me for keeps.'

But by October 1969 – soon after Maxwell had lost Pergamon – Betty's attitude had changed. Now, her exasperation had gone; instead she wearily acknowledged what she believed had become an inescapable fact: 'For some years now I have realized, at first with bellicose sadness, then with hurt pride and at last with victorious serenity, that my usefulness to you has come to an end. I am now certain that I am in your way. You are still a very young man, you are really incredibly healthy. Because of the unfair treatment you have received at the hands of the most hypocritical of societies, you have been denied the laurels you so richly deserved. You are now poised at the peak of your intelligence, made wiser by your experience of men and matters, with the whole wild and mad world around you tearing at your soul . . .

'I have searched night and day in my head and heart and now understand that the only present that can prove my love to you after twenty-five years is, paradoxically, that I should give you your freedom. I have not reached this decision lightly. More than half of me has fought it tooth and nail, but believe me when I say that I offer it with serenity, with no strings attached whatsoever.'

Although Maxwell showed no desire to take his freedom, he did continue to have affairs. One was with a woman called Wendy Leigh, the author of a number of sex manuals, including *What Makes a Woman Good in Bed*, as well as a novel, *Unraveled by Him*, a lightly fictionalized account of her affair with Maxwell.

He appears as a character called Robert Hartwell – 'the number one publisher in the world'. As well as being the owner of Hartwell Castle and a 480-foot luxury yacht, the *Lady Georgiana*, Hartwell has a well-nigh unquenchable appetite for flagellation – something that rouses the narrator, Miranda, to hitherto undreamed-of heights of passion: 'For what seems forever, he spanks and spanks, then spanks more . . .'

Afterwards a surprised Hartwell asks why she's not crying. 'Because I can't, Master,' Miranda tells him. 'And no one has ever been able to make me.'

'Give me time,' says Hartwell, 'with a twinkle that undercuts the menace.'

It's possible that Leigh was letting her imagination run away with her. She told her friend Roy Greenslade, later Editor of the *Daily Mirror*, that Maxwell was a very considerate lover:

'Wendy said that he was always gentle, courteous, and despite the fact that he lacked any manual dexterity, very dainty in his habits.' What's more, he could be unexpectedly old-fashioned, even prudish. 'Apparently he was very shocked once when she started talking dirty to him, and asked her never to do it again.'

Under no illusions about Maxwell's fidelity, Betty herself had never been tempted to stray. But that too was about to change. Cooped up in Headington Hill Hall, she yearned for something to give her back a sense of purpose. After taking an A level in English at the Oxford College of Further Education, she was accepted into St Hugh's College as a mature student studying Modern Languages.

While Betty, now aged fifty-three, was revising for her finals in the summer of 1974, she met a friend of her daughter Isabel's – an American man called Greg. 'He was thirty, dashingly good-looking, sensitive and cultured. I had invited him home to meet Bob one weekend and he had unfortunately witnessed one of Bob's disgraceful outbursts, accompanied by the usual humiliating comments about my character and intelligence.'

Soon Greg became Betty's constant companion, helping her with her revision, taking her to her finals and doing wonders for her confidence. Before each exam he would stand her in front of a full-length mirror, point at her reflection and say, 'Just look at yourself! You look like any other kid taking her exams, except that you're beautiful, knowledgeable and wise.'

As well as being twenty-three years younger than her, Betty realized that Greg was the same age that her son Michael would have been. Although she kept telling herself the whole thing was absurd, she did nothing to discourage him. One evening Greg took her out to a pub by the river and told her that he loved her. He went on to say that he loved her just as she was: 'I don't want you to be different. All I want is to see things as you see them.'

For a moment Betty said nothing; she just sat silently repeating to herself what he had just told her – 'I had to admit that it was sweet music.' Then, gently but firmly, she told him they could never have a future together. That as far as she was concerned, marriage was for ever, no matter how difficult and unrewarding it was. But the flirtation, however innocent, was to have a lasting effect on her. In future, Betty resolved to stand up to her husband – not to let herself be cowed or denigrated.

Any illusions she had once had about Maxwell were now gone. In their place was an almost academic curiosity about what had happened to him to make him the way he was. Why, she wondered, couldn't he tolerate any kind of competition? Part of the answer, she felt, was because he had never learned humility. Doted on by his mother and then forced, prematurely, to become an adult, he had always remained emotionally immature, apt to fly off the handle if he didn't get his own way.

Plainly there was more to it than that. A lot of people never grow up emotionally, but Maxwell seemed to be growing ever more childish and unreasonable the older he became. Betty suspected that he had a Jekyll and Hyde personality – something that made him reserve the worst aspects of himself for those he claimed to care most about. That was why he turned on her and their children with such ferocity, never praising, only ever condemning. Constantly pushing them towards some image of perfection, then rounding on them when they – inevitably – fell short. She was particularly disturbed by how badly he treated his sons, Kevin and Ian, both of whom were now working for him – 'Bob was especially hard on the two younger boys and drove them mercilessly.'

Yet even this didn't explain the relish he took in humiliating people, publicly grinding them into the dust. Like the Hydra of Greek myth, it was as if he needed to devour his victims on a regular basis in order to replenish himself. The more they winced and squirmed, the better he felt about himself. Like a perpetually squalling child, Maxwell had also become addicted to drama – a drama in which he naturally played the lead role, wildly overacting, impossibly histrionic and always displaying a compulsive need to be centre stage.

However isolated Betty was feeling, she tried to keep her unhappiness from the children, to pretend they were still one big happy family. At Christmas time, she always took great pains to ensure the atmosphere was as festive as possible. Every year an enormous tree – around forty feet high – would be put up in the galleried hall at Headington Hill Hall. The tree was so tall that it took eight men all day to erect it.

At 10.30 on Christmas morning, the whole family would gather at the foot of the tree, where, with great ceremony, Maxwell would read out a passage from the Bible in his dark booming voice. Then they would all sing two carols. Only after the singing was over would presents be opened. To compensate for the fact that Maxwell had never been given any presents as a child, Betty always made sure he had more than anyone else. 'Mummy would give him new shirts, new shoes, a new watch, all kinds of things . . .' Ian Maxwell recalls. 'He loved getting presents. Absolutely loved it.'

While Maxwell usually bought Betty a piece of jewellery, he took a less personalized approach to the children's gifts. 'Dad's idea of giving presents was to go to his desk and write out cheques. He would stick them in envelopes, write "Love Dad" on the front and just flip them into the tree. They could be for £100, £200, or even £500.'

Present-opening would be followed by lunch. Despite the size of the Christmas turkey – often in the region of forty pounds – there was another golden rule no one dared disobey: Betty always gave half the turkey to Maxwell; everyone else had to share the rest. Then, when their father had finally eaten his fill, came the moment all the children dreaded. Each of them had to deliver a speech offering their predictions for the year ahead – what they thought was likely to happen in the world, and how they planned to become better, more useful people.

To begin with, this didn't cast too much of a cloud over the day, but slowly everything changed. 'Increasingly, Dad was in a terrible mood,' Ian remembers. 'When I was a little boy in the 1960s the Christmases were great, but then, when we get into the 1970s, everything became very different. Time and time again Christmas Day was ruined because Dad was in a filthy temper for reasons that no one could work out.

'He just seemed to get up in a bad mood, and it went downhill from there. I noticed that food seemed to calm him down and he always appeared to make an effort over lunch. But even then everything had to be perfect. If, say, the turkey was burned – then Bam! That was it for the rest of the day.'

There was worse to come. In the summer of 1980, Ian Maxwell, then aged twenty-four, was fired by his father. At the time he was running the Pergamon offices in Paris and Frankfurt. Maxwell had told Ian to collect him at Orly airport one Sunday evening and drive him to the family's apartment in the centre of Paris. This involved Ian catching a flight from Montpellier, where he was spending the weekend.

After missing the flight, he decided to hire a car to drive to Paris, 750 km away. 'Knowing I wasn't going to make it, I called my father to explain what had happened. When I'd finished, Dad said, "I'm speechless. You can't even get it together to meet your own father. I can't trust you with a burned-out box of matches. I'm relieving you of all your duties with immediate effect."'

Assuming that his father hadn't been serious, Ian turned up for work the following morning. 'The first person I saw was my deputy wearing a black tie.' The man told him Maxwell had called up at midnight to say that Ian had 'been resigned'. Along with his disbelief,

Ian was aware of an enormous sense of relief. 'I thought, thank Christ. I'm finally out of the madhouse.'

In Oxford, he went to see his mother. Maxwell, it turned out, had spoken to her too. 'He'd told her that it was the only way I was ever going to learn. That I had a ring of steel around my heart and it had to be broken into.'

Just like his older brother, Philip, who had gone to live in Argentina, Ian decided to get as far away from his father as possible – he went to California to stay with his sister Christine. 'For the next three months I twiddled my thumbs and half-heartedly wrote my CV.' He and his father didn't speak. 'Then one day I got a phone call. Dad was in Beijing and flying out to San Francisco the next day. He said I should meet him at his hotel at 8 p.m.'

If Ian had any hesitation about going, it didn't last long. 'I felt he was reaching out to me, and that I wasn't kowtowing to him. Somehow that felt important.' He duly flew to San Francisco and – on time – walked into his father's hotel suite. 'One of the things about Dad was that he had this very distinctive smell: it was a combination of aftershave and cigars. To me, it was always the smell of power.

'Straightaway, he said, "Let's stop this fucking holiday. Three months is quite long enough. What are we going to do with you?"' When Ian said that he was enjoying being in America and would like to stay longer, Maxwell suggested he should work in Pergamon's New York office as Director of Marketing. But while he was prepared to welcome Ian back into the fold, there would have to be an appropriate punishment for his misbehaviour.

'"There must be a penalty," he said. "So I'm going to put you on half salary."'

As Ian knew already only too well, in his father's world every perceived offence had to have consequences: 'The more serious the offence, the greater the consequences. After he had told me what he was going to do, I can remember saying to him, "Dad, is it always going to be like this?"'

★

For his Christmas card in 1983, Maxwell chose a photograph of himself that had been taken at his birthday party at Headington Hill Hall in June. The photograph showed Maxwell and Betty standing in the foreground while behind them a firework display spelled out the words 'Happy Birthday Bob' in enormous letters.

Among the recipients was Brian Basham, then head of the City PR firm the Broad Street Group. 'I remember looking at this thing and thinking, Christ, that's a bit weird.' A few days later, Basham ran into Maxwell. 'I thanked him for the card, but told him, "Bob, you really can't say that, you know."'

Maxwell looked puzzled and asked why not.

'Because it's a Christmas card,' Basham explained. 'It's not supposed to be "Happy Birthday Bob." It's supposed to be "Happy Birthday Jesus."'

13.

Written in the Stars

As he was having his breakfast, Clive Thornton, the mild, bespectacled, one-legged Chairman of the *Daily Mirror* – he'd lost the other leg in a tramcar accident – liked to read his copy of the paper. On 9 July 1984, as he always did, Thornton turned to the horoscope and looked under his star sign – Cancer – to see what the day held in store.

Normally, newspaper horoscopes are written in as wishy-washy language as possible, but to his surprise Thornton saw that this one was unusually specific: 'Unless you have written guarantees and solid promises, then leave financial matters alone for a while,' it advised. 'Others may seem plausible and reliable, but the chances are you are being manipulated in some way, or worse.'

Someone, it seemed, was trying to tell him something.

Ever since he'd seen the *News of the World* snatched from under his nose, Robert Maxwell had been obsessed with owning a newspaper. But whenever he made a move, he seemed fated to run into the same figure blocking his path. Rupert Murdoch, he became convinced, was out to thwart him at every turn.

In early 1969, at the same time as he was claiming to be the greatest encyclopedia salesman in history, Maxwell learned that the *Sun* was up for sale. Once known as the *Daily Herald*, the *Sun* had been losing money ever since it had changed its name five years earlier. The paper's proprietors, IPC, announced that if a buyer couldn't be found, the paper would have to close down. Although nobody said so directly, the general feeling in the City and on Fleet Street was that anyone who wanted the *Sun* was welcome to it, but may well need their head examining.

With his usual fanfare, Maxwell announced that he was mounting a bid. Desperate to get it off their hands, IPC offered it to him at a knockdown price – just £50,000 up front – on condition that he did a deal with the print unions. Few people held out any hope the bid would come to anything. 'Maxwell is a strange, roguish man and I can't really believe he is going to make this thing a success,' wrote Richard Crossman in his diary.

Negotiations dragged on. Maxwell declared there would have to be large-scale redundancies. The unions refused; deadlock loomed. As always, Maxwell assumed he had the upper hand; that it was only a matter of time before the unions threw in the towel. What he didn't know was that he had a competitor. By now installed as the owner of the *News of the World*, Rupert Murdoch found himself with printing presses that were only in use once a week. What Murdoch wanted above all was an opportunity to keep them turning every night. 'I thought, I'd really love a daily paper – that's where the action will be. I had read all about how Maxwell was talking to the unions, but nothing seemed to be happening.'

Then one day Murdoch had an inspiration. 'I wrote to IPC saying I don't want to interfere at all, but if Captain Maxwell can't work it out, will you give me a chance? I also sent a copy of the letter to the unions, and that same afternoon they broke off negotiations with him.' More than half a century on, Murdoch can't resist a small smile at the memory.

After agreeing a – much smaller – redundancy package with the unions, Rupert Murdoch was confirmed as the *Sun's* new owner. This was the second time he had bested Maxwell.

Another twelve years would go by before Maxwell's chance came again. In October 1980, the *Times* was put up for sale. On the face of it, the *Times* seemed an even more unattractive proposition than the *Sun*: it was losing around £15,000,000 a year and hopelessly bedevilled by union disputes.

None the less, Maxwell wanted it. So did Murdoch. Maxwell's

bid was treated as an impertinence by the paper's owners, who made it plain they doubted he had the money to buy it – and even if he did, he wasn't a fit person to own the 'Top People's Paper', as it liked to style itself. Once again Murdoch won the day.

That made it three times in a row.

At the beginning of 1984, Reed International, publishers of the *Daily Mirror*, the *Sunday Mirror* and the *Sunday People*, discreetly let it be known that the entire company might be for sale. This time no one, not even Maxwell, expressed a flicker of interest. Like everybody else, he appeared to have been put off by the papers' soaring costs and plummeting profits.

But what none of the Reed directors knew was that Maxwell had a mole inside the company. Bob Edwards was a director of Mirror Group newspapers, as well as an incorrigible gossip. Rather unusually, considering that he didn't own a dog, Edwards would take his lunch every day in the headquarters of the Kennel Club. He was also one of the few people who had carried on sending Maxwell a Christmas card after he'd been branded unfit to run a public company.

Whenever Edwards heard any interesting snippets of information, he would pass them on to Maxwell. This included the news that the *Mirror* board couldn't agree on what to do next. Some of them were still hoping for a sale, while others, like Clive Thornton, wanted to float the *Mirror* on the Stock Exchange. But estimates of how much the paper might be worth had been falling steadily: they were down to around £50,000,000.

Maxwell was almost sixty-one. By now he owned a football club, Oxford United, as well as the largest printing company in Europe – the British Printing Corporation. The BPC had been fast heading for bankruptcy when he took it over in 1981; Maxwell had restored it to profit within two years. Once deemed unfit to run a public company, he had not only proved his detractors wrong; he'd won back the respect of the City.

But still he didn't have what he yearned for more than anything else. Three times Maxwell had tried to buy a Fleet Street paper, and three times he'd failed. If he didn't strike now, his chance might never come again. The stakes could not have been higher. The *Sun* and the *Daily Mirror* were the UK's most popular tabloid newspapers. As the owner of the left-leaning *Mirror*, Maxwell would wield enormous influence; essentially, no Labour government could be elected without the paper's support. There was another incentive, of course: it would bring him into direct competition with Rupert Murdoch. As the owner of the right-leaning *Sun*, Murdoch held the same sway over the Conservative Party. Between them, they would be the two biggest powerbrokers in British politics.

Slowly, stealthily, Maxwell began to circle Clive Thornton. During a lunch at the House of Commons they both attended, he paid him elaborate court, laying on the blandishments with a trowel. One observer was reminded of 'a salivating, handsomely-ruffed wolf descending on a perspiring City-suited pig'.

On 4 July 1984, Maxwell pounced. He called a press conference where he announced he was making a formal offer of £80,000,000 for Mirror Group Newspapers. The news was greeted with horror by Reed International. Immediately, they turned the offer down, at the same time making it clear that they would rather put their families on the street than sell to Maxwell. But, thanks to Bob Edwards, Maxwell knew that cracks were starting to appear in their resolve.

As always, he revelled in the attention. The Max Factor, as it would later become known, was turned up to full blast. So too was Maxwell's inner Mr Toad – never far from the surface when he was anywhere near a car. Hoping for an interview, a female reporter from the *Financial Times* jumped into the back of his Rolls-Royce. At a set of traffic lights, they pulled up beside a Porsche.

'Think he'll beat us, do you?' Maxwell asked her.

No doubt about it, she replied – whereupon he wound down his window and shouted to the Porsche driver that there was something wrong with his back wheel. As the driver pulled over to investigate, Maxwell roared away.

Over the next three days he bombarded Reed with phone calls. All of them went unanswered. He then took the fight to Reed's doorstep by moving into a suite at the Ritz Hotel, just over the road from their headquarters. That weekend, Maxwell increased his offer to £100,000,000.

This time there was no response at all.

The Reed board weren't the only ones appalled at the idea of selling out to Maxwell. So were the *Mirror* journalists. The paper's veteran leader writer, Joe Haines, declared, 'The man is a monster.' Maxwell, said Haines, was 'a liar and a crook and I can prove it'. What's more, if Maxwell ever came through the front door of the *Mirror*, he was heading straight out the back.

By now, though, further cracks had begun to appear in the Reed board – cracks Maxwell was increasingly confident he would be able to squeeze through. On Monday, 9 July, he made a move whose apparent air of gentility fooled nobody: he invited Reed's Chief Executive, Les Carpenter, to come to his suite at the Ritz for tea and cucumber sandwiches the following afternoon.

But when Maxwell's son Ian went into work the next morning he found his father in a highly agitated state. 'He knew this was a day that was going to change his life and he was very touchy. As soon as I came in, Dad said, "I've got a problem."

' "What problem?" I asked.

'The problem,' Maxwell told him, 'is Ryōichi Sasakawa.'

Although Maxwell could be wildly indiscriminate in his choice of friends, Ryōichi Sasakawa still seems a strange choice of bedfellow. During the Second World War, he had been the leader of a group of Japanese fascists called the Patriotic People's Party, whose members idolized Hitler and dressed in black SS-style uniforms. Imprisoned as a war criminal, Sasakawa whiled away his time by reading obsessively about powerboat racing. At the time the only legal forms of gambling in Japan were bicycle racing and horse racing. And then in 1951 another sport was added to the list – powerboat racing.

Immediately Sasakawa was released from prison, he set about

turning himself into the powerboat king of Japan. Over the next twenty years, he made so much money from powerboat racing that he once said proudly, 'I am the world's richest fascist.' In an attempt to buff up his image, he launched the Sasakawa Peace Foundation and tried – unsuccessfully – to buy himself the Nobel Peace Prize by bribing the judges.

At eighty-six years old, Sasakawa had one remaining ambition: he wanted to meet the Queen. Maxwell had promised to fix it and arranged an invitation for them both to go to a garden party at Buckingham Place. But the garden party was that afternoon – at exactly the same time Maxwell had invited Les Carpenter to tea and cucumber sandwiches at the Ritz.

'Dad said, "What are we going to do? He's flown in all the way from Japan specially to meet the Queen. How the fuck are we going to deal with it?" '

Ian asked to see the invitation. 'When I looked closely, I saw it was made out to Ian Robert Maxwell. Whoever had written it had put the anglicized version of Dad's original first name – Jan – as well as the one he had taken – Robert. I said, "But, Dad, I'm also Ian Robert Maxwell. Why don't I go instead and take him as my guest?" '

At first Maxwell dismissed the idea out of hand – 'It'll never work; they'll know you're not me.'

But by now the pressure was getting to him. After pacing around his office for another few minutes, he began to change his tune.

'I suppose it might be worth a try . . .'

At three o'clock that afternoon Reed's Chief Executive, Les Carpenter, knocked on the door of Maxwell's suite at the Ritz. Fearful that Maxwell would make a promise and renege on it later, the Reed board had told Carpenter that if they were going to accept his offer, Maxwell must stump up the £100,000,000 in cash – by the end of the day.

But first of all Carpenter had some haggling of his own to do. He told Maxwell that he wanted more than £100,000,000.

Reluctantly, Maxwell raised his offer to £107,000,000.

It was not enough.

'I want a hundred and thirteen million,' Carpenter told him. Maxwell refused.

Standing up, Carpenter walked towards the door. Before he opened it, he turned around and said, 'It's a hundred and thirteen million or nothing.'

Maxwell protested that he didn't have another £6,000,000. Carpenter told him he needed to consult with his board before going any further. When he arrived back at Reed headquarters, Carpenter learned that the latest estimate of how much a flotation might raise had fallen again – to below £50,000,000.

Carpenter informed the board that he had held out for £113,000,000, but that Maxwell claimed that he didn't have the extra £6,000,000. In the last twenty-four hours, the attitude of the Reed board had gone through a complete about-turn. Having initially declared that they would never sell the Mirror Group to Maxwell under any circumstances, they were now so desperate to get the newspapers off their hands that they came up with an unusual plan – they offered to lend him the extra £6,000,000 themselves, at an extremely favourable rate of interest.

When Ryōichi Sasakawa stepped out of his chauffeur-driven Rolls-Royce Phantom VI – the largest car the company had ever manufactured – Ian Maxwell saw that he was not wearing a suit – standard attire on such occasions. Instead, he was dressed in full Japanese formal dress, with a long pleated skirt and a kimono jacket. He also turned out not to speak any English – he and Maxwell always communicated through an interpreter.

At the gates of Buckingham Palace, the invitation was carefully scrutinized. To Maxwell's relief, the two of them were waved through. However, his relief didn't last long. As they walked into the main reception room at the Palace, Maxwell looked out of the window and saw hundreds of people milling about in the Buckingham Palace garden.

His heart sank. 'All I can think is, how the hell am I ever going to get Sasakawa to meet the Queen?'

But, at this point, he had a stroke of luck. 'This man comes up to me and says, "Is this by any chance Ryōichi Sasakawa?"' He turned out to be the Vice-President of the National Society for the Prevention of Cruelty to Children – a charity that Sasakawa had recently donated £2,000,000 to in his role as a born-again philanthropist.

Would Sasakawa care to meet the charity's patron, Princess Margaret, the man asked.

Yes, said Maxwell. He'd like that very much indeed.

'We go into the garden and we're told where to stand. After a few minutes Princess Margaret arrives and I'm introduced as Robert Maxwell. I start to tell her that actually I'm Ian Maxwell, Bob's son, but before I can introduce her to Sasakawa, there's this commotion in the background.'

The crowd parted and around the corner came the Queen. 'When she sees her, Princess Margaret turns away from us and says, "Lilibet, come and meet Bob Maxwell's son."' As soon as Sasakawa laid eyes on the Queen, something unexpected happened: he fell to the ground and started emitting a high-pitched wailing sound.

The Queen looked at him.

'What have we here?' she asked.

Maxwell told her that this was Ryōichi Sasakawa, the noted Japanese philanthropist. By this point the Queen had been on the throne for more than three decades and must have become used to people reacting oddly in her presence. Even so, it's doubtful if she had ever before seen an 86-year-old former fascist in traditional Japanese costume lying wailing at her feet.

'He can get up, you know,' the Queen said.

Ian Maxwell explained that it was customary in Japan, when meeting royalty, not to look at them directly, and also to prostrate oneself on the ground. The Queen continued to stare at Sasakawa. Then she abruptly changed the subject.

'How it's going with the *Mirror*?' she asked.

Maxwell told her that everything was still up in the air, but he thought his father's bid would be successful.

'I do hope so,' said the Queen.

★

At 5.30 p.m., Carpenter went to the Ritz, where Maxwell was waiting in his suite. The two of them shook hands before walking over the road to go through the necessary paperwork. Maxwell, as he was fully aware, had got a terrific deal. While the newspapers may have been doing badly, the value of the *Mirror* building and its shareholdings were worth what he had paid for the entire group.

By the time lawyers on both sides had gone through all the paperwork and the contracts had been signed, it was just before midnight.

'Are you going home now?' Maxwell was asked.

'Yes, off to bed,' he replied.

Before he left, Les Carpenter had one last request. 'Bob, do me a favour. Don't go to the *Mirror* tonight. Let's be tactful and break the news in the morning.'

This was an excellent idea, agreed Maxwell; he had no wish to cause any unnecessary ructions. Going back to his suite at the Ritz, he phoned Bob Edwards at ten past midnight. Already asleep in bed, Edwards stumbled naked to the telephone. When he picked it up, he heard Maxwell announce, 'We have lift-off!' Maxwell then told Edwards to phone all the members of the *Mirror* board and summon them to a meeting starting at 2.45 that morning.

'Get there at one o'clock yourself,' he said, 'and we'll have a drink.'

Outside, Maxwell's Rolls-Royce was waiting by the Ritz entrance.

'Where to, sir?' asked his chauffeur.

'Where the fuck do you think?' he said. 'To the *Mirror*!'

Bob Edwards spent the next hour phoning up the astonished *Mirror* directors, rousing them from their beds and telling them to head straight to the *Mirror* for a board meeting. But when he arrived, he found the place in darkness. By this point a thunderstorm had broken. As Edwards stood there with the rain drumming on his umbrella and lightning crackling overhead, he found himself gripped by a sudden sense of unease.

'I decided that my role in the developing drama would be similar to that of the music critic friend of Citizen Kane, played by Joseph

Cotten, whose newspaper was taken over by Kane and who became a disillusioned employee swamped in drink and self-pity.' Edwards's musings were soon cut short. 'I gradually became illuminated in the shadows by the approaching headlights of a Rolls-Royce.'

Maxwell's arrival at the *Mirror* caught everyone on the nightshift off-guard.

'Who are you?' the doorman asked.

'I'm the new owner,' Maxwell told him, walking straight into the leather-lined executive lift. Up on the third floor, the panic-stricken editorial staff learned that he was on his way. The *Mirror*'s Editor, Mike Molloy, a dapper bow-tied man with carefully coiffed blond hair and an equally well-tended moustache, decided there was only one thing he could do.

'It's my duty to go and greet him.'

Molloy had first met Maxwell ten years earlier at a Labour Party Conference in Blackpool. It was an encounter he had never forgotten: 'The strangely orange colour of his complexion, his ink-black hair and enormous eyebrows gave him the look of a music-hall comedian; but his smile was like that of Richard III.'

Now Maxwell strode into the Chairman's office, headed straight for the drinks cabinet and poured himself a large Scotch. Afterwards, he held up the bottle.

'Anyone else want one?'

As he looked on, Molloy found there was an image in his head that he couldn't dislodge. 'He looked just like an animal laying down its scent.'

By the time the board meeting was over, the thunderstorm had passed and the sky was starting to lighten. Shell-shocked and bleary, the *Mirror* executives staggered out into the dawn. Five hours later, Clive Thornton arrived to clear out his office. As he was leaving the building for the last time, Thornton was asked if he'd had any contact with Maxwell.

'I could hardly miss him,' he said glumly. 'He was sitting behind my desk.'

That morning, Maxwell called a meeting of the paper's union

leaders – the Fathers of Chapel, as they were known. He explained that he planned to topple Rupert Murdoch's *Sun* as the most popular paper in the UK and restore the *Mirror's* fortunes to their former glory. From the union leaders' reaction, it was plain that they were sceptical – both of his plans and of his motives.

Maxwell was affronted.

'Do you think I'm just on an ego trip?' he asked.

'Yes!' they bellowed back in unison.

However, he had better luck wooing the paper's senior editorial staff. At lunchtime Maxwell took them to the Royal Suite in Claridge's hotel. Bob Edwards offered Maxwell a lift in his own chauffeur-driven car. It proved to be an eventful journey. 'His attitude to the driver was extraordinary,' Edwards recalled later. ' "Go to the left!" he would shout. "Nip in front!" "Jump the lights!" '

By the time they arrived, Edwards noticed that his chauffeur's hands were shaking so much that he could barely hold the wheel. Not only that: 'We had also gone the worst possible way.'

At Claridge's, champagne and Buck's Fizz were served, along with an enormous cheese soufflé. But as they were leaving another event occured – one that several of those present would look back on as a foretaste of things to come. Outside the hotel, Maxwell was pursued by the manager. 'Mr Maxwell, Mr Maxwell, come back,' he cried. 'You haven't paid.'

Waving a hand, Maxwell told the man to send the bill to his office.

The manager was having none of it. 'You always say that, and you never pay. You must pay now!'

Reluctantly, but with no sign of embarrassment, Maxwell took out his wallet and settled the bill.

The first edition of the *Mirror* under Maxwell's ownership came with a banner headline reading 'FORWARD WITH BRITAIN!' and an editorial that had been written by Maxwell himself: 'We stand for a modern Britain – a country which truly needs modernizing, with industry and trade unions alike prepared to face the hard facts of survival in the Eighties. I have been in a position to buy the *Daily Mirror*. But what I cannot buy is the loyalty of its readers. That will have to continue to be earned. To me, the *Mirror* has always meant something special. I believe it means something special to those who work for it and you who buy it. The British people. That is why the *Mirror* today carries our new slogan: "Forward with Britain!" That slogan is my policy.'

Although Bob Edwards's sense of unease hadn't gone away, it grew a little fainter after he read Maxwell's horoscope – Gemini – in the next Monday's *Evening Standard*. Just as Clive Thornton's demise had been foretold in the stars, so too, it seemed, had Maxwell's triumph. 'A career change must add to your long-term security,' the horoscope declared confidently. 'Although the coming months will at certain times be demanding, not for one second should you think you are doomed to fail!'

14.

Madness

At last Maxwell had what he had always wanted: a newspaper of his own. At last he could go toe-to-toe with his greatest rival. Together, he and Rupert Murdoch would slug it out in a fight to become the most powerful newspaper baron in the country. But Maxwell had another, even loftier, ambition: he wanted to be the greatest media mogul the world had ever known.

By now he had become a figure of fascination, regarded with a constantly shifting mix of awe, fear and derision. At a reception at the French embassy, Prince Charles bombarded Mike Molloy with questions about his new boss: 'What an extraordinary man. What's he like to work for? Where does he get all his money from?'

At the same reception, Bob Edwards was approached by Princess Margaret's former husband, Lord Snowdon. 'I must see him,' Snowdon said. Edwards offered to introduce them, but this turned out to be the last thing on Snowdon's mind.

'No, no,' he said. 'I don't want to meet him. I just want to look at him.'

On the day after he took over the *Mirror*, Maxwell called a press conference where he announced that the paper would gain an extra million readers within a year. By any standards, this was a wildly ambitious plan; at the time the circulation stood at 3.5 million. Few, if anyone, on the *Mirror* believed it was possible. Undeterred, Maxwell decided that what the paper needed was a game to encourage new readers. A game that would encourage them to keep buying the paper day after day.

There was a certain amount of logic in this; after all, Rupert

Murdoch had a game – Bingo – in the *Sun*, so why shouldn't he? But while there may have been logic here, there was also reckoned to be a large amount of lunacy. Not only was any game bound to be very costly, but history had shown that new readers tended to melt away as soon as the prize had been won. Various *Mirror* executives pleaded with Maxwell to change his mind.

He ignored them.

His game, he declared, would be 'The Game of the Decade'. Two rival advertising agencies were told to come up with some ideas and report back within a week. The winning proposal aimed squarely at two of the most glaring chinks in Maxwell's armour: his vanity and his lack of any sense of absurdity.

'You are the biggest celebrity around, Bob,' the boss of the advertising agency told him. 'You should be fronting this campaign. You are the unique selling point. That is why we are calling it "Who Dares Wins". You have dared and you have won.'

Gravely, Maxwell nodded, then gave his verdict. 'I have come to the conclusion that you are right.'

Listening to this, Richard Stott, then Editor of the *Sunday People*, thought it was the most flagrant display of toadying he had ever witnessed. He was also reminded of something that he had noticed before: how there tended to be a big difference between people's behaviour in front of Maxwell and their recollections of it afterwards. In Maxwell's presence, normally bullish, swaggering people – usually men – would often became sycophantic to the point of spinelessness. Yet afterwards they would be full of stories about how they had fearlessly stood their ground, refusing to have any truck with Maxwell and his disgraceful ways.

Who Dares Wins – Bingo in all but name – was to be launched with a slogan: 'Do you sincerely want to be rich?' Again, people begged Maxwell to reconsider. Was this really the sort of question a socialist paper should be asking its readers?

He took no notice.

As well as featuring in television adverts to launch the game, Maxwell's face began appearing in the *Mirror* ever more frequently – over a hundred times in the first six months of his ownership. This didn't escape anybody's attention, least of all Rupert Murdoch's. 'I could see the way he was running the *Mirror* was a joke. Always putting himself on the front page. My picture never appears in my papers, and preferably no quotes either. But, of course, his ego was enormous.'

The former Chairman of Mirror Group Newspapers, Hugh Cudlipp, was particularly alarmed by all this self-advertisement. As he wrote in his diary, 'In 1984, it is true to say that anyone in the United Kingdom not aware that all the Mirror Group Newspapers are now published by Robert Maxwell must be deaf, dumb, blind, or all three.'

To make sure he was always seen looking his best, Maxwell even appointed his own 'Personal Photographer'. Mike Maloney was a junior photographer on the *Mirror* when he was asked to take some flattering shots of the new proprietor. As brash as he was eager to get ahead, Maloney, like Maxwell, drove a Rolls-Royce with personalized number plates – his, however, was second-hand and had taken him years to save up for.

Quickly, Maloney worked out there were some key dos and don'ts here. The first was the most important of all: 'Disguise his paunch.' This was easier said than done, but he devised a way of shrinking Maxwell down to an acceptable size: 'His best angle was taken from above, looking down, and using a wide-angle lens to make him look taller and slimmer.' Maloney was also careful never to shoot Maxwell with the flash below the camera pointing up. 'This gives a dreadful ghoulish effect, highlighting the wrong features and making the subject look like Dracula.'

Just as the Who Dares Wins slogan had been 'borrowed' from the SAS, so Maxwell also helped himself to Metro Goldwyn Mayer's roaring lion as his new logo. In future, the lion's head would appear on all the letterheads and company literature of MGN – as Mirror Group Newspapers had been rechristened. A specially woven blue and gold carpet bearing both the lion's head and the letters MGN was laid on the editorial floor.

The Who Dares Wins prize was to be one million pounds – the highest in newspaper history. It was launched with an extra large photograph of Maxwell standing in front of one million pounds in bank notes – nervously lent for the occasion by the Queen's bankers, Coutts. 'Mr Maxwell's pretty daughter, Ghislaine, 22, was on hand to see the cash in all denominations wheeled out under the watchful eyes of police and bank security staff,' the *Mirror* reported. Ghislaine also made a – rather regal – statement of her own: 'It pleases me to know it will make one of our readers very happy soon.'

Five days later – before anyone had had a chance to win the prize – the *Sun* announced that it had just created the first 'Bingo millionaire'. Murdoch had done it again. Television pictures of Maxwell being told the news showed him looking more Dracula-like than ever.

When Clive Thornton had been Chairman of the *Mirror*, he decided that his vast, oak-panelled office sent out quite the wrong message. Such grandeur, such ostentation, had no place in a newspaper that claimed to speak for the working class of Great Britain. He decided that a wall should be symbolically erected in the middle of his office, dividing it in two. This proved trickier than he had anticipated. Several different unions had to be consulted and negotiations went on for more than three months before agreement was finally reached.

The moment Maxwell took over the *Mirror*, he decided that – just as symbolically – the wall should be torn down. By the time Joe Haines went to see Maxwell on the morning of Sunday, 15 July, demolition work had already begun. Born and brought up in a Rotherhithe slum, Haines had left school at fourteen, and joined the *Glasgow Herald* as a copyboy. After a stint as Harold Wilson's Press Secretary at 10 Downing Street, he became Chief Leader Writer at the *Mirror*. Haines proved brilliant at distilling the essence of a complex political argument into a few punchy sentences. A lifelong socialist, he was widely regarded as the moral conscience of the paper.

While his abilities were not in doubt, Haines was also reckoned to be someone you crossed at your peril. A small, balding man with steel-framed spectacles, he had a reputation for being extremely touchy, and also for possessing photographic recall of every slight he had ever suffered. Having denounced Maxwell as a crook and a monster, Haines assumed that his days were numbered.

While he was clearing his desk, his phone went. Would he come up to the ninth floor?

Haines had no doubt what was in store. 'It was a moment of high tension to me. A public execution was expected.'

When he came in, Maxwell immediately got to the point. Was he staying or going?

'I said, "That depends on whether you accept my conditions or not."'

Haines proceeded to lay out his terms: he would only stay if the *Mirror* remained committed to the Labour Party; if Maxwell never told him what to write, or tried to interfere with anything he had written.

As soon as he'd finished, Maxwell said, 'I agree to all your terms.'

Too late, Haines realized he had been outmanoeuvred. Maxwell, as he'd so often proved in the past, was a master at the art of giving people everything they wanted. Or at least appearing to – what they actually received tended to be another matter.

'It was my own fault,' Haines admitted later. 'I had walked into a trap of my own making.'

One of Haines's first pieces under Maxwell's ownership was a characteristically fierce condemnation of corrupt union practices, and the expenses-fuelled lifestyles of many of the paper's senior journalists.

'The gravy-train,' he wrote, 'has hit the buffers.'

Later on, Rupert Murdoch would get the credit for revolution-izing Fleet Street, but it was Maxwell who set the process in motion. Over the next two years, he forced the print unions to accept widespread redundancies, repeatedly threatening to shut down his papers unless they agreed to his terms. However, Murdoch did – inadvertently – do Maxwell a favour. In the course of a single night in January 1986, he transferred production of his papers to a fortified stockade in Wapping where no printers, only electricians, were required to print them. Facing the prospect of imminent extinction, the unions at the *Mirror* swiftly caved in.

But while Maxwell happily whacked his adversaries with any stick that came to hand, he also knew how to wield the carrot to maximum effect. Among the cost-cutting measures introduced by Clive Thornton had been one of the *Mirror*'s most sacred traditions: the distribution of free alcohol to journalists during working hours. As well as costing hundreds of thousands of pounds each year, this arrangement was held to be largely responsible for the fact that the *Mirror* had the highest level of alcoholism in Fleet Street.

Not only did Maxwell restore the practice – he added a little twist of his own. Every Thursday afternoon an elderly man wearing a once-white linen jacket would push a trolley around the editorial floor handing out the weekly alcohol ration. How much each journalist received depended on their level of seniority. Peter Miller, Deputy News Editor of the *Sunday Mirror*, was given a weekly allocation of six bottles of red wine and six bottles of white wine – 'and it was good stuff too.' He was also provided with a fridge to keep it in. As far as anybody knew, there was no maximum allowance. Or, if there was, no one ever managed to exceed it.

In the hallway outside Maxwell's office, people waited for hours – sometimes, it was reputed, for days – in the hope of being granted an audience. The atmosphere was like that of a medieval court, with a constant stream of supplicants seeking the monarch's bounty. Some sat clutching papers they wanted him to sign – Maxwell insisted on making all decisions himself, however minor. The more experienced brought books to read. At times there were so many people waiting that there weren't enough chairs for them to sit on. Instead, they shuffled about disconsolately, hoping against hope to hear their name announced.

But still they came, from dawn until long after dusk: personnel managers with hit lists of people to be fired, journalists wanting an interview, down-on-their-luck peers looking for a job . . . Periodically, trays of snacks would be handed round to those who had been waiting the longest. One man who had been summoned for a job interview finally got to see Maxwell twenty-six hours after he had arrived.

Meanwhile, Maxwell rushed about in an ecstasy of excitement, keen to show off his new purchase to as many people as possible. Among the early visitors was Margaret Thatcher, who was invited to lunch in the newspaper's executive dining room. Mike Molloy was also there. 'The lunch was a lively occasion as both had a lot to say,' he recalled. 'The trouble was they both said it at the same time, so it was impossible to hear the points each of them was making.'

As Molloy soon discovered, there was a further hazard to dining with Maxwell. 'I was the first to be served by the butler. It was leg of lamb, and I helped myself to the meat cut from around the knuckle. I began talking to the person on my left and when I turned back I found Bob finishing the last of the choice morsels of meat from my plate. He obviously liked the same cut as well and couldn't wait until the butler got around to him.'

The Deputy Leader of the Labour Party, Roy Hattersley, was another early visitor, along with his political adviser, Dave Hill. When they were shown into the dining room, Hattersley found Maxwell sitting at the head of 'a huge dining table drinking from a silver goblet. He did not get up.'

Shortly after the meal started, Maxwell told the butler to leave and close the door behind him. Once the butler had gone, Maxwell explained what he had done. ' "I feared that you were going to discuss intelligence reports. And that man" – he pointed at the door – "is a spy planted by Rupert Murdoch." '

When Dave Hill, not unreasonably, asked why Maxwell continued to employ him, 'the response was a mixture of contempt and incredulity. "That just goes to show how little you know about business," Maxwell said. "I don't waste my time worrying about who is appointed as my butler." '

By this point Who Dares Wins had been running for several weeks and no one had won the million-pound prize. Now that the novelty had worn off, the *Mirror*'s circulation had started to slide back to what it had been before the prize had been announced. But once again this wasn't the whole story. In fact, there had been several winners. Maxwell, however, didn't consider any of them to be worthy recipients of his money. Either they were too middle class, or too undeserving, or just not appealing enough.

Having rejected all the winners so far, Maxwell finally found one who ticked all the right boxes. Maudie Barrett was an elderly widow from Harwich in Essex who had spent her entire working life as a cleaning lady. As well as heroically providing for a large family, Mrs Barrett also had a dog – a spaniel – called Thumper. The dog, Maxwell felt, would go down especially well with readers.

Mrs Barrett and Thumper were driven up to Blackpool, where Maxwell, accompanied by his editors and senior members of staff, would present her prize at the Town Hall. It just so happened that the Labour Party Conference was going on at the same time – an event Maxwell had calculated would ensure him even more publicity. But not everything went according to plan. First of all, Mrs Barrett, unused to long car journeys, was sick by the roadside on the way to Blackpool. Then the *Mirror*'s gossip columnist stood on Thumper's paw, putting an already nervous Mrs Barrett even more on edge.

Installed in a suite at the Imperial Hotel, she sat on a bed chain-smoking.

When Maxwell finally appeared, he made a great fuss of the now-limping Thumper, before plonking himself down beside Mrs Barrett – causing, as Mike Molloy recalled, 'the bed to rear like a boat in a heavy sea'. Having congratulated her on her win, Maxwell proceeded to lecture Mrs Barrett on what to do with the money; essentially, this involved her giving it straight back to him. 'Do you realize this is a tax-free sum and if you let me invest it for you it will bring you an income of a thousand pounds a week without any reduction in the capital sum?'

Afterwards Mrs Barrett was driven in an open-topped tram along the seafront to the Town Hall. Before the cheque could be presented, there was another hitch: the paper's veteran agony aunt, Marje Proops, sat on the luckless Thumper. Richard Stott looked on in disbelief. 'Marje sat down, not knowing that Thumper's rear end was already occupying part of the seat. As she did so, she pinioned him, but as neither could move, the squeals of Thumper and the protestations of Marje held up the ceremony for several minutes.'

Within a few days of promising Joe Haines that he would never interfere with anything he had written, Maxwell went back on his word. Once again Haines threatened to resign. Although Maxwell backed down, Richard Stott saw that he had already homed in on Haines's own Achilles heel: 'Joe always loved power; it was an aphrodisiac and the powerful men who exercised it fascinated and mesmerized him.'

Maxwell not only rewrote articles: he chose photographs – frequently of himself – and commissioned pieces extolling the virtues of places where he had, or hoped to have, business interests. Puzzled *Mirror* readers now found themselves confronted by headlines such as: 'Burma, A Country We Have Ignored For Far Too Long.'

At the same time, Maxwell clearly believed that owning a newspaper gave him a licence to act as a kind of international superhero, jetting round the world dispensing money and advice as he saw fit. The 1984/5 famine in Ethiopia claimed the lives of more than a million people and left more than twice that number homeless.

Infuriated by what he regarded as a tardy and ineffectual response to the crisis, Maxwell ran an appeal in the *Mirror* which raised £2,000,000 from readers and well-heeled friends. Still reeling from his introduction to the Queen, Ryōichi Sasakawa stumped up £100,000. Maxwell also persuaded the country's military government to allow an RAF transport plane loaded with food and medical supplies to land in Addis Ababa. He insisted on travelling in the plane and took along a number of journalists to record what was dubbed 'The *Mirror*'s Mercy Mission'.

Among the journalists on the plane was the paper's Political Editor, Alastair Campbell. 'If I read back my stuff today, I have to say I'm ashamed. It really was "Starving children were saved yesterday thanks to the intervention of *Mirror* publisher, Robert Maxwell."' One evening, Campbell returned to his hotel to find Maxwell had left a note for him. 'My work here is done,' he had written. 'I have returned home to resolve the miners' strike.'

The next year Maxwell stepped in to – as he put it – save the 1986 Commonwealth Games in Edinburgh. Dogged by financial mismanagement and facing a political boycott, the games were on the verge of collapse. Maxwell promised £2,000,000 of his own money. Once again, he turned to Ryōichi Sasakawa to help him out. At a joint press conference, Sasakawa caused considerable surprise by claiming to be twenty-seven years old and predicting that he would live until he was 200. In fact, he had recently celebrated his eighty-seventh birthday.

When the Queen arrived to open the games, Maxwell gave her a set of commemorative coins, saying, 'Permit me to present you with a token of this great event which I have orchestrated.' But once the games were over and the dust had settled, the organizers complained that, of the £2,000,000 Maxwell had promised, only £250,000 ever materialized.

If the public Maxwell radiated brightness and beneficence, the private Maxwell was much darker, especially where his children were concerned. Joe Haines once went into Maxwell's office to see his son Kevin standing in front of his father's desk. 'As I walked in, he said to Kevin, "Get out. I want to talk to Joe." What struck me most of all was how he treated the boy. Not "Excuse me, son", or anything like that, just "Get out." It was incredible.'

But, as Haines came to see, alongside Maxwell's ballooning messianic complex ran an almost equally large sentimental streak. In Berlin, Maxwell had doted on Barry, his German shepherd; in Blackpool he'd made a great fuss of Mrs Barratt's Thumper, and when he learned that Haines and his wife had just bought a new puppy, he reacted in a way that neither of them could have predicted. The next day Maxwell gave him a present he had bought for the puppy: a fluffy toy. That evening, Haines took the toy home and gave it to the puppy – who promptly tore it to pieces.

The following morning Maxwell asked how the puppy had liked it. Diplomatically, Haines said that it had been a great success. Maxwell was delighted. Perhaps Haines wouldn't mind doing him a favour? Would he take a photograph of the puppy with the fluffy toy?

Rushing home, Haines and his wife fished out the remains of the toy from their rubbish bin. After sticking it back together as best they could, they took a Polaroid which Haines duly gave to Maxwell. This too was to have unexpected consequences. Normally, Maxwell had just one framed photograph on his desk – of his daughter Ghislaine. But the next time Haines went into Maxwell's office, he saw that it had been replaced by the photograph of his dog. 'He kept it there for months. The whole thing just seemed very odd to me, especially when he treated his own children so badly.'

Yet, however appealing Mrs Barrett and Thumper may have been, however enormous the *Mirror*'s cash prizes, however many photos of Maxwell they ran, or starving children they saved, these failed to have the desired effect on the paper's sales. Within a year of his taking over, the *Mirror*'s circulation was down to 3,102,427, a loss of almost 450,000 copies a day. Even though all Fleet Street papers were going through a rough patch at the time, nearly one million readers had deserted Maxwell's three national papers – the fastest fall in their history.

Soon after returning from Blackpool, Mike Molloy met a friend of his – a psychiatrist called Tom Pitt-Atkins – who asked how he was getting on with Maxwell.

'He's pretty eccentric,' Molloy told him.

'He's not eccentric – he's mad,' said Pitt-Atkins bluntly. 'I've got people inside who are less crazy than him.'

'You actually think he's clinically mad?' said Molloy.

Pitt-Atkins nodded.

'Does he have a group of executives who are bitter rivals and only answer to him directly?' he asked.

Molloy said that he did.

'Does he micro-manage trivial matters, but leave important decisions deliberately vague and then blame others when things go wrong?'

Again Molloy admitted that he did.

'Does he make grandiose claims for all his business motives?'

'He says he went into scientific publishing when he saw the first atomic explosion, and he knew that science was the only hope for mankind to avert nuclear Armageddon,' Molloy said.

'That'll do. How does he treat his family?'

'Like slaves.'

'The man's off his head,' said Pitt-Atkins. 'He'll end up bringing his whole empire down around him.'

As for Maxwell himself, Pitt-Atkins felt the future was equally bleak. 'He'll probably die unexpectedly, perhaps in some sort of explosion.'

When Molloy pointed out that Maxwell had claimed that he wanted to leave a great heritage for his children, Pitt-Atkins offered a prediction of his own:

'He'll leave nothing to them,' he said. 'Just ashes.'

15.

In the Lair of the Black Bear

Two years after buying the *Daily Mirror*, Maxwell bought the building next door, Strand House, previously the headquarters of the Goldman Sachs bank. He promptly rechristened it Maxwell House – just as he'd done with his office on the Marylebone Road thirty-five years before. The top floor was converted into a luxury apartment where in future Maxwell would spend most of his time.

Now that he had a grand apartment, he wanted a suitably grand entrance to go with it. Two nine-foot-high doors of darkly polished wood, more suited to a doge's palace than a newspaper proprietor, were installed. Once the work was finished, Maxwell asked Eleanor Berry to come and have a look. She was enormously impressed: 'The lift ascended to the top floor. When it opened, I saw an entirely new world. I am not an authority on interior decoration, but the room I had been left in looked majestic and was adorned with seventeenth and eighteenth century paintings. The furniture might have belonged to kings and the carpets were embroidered with the letter M.'

Maxwell also wondered if Berry would like to watch the paper being printed. With its clanging hot-metal presses and streams of newspapers flying by on overhead conveyor belts, this too was an entirely new world – although possibly no one had ever seen it in quite such apocalyptic terms: 'I saw before me a river of volcanic lava sent by the gods in colours of red and white, purifying the earth and the fleece of freshly-shorn lambs and newly-fallen snow. Beside me stood the black bear, taking me by the hand.'

Maxwell had a lot to feel proud of. By pruning the workforce and driving costs down, he had turned Mirror Group Newspapers into a colossal cash cow. While circulation may have continued to fall, profits were soaring: up from £5,000,000 a year to £70,000,000 within eighteen months of his arrival.

Having recently bought the British Airways helicopter division for £12,500,000, he now owned more helicopters than anyone else in Europe. As Maxwell House had at one time been an HM Customs & Revenue building, the new owner still had the right to use the flat roof as a helipad – one of only three places in London where private helicopters could land and take off. Maxwell's personal helicopter was a twin-engined Eurocopter Squirrel. Before getting on board, he had a little ritual he would perform: he would stand on the roof of Maxwell House, unzip his fly and urinate over the side of the building. Subsequently, people would claim that he liked to do so directly on to the heads of the people below, an impression Maxwell did nothing to dispel; in fact, there was an internal gutter that ran around the roof of the building.

The child in Maxwell – bubbling ever closer to the surface, as Betty had realized – exulted in having another new toy. He took particular pleasure in the call sign given to the new helicopter: VR-BOB – he liked to say it stood for 'Very Rich Bob' – and would eagerly invite guests to join him on a spin over the rooftops of London. Sometimes when he went further afield he liked to drop in on people unexpectedly, descending from the skies and landing in their back gardens.

Maxwell could be an exacting guest. Arriving at a party that a *Mirror* employee and his wife were having, he held court in their living room. A small girl was brought forward to be introduced to the famous publisher. After chatting to her for a few minutes, Maxwell stared more closely at the girl's mouth.

'Why don't your parents do something about your teeth?' he asked.

Apologetically, the girl's mother admitted they had been meaning to take her to a dentist.

Later, Maxwell quietly paid her dental bills. Rather more often, people would come to see him. On one occasion, Mother Teresa arrived unexpectedly in Maxwell's apartment accompanied by an interpreter and, according to Mike Molloy, 'clothed in garments that appeared to have been made out of old tea towels'. She had come specially to bring him a message from God, she said.

If this struck Maxwell as unusual, he gave no sign of it. Mother Teresa then launched into a lengthy speech in her native Albanian, sounding 'like someone cracking nuts with their teeth'. When she had finished, the interpreter declared, 'God wants you to give Mother Teresa a million pounds to start a hospice in England!' In the silence that followed, observers noticed that the grin on Maxwell's face appeared to be rather more fixed than it had been before. Glancing at his watch, he announced that he had urgent business to attend to. A few minutes later, the clatter of rotor blades was heard overhead.

Over the next year, two men started working for Robert Maxwell – men from very different backgrounds and possessed of very different skills. Each of them would bring out very different sides of Maxwell's character.

Peter Jay was one of the golden boys of his generation. The son of two prominent Labour politicians, he went to Winchester College – where he was Head Boy – then Christ Church College, Oxford, where he gained a first-class degree in PPE. He was also President of the Oxford Union. Jay went on to become the Economics Editor of *The Times* and to marry Margaret Callaghan, daughter of the Labour politician Jim Callaghan.

In every magazine profile, he would be referred to, without fail, as 'the cleverest man in Britain'. As if this wasn't enough, in 1974 Jay was tipped by *Time* magazine as a future world leader. Three years later his father-in-law, Jim Callaghan, succeeded Harold Wilson as Prime Minister. Then, just when Jay's path to the top seemed assured, everything began to fall apart. Despite having no experience as a diplomat, he was appointed British ambassador in Washington.

With accusations of nepotism ringing in his ears, Jay headed across the Atlantic to take up his new job. Once in Washington, his wife, Margaret, started an affair with the journalist Carl Bernstein, co-author of *All the President's Men*. Meanwhile Jay had an affair of his own – with their children's nanny. To complicate things further, Bernstein was also married, to the writer Nora Ephron, who wrote a comic novel, *Heartburn*, based on the whole tangled business. The book was turned into a hit film with Meryl Streep and Jack Nicholson.

All this was related with enormous glee in the British tabloid press – Rupert Murdoch's *Sun* ran the story under the headline 'How the Know-All Came a Cropper'. When Jay came back to London after two years, he found he was no longer the golden boy; instead, he had become a pariah.

At this point Maxwell swooped. He'd always had a peculiar knack for homing in on once grand people who had fallen on hard times, and Jay, however tarnished he may have become, was still grander than most. Maxwell offered him a job as his 'Chief-of-Staff' – a job title normally reserved for the armed forces, or the White House. While no one, least of all Jay himself, was sure what this involved, it sounded prestigious and carried a hefty salary. Eagerly, he accepted.

But before Jay started, there was something he needed to find out. Like practically everyone else, he'd heard rumours that Maxwell was working for the KGB. Clearly, it would be awkward for a former British ambassador to work for anybody in the pay of a foreign government. Jay therefore took soundings from his contacts in the Foreign Office, and was reassured that, while Maxwell plainly loved passing snippets of information back and forth between world leaders, there was no evidence to suggest he was a spy.

Back in 1977, Jay had written an essay for a book entitled *The Future That Doesn't Work: Social Democracy's Failures in Britain*. His essay was called 'Englanditis' and began: 'We in Britain are a confused and unhappy people.' The two years Peter Jay spent working for Maxwell were to bring him more confusion and unhappiness than he would have imagined possible.

Simon Grigg was born into a working-class family who lived on a council estate in Reading. Leaving school at fifteen, he went to work for his father, a builder, but never much cared for it. One day he was reading a newspaper and saw an advertisement for Ivor Spencer's International School for Butlers – Spencer was a former Toastmaster to the Queen. Grigg spent the next year saving up the course fees, and by the time he left, nine months later, he'd acquired a whole range of new skills – including 'dealing with greedy guests', 'answering the door to tradesmen' and 'polishing very high-end shoes'.

After a spell working for the son of the richest man in Austria, Grigg, then aged twenty-one, came back to Britain with the growing suspicion that he'd made a big mistake. But Ivor Spencer arranged for him to go for an interview as assistant to Robert Maxwell's butler, and, much to Griggs's surprise, he got the job.

'I wasn't really prepared for it at all. I'd just done this course, but I was very young, incredibly shy and had no real experience of the world. I was winging it really – completely winging it.'

Dressed in his uniform – a morning suit and a grey tie – Grigg did his best to keep as busy as possible. Naturally discreet and light on his feet, he also had a knack for making himself inconspicuous. At first, Grigg hardly ever saw Maxwell; occasionally a large, black-haired figure would sweep by on his way to yet another meeting. Then, after a few months, Maxwell's butler was moved to another job; his replacement turned out to have a criminal record and all at once Grigg was bumped up the line to become his valet.

'Even though I was shy, I wasn't nervous in his presence; for some reason he didn't frighten me. I think he liked the fact that I wasn't pretending to be anything I wasn't. He needed people who he could trust, whose loyalty wasn't in any doubt. Clearly, I wasn't any threat to him. He also liked having young people around him; they energized him. And while I may have been inexperienced, I was very keen and determined to do well.'

Grigg's duties included everything from serving Maxwell breakfast – orange juice, Corn Flakes and strong coffee, served in an enormous cup with 'Very Important Person' printed on the side – to dabbing his face with a powder puff so that he never looked sweaty in photographs.

As he settled into his job, Grigg began to pay more attention to Maxwell's foibles – partly so he could anticipate his demands, and partly because he had never met anyone remotely like him before. Like Betty, he noticed how childlike Maxwell could be. 'If you showed weakness, you'd had it. But if you stood up to him, he tended to crumble. I remember once he was firing off all these different orders. I think I must have been really tired at the time because after a while I just said, "Right, what the fuck do you want me to do first?" He just looked at me for a bit, then he started to laugh. The strange thing was that at times like that there was this incredible innocence to him; he became just like a little boy.'

It wasn't just Maxwell's behaviour that was childlike; so were his tastes. Wherever they were in the world, he would send Grigg out to buy boxed sets of his favourite films. 'He used to like watching James Bond movies more than anything else. Even though he must have seen the same films time and time again, he never seemed to tire of them.'

In the four years Grigg spent working for Maxwell, he accompanied him to sixty-four countries, sometimes travelling on his private jet, sometimes on Concorde and sometimes – though much less often – on regular commercial flights. As they sped through one border control after another, Grigg noticed something else about Maxwell: how carefully he guarded his passport. 'He was very protective about it in a way he wasn't protective about anything else. Although he'd lived in this country for most of his adult life, I think somewhere inside him he felt that, as an immigrant, it could be taken away from him at any moment.'

In his own way, Peter Jay was also winging it. His job, as he saw it, was to make sure that Maxwell's life ran as smoothly as possible. Seeing the teetering piles of unopened envelopes on Maxwell's desk, he instigated a filing system whereby all the post would be put into different boxes depending on importance. But it soon became clear that this was the last thing Maxwell wanted; instead, he was determined to remain in charge of everything himself. That way, he, and he alone, knew what was happening.

While Maxwell would frequently reduce people to quivering wrecks, Grigg saw that he took particular pleasure in humiliating Peter Jay. The combination of Jay's reputation for cleverness, his Establishment background and his air of fleshy self-assurance brought all Maxwell's resentment – and insecurities – surging to the fore.

At the fortnightly lunches Maxwell held in the *Mirror* dining room, he would sneeringly refer to Jay as 'Mister Ambassador' – insisting that he take down verbatim notes of what was being said, or sending him off on mundane errands. Visitors winced with embarrassment. Peter Mandelson, the Labour Party's Director of Communications and the man widely credited with reviving the party's fortunes, remembers Maxwell treating Jay appallingly – 'just like the office boy'. Maxwell also took to phoning Jay up in the middle of the night with absurdly trivial questions. He once called him at four o'clock on a Saturday morning to ask him what the time was.

On another occasion he told Grigg that he needed to speak to Jay immediately. At the time, senior staff at the *Mirror* had just been issued with early mobile phones. When Grigg finally tracked him down, Jay turned out to be in the middle of an important family occasion: 'I remember Peter saying, "Look, Simon, it's my daughter's wedding and I'm just about to walk her down the aisle. Does he really want to talk to me?" I said, 'I'm afraid he does."' Faced with a choice between discharging his paternal duties and answering his master's call, the ever-obliging Jay decided that his daughter would have to wait.

Jay himself claimed to be more bemused than upset by Maxwell's behaviour. 'From the moment I took the job, I very consciously decided to surround myself with an impermeable glass bubble so that nothing he did ever got to me. That said, I often found myself laughing hysterically at the bizarre nature of what we were all doing.' But when he wasn't laughing hysterically, Jay, like Simon Grigg, was observing Maxwell and coming to his own conclusions:

'It seemed to me that there was something not so much amoral about him, as pre-moral. It was as if he was literally uncivilized, like some great woolly mammoth stalking through a primeval forest wholly unaware of things like good and evil.'

At night, as he replayed the events of the day in his mind, Jay would sometimes wonder how Maxwell spent his own spare time up in his apartment at the top of Maxwell House. 'I came to see that he was terrified of boredom. He had no hobbies, no private activities and no friends. I think what drove him more than anything wasn't greed, or money, or even notoriety, but the desire to generate activity – no matter how pointless it was. Above all, he dreaded being on his own with nothing to do. That's why he would do things like call me up at four o'clock on a Saturday morning. The weekend was always an agony. Every Friday night it must have stretched before him like a vast desert of boredom.'

Although Eleanor Berry was very taken by Maxwell's new apartment at the top of Maxwell House, not everyone was so impressed. As Mike Molloy looked at the mahogany furniture, the pink marble fireplace that had been specially imported from Siena, the silk curtains, gilt mirrors and marble urns, he thought it tried – none too convincingly – to evoke the home of a country squire.

Molloy was intrigued by the Doric columns that had been erected in the entrance hall. Something about them didn't seem right, he felt, although he couldn't say what exactly. One day when nobody was looking, he tapped one.

It was hollow.

16.

An Enormous Spread

Whenever a new chef started work for Robert Maxwell, they would be handed a six-page list by his fiercely protective PA, Jean Baddeley. The list was headlined 'Robert Maxwell's likes' and contained very specific instructions about the food that Maxwell was to be served. It began with the most important instruction of all – so important that it was printed across the top of the paper in capital letters:

'IN NO CIRCUMSTANCES SHOULD GARLIC OR ONIONS BE USED.'

While garlic and onions topped his list of dislikes, they were by no means the only ones. Mr Maxwell did not care for 'small apples or oranges' – or indeed for small anything. 'In most instances, the largest sized fruit available should be sent of the best quality.' Sliced brown bread 'should never be buttered'. Similarly, no butter should ever be used in cooking – 'peanut oil may be used as an alternative'. On no account was deep-fried fish ever to be served. Caviar should always be Beluga and served with half-slices of brown bread or toast – again with the key proviso: 'NO BUTTER'. Mediterranean king prawns were to be accompanied by 'a plain yoghurt dip'.

Beef was to be cooked medium – 'trim off fat where possible'. Steak should be 'grilled only. Medium, sirloin fillet only. Brush with oil, trim fat.' When it came to lamb, Maxwell liked the 'knuckle end of a roast leg of lamb' and 'the end next to the tail' of a saddle. He was also fond of offal – in particular grilled calves' kidneys and veal kidneys in cream sauce. Other 'likes' included Chinese takeaway meals.

Coffee was to be poured into 'RM'S VIP cup which should be

warmed first'. Sugar should not be served 'unless asked for'. As for alcohol, he preferred vodka: 'RM only drinks Stolichnaya which should be kept very cold and served on its own.' Whisky should be Chivas Regal, brandy Exshaw's Vintage, champagne Mumm Cordon Rouge – 'served in tumblers' – and beer Löwenbräu. Mixers were 'all to be slimline'.

With the possible exception of Chinese takeaways and veal kidneys in cream sauce, all this amounted to a pretty healthy diet. Yet, by the mid-1980s, even the most casual of observers could hardly fail to notice that Maxwell, always a large man, was getting considerably larger.

Maxwell's weight was a constant source of mystery to his chefs. However dutifully they followed Jean Baddeley's instructions, he continued to pile on the pounds. What was going on? It seemed that whenever Baddeley wasn't around with her reproving finger and list of instructions, Maxwell's self-control went out of the window.

Even as a youngish man, he had always been a big, as well as an unorthodox, feeder. Gyles Brandreth remembers seeing Maxwell at a buffet lunch in the late 1960s to launch the Buy British campaign. 'He was going down the table eating everything with his hands, piling it into his mouth. I've never seen anything like it before. It was as if he was hungry for life, as if he just couldn't get enough of it.'

Fifteen years later, Eleanor Berry was a frequent guest at mealtimes in Headington Hill Hall. On one occasion she noticed that there was a padlock on the larder door. When Berry asked Betty why the larder was locked, she told her that it was to keep Maxwell out. 'Otherwise he breaks in and eats everything there is,' said Betty. 'He broke in the other day I'm sorry to say. He ate a pound of cheese, a jar of peanut butter, two jars of caviar, a loaf of bread and a whole chicken in one go.' She went on to say they had had to change the padlock a few weeks earlier as Maxwell had broken the last one. 'He's so strong he can break any door down . . . he's so naughty sometimes.'

When they sat down to lunch, Jean Baddeley was on hand to ensure that any outbursts of gluttony were kept in check. After the joint had been carved, a maid went round the table with a dish of potatoes. Berry helped herself before the dish was passed to Maxwell, 'who took even more potatoes than I had'.

Furiously, Baddeley rounded on the maid.

'I thought I told you that Mr Maxwell was *not* to be offered potatoes!' she told her.

She then spooned the potatoes off Maxwell's plate and back into the serving dish. To Berry's surprise, Maxwell did nothing; he just sat there meekly. At the end of the meal, his daughter Isabel took her to one side. 'My father has an eating disorder,' she explained. 'And we all have to struggle to prevent him from harming himself. Once he starts to eat carbohydrates, he can't stop.'

On another occasion, the journalist and editor Nicholas Coleridge was a guest at Sunday lunch, where roast chicken was served. Coleridge was particularly keen on breast meat and eagerly looking forward to a decent helping. But so too, it turned out, was his host. Glumly, Coleridge watched as Maxwell carved several chickens, putting every piece of breast on to his own plate in an enormous pile which he then topped off with a gherkin on a cocktail stick.

Betty believed that the roots of Maxwell's food consumption went back to his childhood – to when there was never enough to eat and he was always hungry: to when, as he told one of his secretaries, he had once been reduced to eating a dog. Ever since food had always represented security, a clear dividing line between his past life and his present.

As Maxwell grew older, his eating habits became even more unconstrained. Now it was if nothing ever satisfied him, nothing ever made him feel full. The *Mirror*'s Foreign Editor, Nick Davies, was with Maxwell on a trip abroad when he walked into Maxwell's suite one morning and saw him stuffing himself with sandwiches: 'It was like watching a starving man, driven mad by hunger, unable to control himself as he forced handfuls of food into his mouth. He must have sensed me there, because he turned and saw me standing in the doorway. For a split second, he was like a cornered animal, as though I had caught him thieving.'

Every year the disparity between pigginess and pickiness grew more pronounced. And, every year, Maxwell's waistband continued to expand. During the late 1970s and 1980s, Betty would send him to specialist slimming clinics – in one clinic in Switzerland, he was put on a sleep regime for several days, presumably on the grounds that this would be the only time when he was unable to eat. Nothing, though, seemed to have any effect.

When Martin Cheeseman, who had previously cooked for Harold Wilson in Downing Street, became Maxwell's private chef in October 1987, Baddeley duly presented him with her six-page list – by now, one suspects, more in hope than expectation. Each morning at seven o'clock Cheeseman would prepare his breakfast. 'He would have showered and dressed by then. For breakfast I would give him Corn Flakes and orange juice. At lunch, he would usually have a homemade soup, unless he was having lunch with his board. At five o'clock, he might have some smoked salmon or caviar. That said, he could be quite choosy. He hated the smell of cooking and I remember I once cooked him some white asparagus. He called me into the room and said "Mr Martin" – that was what he always called me – "what are these?"

'I said, "They're white asparagus, Mr Maxwell."

' "No, they're not," he said. "They're pigs' pricks." '

Seeing Maxwell at the 1987 Cannes Film Festival, the writer and critic Clive James was reminded of 'a ton and a half of half-cured ham wrapped in a white tuxedo'. At the time, James had just been introduced to Princess Diana, who turned out to share his antipathy. 'She made a face as if she had just sucked a lemon. "Ooh. There's that odious man Maxwell over there. Don't want to meet *him* again." '

It was his valet, Simon Grigg, who worked out why Maxwell's girth kept expanding: at night, he was going to the kitchen and helping himself to food. 'I'd come in in the morning and see that he'd raided the fridge. There would be all this mess everywhere.'

Meanwhile Maxwell's manners, always erratic, had also gone haywire. Staff became used to finding plates encrusted with food hidden underneath the furniture. If he was eating a watermelon, he would simply spit the seeds on to the floor for someone else to clear up. Plates would be swept on to the floor if he didn't like what was on them.

All this of course was a long way from 'The Three Cs' and 'How To Make Friends Among Young and Old' – 'Try to be considerate and helpful; avoid selfish and provocative acts.' But by then something had snapped. However restrained Maxwell attempted to be, the war had been lost. Excess had won the day.

In 1986, Maxwell's 'Personal Photographer', Mike Maloney, accompanied him to Edinburgh. That evening, Maxwell invited Maloney to come and have dinner with him in the penthouse suite of the Sheraton Hotel.

'He asked me, "What do you like to eat?" '

Maloney told him that he liked most things, but was particularly partial to Chinese cuisine. Excellent, said Maxwell; he was fond of Chinese food himself. Calling up what he had been assured was the best Chinese restaurant in Edinburgh, Maxwell ordered food for fourteen people. When the restaurant protested they couldn't handle that big an order, he threatened to close them down unless they did as they were told.

Arriving in Maxwell's suite, Maloney saw that the food had already been delivered and was sitting on the dining table.

'Right,' said Maxwell, 'Let's eat.'

'But what about the other guests?' Maloney asked.

Maxwell looked at him in surprise.

'What other fucking guests?' he said, 'It's just the two of us.'

17

A Very Happy Person

In July 1987, Robert Maxwell was a guest on the long-running BBC radio programme *Desert Island Discs*, where he was interviewed by the show's presenter, Michael Parkinson. After describing Maxwell's life story as 'more exotic than fiction', Parkinson went on to depict him as 'a big-league player with the resources and the bravado to walk where angels fear to tread. He is Robert Maxwell.'

MP: 'Bob, have you ever been tempted to write this remarkable life story of yours?'

RM: 'I have been tempted – and induced – and I'm still hoping to get it down. I'm a very happy person. I have a large family. My wife and I have been married – happily married – for forty-two years. We have seven children. We're very proud of them. Yes, it would be a happy book and I hope that if I do get it written, it would be of both value and amusement to lots of people.'

MP: 'When you look back on your life, you must at times disbelieve that it actually happened?'

RM: 'That is certainly true, but I'm so busy that I do not have the time in recent years to look back on anything. All I've got the time for is to deal with the issues of the day, and plan forward a little in order to Get Things Done.' (This is said with great emphasis.)

MP: 'Has music played a large part in your life?'

RM: 'Yes, music has played a great part in my life. The records I've chosen contain memories. They have moved me when I first heard them and I'm happy to take them

along as loving companions on to the desert island. Fur-
thermore, I consider people who write music to be the
greatest geniuses of all.'

MP: 'Bob, you were born in Czechoslovakia. Can you tell me
exactly what sort of background you come from?'

RM: 'I come from a very poor family indeed. My father was
an unemployed farm labourer. We didn't have enough
to eat . . .'

MP: 'What sort of effect did that have on you in later life?'

RM: 'All I remember is being hungry most of the time. It has
had no effect on me in any way.' (Again this is said with
great emphasis.)

In between his choices of music, Maxwell gives an account of his
war years: his being sentenced to death as a spy; his overpowering
of the one-armed guard (there's no mention of the gypsy woman
who removed his handcuffs); his arrival in England – 'with a rifle in
my hand' – and his discovery that most of his family had been
wiped out in Auschwitz.

MP: 'How do you feel about it now?'

RM: 'The sorrow of those losses is ever before me.'

MP: 'And your own hatred?'

RM: 'I don't hate as I did during the War, but I cannot forgive
or forget.'

So far Maxwell's choice of records has included Mozart, Gersh-
win's *Porgy and Bess* and Winston Churchill's 'We shall fight them
on the beaches' speech, which he describes as one of the main reasons why he came to England. For his fourth record, Maxwell
chooses 'On the Street Where You Live', from the musical *My Fair
Lady*.

MP: 'Why have you chosen that?'

RM: 'Because it's cheerful.'

MP: 'Bob, one of the things that fascinates people about you is this business of being an exceedingly rich man who has made it from nowhere. Is there a trick to making money?'

RM: 'No, there is no trick other than hard work, creativity and recognizing that duty is more important than love.'

MP: 'Would you care to expand on that?'

RM: 'Whatever you do, you must give it total concentration and commitment. If you are out selling and it's five o'clock and you have a date with your girl, but if you stayed and walked an extra mile you may talk to a customer and fulfil their requirements – then you'd better do that rather than going on your date.'

MP: 'Really? Is that what you've done all your life?'

RM: 'That's what I've done all my life. And that's what I've tried to teach my children. It separates the Achiever from the Talker.'

MP: 'Does that involve, of necessity, sacrifices to family?'

RM: 'It does involve, above all, sacrifice to yourself. I have not seen as much of my family as I should have done. But all life is a choice. And if you want to succeed then you have got to commit yourself in order to' – once again – 'Get Things Done.'

MP: 'At the end of the day what is the achievement?'

RM: 'The achievement at the end of it is that I feel that my life, which I am continuing to live to the full and will do so until the day I die, I will have left the world a slightly better place by my having lived in it.'

For his seventh record, Maxwell picks *Finlandia* by Sibelius – 'Very uplifting' – and for his eighth and last *Má Vlast* (My Homeland) by the Czech composer Smetana. His choice of book is the *Works of Plato* and his luxury a computer program to play chess.

MP: 'Bob, you're on your desert island. Are you going to enjoy the experience, do you think?'

RM (unhesitatingly): 'Yes.'
MP: 'Would you try to escape?'

Maxwell thinks about this. For the first time, a note of wistfulness comes into his voice.

RM: 'No, not for a little while . . . I could use the luxury of
     having time to think . . .'

He seems about to say something else, then changes his mind, taking Parkinson by surprise. There is an awkward silence.

MP: 'Robert Maxwell, thank you for letting us hear your
     Desert Island Discs.'

Anyone who didn't know much, or anything, about Maxwell before listening to this would have been left with certain impressions. Above all, that he was a very happy man with a rock-solid marriage and children he adored. A natural optimist who had managed to put the trauma of his childhood firmly behind him. Yet none of this was true. Effectively, his marriage was over and he hardly saw his children unless they happened to work for him. He was also haunted by guilt over what had happened to his family.

As for Maxwell's claim that music had played a great part in his life, he may have been telling the truth here. However, he hadn't actually chosen his own records for the programme; instead, he told Betty and his son Ian to do it for him.

Maxwell himself was far too busy.

18.

Battle Rejoined

Sometimes when he was waiting in Maxwell's office, half braced for yet another tongue-lashing, Peter Jay would listen to him talking on the phone. Every once in a while Maxwell and Rupert Murdoch spoke to one another. Whenever they did, Jay noticed that a particular note came into Maxwell's voice. 'I could see that he was obsessed with Murdoch. And when they did speak, Maxwell would sound almost matey; it was as if he wanted Murdoch to be matey with him. The really odd thing was it was like listening to someone who craved acceptance.'

On Saturday, 28 June 1987, Maxwell called Murdoch up in Los Angeles with some important news – news that he was sure would be of great interest. Maxwell proceeded to tell him that he had bought the *Today* newspaper. Launched just over a year earlier, *Today* had been jointly owned by the multinational conglomerate Lonrho, which had 90 per cent of its shares, and the paper's founder, Eddie Shah, who still had 10 per cent.

A mid-market tabloid, *Today* was the first British newspaper to be printed in colour. As far as most pundits were concerned that was the sum total of the paper's achievements: it was already losing nearly £30,000,000 a year. But having successfully introduced colour printing on the *Mirror* – eighteen months before the *Sun* – Maxwell wanted another colour tabloid to add to his stable. He was particularly keen that Murdoch should be the first to know he'd just brought off another great coup.

'That was the thing with Maxwell; he couldn't stop showing off,' remembers Murdoch. 'And it was always personal with him, whereas with me, it was never personal.'

Possibly not – but possibly there was more to it than that. As Maxwell insisted on describing every detail of what had happened, Murdoch's attention began to wane. Then all at once it picked up. From what Maxwell had inadvertently let slip, it seemed that no contracts had actually been signed. While the deal may have been agreed, nothing had been put in writing. In his eagerness to boast, Maxwell had jumped the gun.

As he always did whenever Maxwell told him about his latest triumph, Murdoch waited until he had finished, offered his congratulations, then calmly thanked him for his courtesy. Only this time he did something he'd never done before. The moment Murdoch put the phone down, he caught a plane to Aspen. There he had a hurried series of conference calls with representatives from his company, News International. Learning that the contract with Maxwell was due to be signed at 10.30 on the Monday morning, Murdoch flew overnight to London. By the time he arrived, News International's lawyers had already put in a bid for *Today*.

A year earlier, Eddie Shah had telephoned Jeffrey Archer, the former Conservative MP turned bestselling novelist. Archer's new novel, *A Matter of Honour*, had just been published to glowing reviews – according to *The New York Times*, 'it sizzles along at a pace that would peel the paint off a spaceship' – and Shah wanted to serialize extracts in *Today*.

Archer wasn't tempted: 'I said to Eddie, "Look, you can't possibly afford me." '

Hoping to change his mind, Shah offered him 1 per cent of the paper in lieu of payment. Archer got in touch with his agent and asked what he thought 1 per cent of *Today* would be worth. Nothing whatsoever, his agent told him confidently. But Archer was amused by the thought of owning a slice of a national newspaper, however tiny, and agreed to the deal. Having done so, he thought no more about it – not until Maxwell called him a few weeks later while he was lying in the bath.

'I've never forgotten it,' Archer recalls. 'Maxwell asked if I would sell him my 1 per cent. I said, "That's very flattering, Bob, but could

I think about it?"' Having dried himself off, Archer called a banker friend to ask what he should do. 'He told me, "Jeffrey, there must be a good reason why Maxwell wants your one per cent. So it isn't really just one per cent you own. In real terms it's far more."'

Archer asked his banker friend what he should do. 'He told me to name a price. I said how about £10,000? "No no, Jeffrey," my friend said, "Go for £500,000 and settle for £250,000."' Archer took his advice and a few days later found himself a quarter of a million pounds richer.

But it soon became clear there was a lot more between Maxwell and Murdoch than Jeffrey Archer's single per cent. Maxwell had offered to pay Lonrho £10,000,000 and promised to take on the paper's £30,000,000 debt. Murdoch offered £38,000,000 upfront. From that moment, the outcome was never in doubt. As soon as he learned about Murdoch's bid, an infuriated Maxwell pulled out, referring to Murdoch as 'that Australian bastard'.

Later, Murdoch would insist that he had no axe to grind with Maxwell. That he'd been looking to buy a middle-market paper for some time, and *Today* plainly fitted the bill. This, though, wasn't quite the whole story. Murdoch had always found Maxwell coarse and boorish, as well as absurdly full of himself: 'You'd switch on the TV in some hotel bedroom and there would be Maxwell in his dark suit and bow-tie telling you about his global communications company. It was all bullshit. I never spoke about him, but he couldn't stop talking about me. Whatever we did, he wanted to do it too. Also I could see that he was ruining everything he touched. He was a total buffoon really.'

For the fourth time, Murdoch had bested Maxwell.

Despite all the evidence to the contrary, Maxwell remained convinced that one day he would outsmart Murdoch. The trouble was that by now almost no one else felt the same way. As he watched from the sidelines, the Editor of *The Times*, Harry Evans, reckoned it was a hopelessly unequal contest. 'Maxwell thought he'd entered the ring with another boxer, but he hadn't. In fact, he'd entered the ring with a ju-jitsu artist who also happened to be carrying a stiletto.'

In 1986, a new contestant came into the ring. When he was eight years old, Conrad Black saved up his pocket money and bought a single share in General Motors for $60. Thirty-four years later, he bought the Telegraph Group for £30,000,000. Shortly afterwards, Black was invited to a lunch of Fleet Street proprietors at the Savoy Hotel where Robert Maxwell was a fellow guest.

This was the first time Black had met Maxwell and he wasn't sure what to make of him. 'He was a huge physical presence and a rather sinister-looking man because of his heavy eyebrows. I knew people in Fleet Street could be flamboyant, but this guy was very strange indeed. It wasn't immediately clear if he was extraordinarily worldly and expansive, or a gigantic charlatan. Or some combination of the two.'

By the time Black went to see Rupert Murdoch in New York a few months later, his opinion had hardened. When Murdoch asked him what he thought of Maxwell, Black said, 'Maxwell is a crook, a thief, a buffoon and probably a KGB man.' According to Black, Murdoch was so amused by this that he wrote it down. In Murdoch's recollection, he – not Black – was the one who came up with the quote.

What's not in doubt is that by then Murdoch was a big player in America – he'd bought his first newspapers there back in 1973. Twelve years later, in 1985, he became an American citizen so that he could buy a number of television stations – non-US citizens were forbidden from owning more than 20 per cent of a broadcast licence. Maxwell on the other hand was an unknown quantity. His address book may have been bulging with the private numbers of world leaders, but scarcely anybody in America had ever heard of him.

All that was about to change. In September 1988, Maxwell went on a spending spree. First, he offered more than two billion dollars for the American publishers Macmillan. The more prudent of his advisers begged him to think again, or at least exercise some caution. Solemnly, Maxwell promised that under no circumstances would he go above $80 a share. A few days later – without telling them – he upped his bid again.

Gerald Ronson, CEO of the property developers Heron International, had no doubt what was going on. 'Maxwell had to be in America, and he had to be bigger than Rupert Murdoch. Bob saw an opportunity to beat Murdoch at being Murdoch and took it.' Ronson too tried to talk some sense into Maxwell. 'I told him because I thought I owed it to him, "Those Americans are going to bid you up." But he still had to have an empire in New York. He was like a child at Hamleys; he had to have his toy right away.'

As soon as anyone made a bid for Macmillan, Maxwell would top it. The final purchase price was 2.6 billion dollars – $90.25 a share. This was roughly a billion dollars more than anyone – including the company's own directors – thought it was worth. And it didn't stop there. At the same time Maxwell also bought the Official Aviation Guide for $750,000,000 – the guide published timetables for the world's airline industry. To raise the combined purchase price of 3.3 billion dollars, Maxwell borrowed money from a total of forty-four different banks and financial syndicates. All of them were only too happy to lend him whatever he wanted.

To make the moment sweeter still, the deal was negotiated, in part, by Rothschild's. Back in 1969, Rothschild's had conspicuously frozen out Maxwell after the Pergamon takeover. This made Betty Maxwell so mad that for fifteen years afterwards she turned her back on Jacob Rothschild, Chairman of the English branch, whenever she saw him.

Now all that had been forgotten. Maxwell was ecstatic. At last he had joined the Big Ten League, an unofficial club of the world's top media moguls. Admittedly, the entry fee was much higher than he had anticipated, but Maxwell was convinced he could pay off his loans within a few years.

On the surface everything looked rosy. Beneath it, though, lay a very different story. A story of falling profits, soaring interest rates and looming recession. In trying to emulate Rupert Murdoch – to prove he could be an equally heavy hitter – Maxwell had set in train a course of events that would lead to his physical and mental disintegration, his downfall and, ultimately, his death.

19

Homecomings

When Gerald Ronson first met Robert Maxwell in the late 1970s, he had not been impressed. Always nattily dressed in tailor-made suits, Ronson took great pride both in his wardrobe and in the opulence of his lifestyle. Maxwell on the other hand arrived for their first meeting wearing a suit that was shiny with wear and driving a clapped-out Rolls-Royce. Ronson felt he was letting the side down.

'I told him, "You can't go around like that."'

In a bid to smarten him up, Ronson first introduced him to his tailor, then sent him over to the luxury car dealers H. R. Owen in Berkeley Square so that Maxwell could buy himself a new Rolls-Royce. He even tried to interest Maxwell in some 'very expensive art', but quickly realized this was going too far. 'Bob said, "I'm not spending a million quid on pictures when I can get some that look real for a few hundred."'

However, Ronson had better luck when it came to a much more expensive purchase. At the time, he was in the process of building himself a yacht, *My Gail III* – named after his wife. Ronson happened to hear that the brother of the Saudi financier/arms dealer Adnan Khashoggi had also been building a yacht, but had abandoned the project halfway through. Perhaps Maxwell might be interested in taking it on, he suggested.

'I helped Bob buy that boat. I think he paid eleven to twelve million dollars for it. He wasn't at all bothered about how it was finished inside and said to me, "You deal with it", so I did. I didn't make money out of it; I did it as a friend.'

For the next few years, whenever Ronson and his family went on a summer holiday on the *My Gail III*, Maxwell would follow close behind in the *Lady Ghislaine*, as he had named his new boat. He could, of course, have named the boat after Betty, or any one of his three older daughters, Isabel, Christine or Anne, but instead he plumped for his favourite child. 'He loved that boat. His private plane was a tool, but his boat was his escape.'

At sea, Maxwell behaved very differently to the way he did on dry land. According to the *Mirror*'s Foreign Editor, Nick Davies, he would often revert to a child-like state when on board the *Lady Ghislaine*, sometimes slipping into baby language. 'He would refer to a swim in the sea as a "twim in the tea"; he would say "trightened" for "frightened", "minkey" for "monkey", "deaded" for "tired", and call his pockets "sky-rockets".'

But, even here, Maxwell was seldom off the phone, Ronson noticed. 'He could never relax. And he didn't have a lot of personal friends. There were plenty of people he could use and abuse, but there weren't a lot of people he could sit down and have a genuine talk with.'

Ronson knew that Maxwell, like him, was a Jew. But he also knew that Maxwell had denied it in the past, or else claimed to have abandoned Judaism long ago. 'He usually told people he wasn't Jewish, but he told me he was and had given it up.'

Again, Ronson was not impressed. 'I said to him, "What's all this crap? How come all of a sudden you're not Jewish any more?"'

Shortly after Maxwell had bought the *Mirror* in 1984, Ronson was due to go to Israel to see the Prime Minister, Yitzhak Shamir. Why didn't Maxwell and Betty come along? Despite being 'nonplussed' by the idea, Maxwell agreed. They flew out on Ronson's private plane. As they neared Tel Aviv, Ronson glanced over at Maxwell and saw he was crying. 'There were tears coming down his face. He kept saying, "I should have come here years ago." It surprised me because he was not the sort of man you expected to see showing such emotion.'

Ronson was even more surprised when he and Maxwell went to see Yitzhak Shamir the next morning. At one point in the meeting Maxwell suddenly announced that he wanted to i̶ in Israel.

Shamir wondered how much he had in mind.

'At least a quarter of a billion dollars,' Maxwell told him.

Both Shamir and Ronson were astounded. 'That was a huge amount of money.' Whether Maxwell actually had it was another matter. 'He certainly wasn't shy when it came to telling people stories that weren't true.' But on this occasion, Maxwell proved to be as good as his word. Over the next four years he became the largest single investor in the Israeli economy, so much so that people began driving around Tel Aviv and Jerusalem with bumper stickers reading, 'Please Mr Maxwell, Buy Me!'

Using Mirror Group funds, Maxwell bought several newspapers, made substantial investments in Israeli high-tech and pharmaceutical companies, and tried to buy a football team. Not only that, he would also pass on any useful information that came his way to Mossad, the Israeli secret service. Now that Maxwell had rediscovered his Judaism, Ronson set about 'guiding him into the Community', encouraging his involvement in various charities he supported.

In December 1984, there was a production of *The Nutcracker* at the Royal Opera House in Covent Garden to mark the centenary year of the National Society for the Prevention of Cruelty to Children, one of the many charities to which Maxwell gave large sums of money. All the senior members of the Royal Family were present: the Queen, Prince Philip, the Queen Mother, Princess Margaret, Princess Diana, Prince Charles and Prince Andrew.

Maxwell and Betty were in the Royal Box; he was placed next to the Queen Mother. Although he would sometimes profess a keen interest in the ballet when asked about his cultural pursuits, to Betty's alarm Maxwell fell asleep as soon as the lights went down and continued nodding off throughout the performance: 'I was constantly poking him in the ribs to wake him up.'

Ronson was under no illusions about Maxwell's motives – or his own for that matter. 'Maybe he was using me for a certain amount of respectability. And maybe I was using him for the money he

to worthy causes. But still we became good
: I was one of the few people he trusted enough to
ıme with. He knew that I'd give him a straight
;s and would also tell him if he was talking bol-
tely for him, he didn't always listen to my advice.'
:ael not only changed Maxwell's life; it changed
Betty's too. On her return, she immersed herself in studying the
Nazi genocide. She started a journal called *Holocaust and Genocide
Studies* – published by Pergamon – and in 1988 organized a conference in Oxford called 'Remembering for the Future', the largest
collection of Holocaust scholars ever assembled.

Having researched her own family tree for her thesis, Betty
decided to do the same for Maxwell's – partly for their children's
sake, and partly to show him how much, despite everything, she
still cared for him. She spent most of 1985 travelling the world in
search of Maxwell's roots, tracking down his distant cousins in
America, Argentina, Switzerland, Belgium and Israel.

When Betty came to compile Maxwell's family tree, she put a
little yellow Star of David in front of all the people who had been
murdered in the camps. It wasn't until she finished that she realized
just how many there were. 'When I unfolded it, it was like a shower
of yellow stars.' But her hopes that this might bring the two of them
closer together came to nothing. At a meeting of the editorial board
of *Holocaust and Genocide Studies* in Jerusalem, Maxwell shocked
everyone by ridiculing her for her lack of experience in publishing,
and belittling her whenever she opened her mouth.

Nobody could understand what was going on – nobody except
Betty herself. 'That episode could not have demonstrated more
clearly that Bob had not managed to reconcile himself with his grief,
or overcome his guilt complex at having married a Christian. Confronted by Israeli Jews, most of them survivors, and dealing with the
subject of the Holocaust, he took his distress out on me.'

In September 1978, Maxwell finally went back to his home town of
Solotvino. Hoping to butter him up for a publishing deal, the

Soviet Minister of Culture extended an invitation to him and Betty. When he had left almost forty years earlier, Maxwell had been sixteen years old and trying to make a living selling bead necklaces. Now dancers lined the streets to greet his arrival. The couple were showered with gifts and at the town hall the Mayor launched into what proved to be an epically long speech of welcome.

Despite all the celebrations, it was a profoundly depressing experience for Maxwell. The house where he had been born was still standing, but even tinier and shabbier than he remembered. There was no one left whom he'd known as a child – all of them had either fled or been killed. That night, he and Betty slept in a local inn. It was bitterly cold. To try to keep Maxwell warm, she wrapped him in a sheep's wool blanket they had been presented with earlier.

He left vowing never to return.

Previously part of Czechoslovakia, Solotvino had been incorporated into Ukraine at the end of the War. While Maxwell may have gone back to his home town, he hadn't visited the land of his birth since his mysterious trips there in the 1950s.

Another eight years would pass until he went to Czechoslovakia on what was described as a 'state visit'. In September 1986, Maxwell flew to Prague accompanied by the *Mirror*'s Political Editor, Julia Langdon. During the flight, he speculated about who would be there to greet him when his plane landed. Given the significance of the event, he expected a suitably grand turn-out – the Czech Foreign Minister at the very least.

But when they arrived at one o'clock in the morning, there was no sign of the Foreign Minister, or anyone else. Instead, their plane was guided to a distant corner of the airport where both of them had their passports confiscated. They were then locked into a large glass box. For the next hour they waited while Maxwell grew more and more angry. 'The problem was the airport officials could only speak Czech and Maxwell's Czech was quite rusty because he hadn't spoken it for so long,' Langdon recalls.

All at once she became aware of a commotion in the distance. 'I could see these people rushing towards us, clearly in a flustered state. There was an entire band, some other people carrying a red carpet and a man who turned out to be the Deputy Foreign Minister.' The carpet was unrolled, the band struck up and profuse apologies were offered; apparently a terrible mistake had been made and their plane had been directed to the wrong part of the airport.

The next morning, Maxwell and Langdon were driven to Prague Castle to see the Czech President, Gustáv Husák. After Husák had been presented with a hefty vellum-bound edition of his speeches, the two men made what struck Langdon as extremely stilted conversation, with each sentence being translated from Czech to English, then back again.

At one point Husák started banging on about great Czech folk traditions. Much to Langdon's surprise, Maxwell suddenly expressed an interested in hunting. It was obvious to her that he'd only done so because he couldn't think of anything else to say.

Husák, however, didn't see it that way.

'Oh, you like hunting, do you?' he said. 'Well, you must go hunting this afternoon.'

Frantic phone calls were made to Maxwell's office in London asking for his measurements. That afternoon he and Langdon were driven to the President's summer palace. There, Maxwell was taken off to change into his hunting uniform – a green hunting jacket and matching hat with a feather in the brim. Unfortunately, his waist measurement was so large that they'd been unable to find him any trousers that fitted, so he had to wear his suit trousers instead.

Normally, the hunters all rode horses, but as Maxwell couldn't ride it was decided they should go in the back of a lorry. Before they left a procession of women wearing white dresses came out with trays of vodka so that everyone could wish them good fortune. Bugles were played and toasts drunk. Then, amid more fanfares, the hunting party disappeared off into the forest.

They were gone a long time, but when at last the party returned they did so in triumph, with a deer which Maxwell had shot. The deer was ceremonially laid on a bed of branches, the women in white dresses reappeared and yet more toasts were drunk – this time to Maxwell the mighty hunter.

When he and Langdon were driven back to Prague that evening, they saw the castle had been specially lit up – something the Czechs only did for their most esteemed guests.

'I remember we got out of the car to look at the view and Maxwell said, "Why do you think they are doing this for me?"

'I said, "I suppose it must be a token of their admiration for you, Bob." I was being ironic, but of course he didn't see it that way; he took it quite literally.'

After dinner with the President, Langdon and Maxwell had a whisky before bed. They were talking about the events of the day when Maxwell made a sudden announcement.

'I didn't shoot that deer, you know,' he told her.

'I said, "What do you mean?"

' "I didn't shoot the deer," he repeated. "I tried to, but I kept on missing. That was why we took so long. In the end, someone else had to shoot it for me." '

This admission made an enormous impression on Langdon. 'He spoke quite casually, but also as though he was getting something off his chest. It felt extraordinarily self-revelatory. What struck me most of all was the honesty, the openness. It was as if for once in his life he didn't have to pretend.'

20.

The Party of the Decade

The dinner-dances hosted by Robert and Betty Maxwell at Headington Hill Hall were considered, even by hardened partygoers, to be in a class of their own. The house itself was an ideal venue for a party. It had been built in the early nineteenth century by a culture-loving family of brewers, the Morrells. They too had been keen party-givers. In 1878, Oscar Wilde was among the 300 guests at one of their fancy-dress balls. For reasons that are not entirely clear, he chose to come dressed as Prince Rupert of the Rhine.

Ever since the Maxwells had moved into Headington Hill Hall, they had continued the tradition of throwing grand parties. But, as guests soon discovered, Maxwell had his own distinctive way of doing things. The writer and future Conservative MP Gyles Brandreth was a guest at one of their parties in the 1970s. At first nothing struck him as out of the ordinary. 'It was only when I went up to Maxwell that I realized he had this apparatus on. There was an old-fashioned microphone attached to the lapel of his jacket with a wind-shield on it. And on his belt was this large box, the size of a hard-back book with a dial in the middle. This was somehow connected to speakers in each of the rooms.'

Maxwell, Brandreth realized, was wearing his own personal PA system, enabling him to address people no matter how far away they were. 'He'd turn the dial down when he was talking to you. Then, as soon as he saw someone he wanted to talk to on the other side of the room he'd turn it up again and this disembodied voice would come booming out of the speakers.'

For all the splendour of his parties, Maxwell himself remained an oddly elusive figure. 'It was as if there was a kind of invisible moat around Maxwell,' Brandreth recalls. 'He was definitely a presence, but whenever he came into a room, instead of the room being more crowded, it always seemed slightly emptier than before.'

As Maxwell's fortune grew, the larger and grander their parties became. Cabinet ministers would rub shoulders with captains of industry, leading scientists with newspaper editors. But the joint party to celebrate Maxwell's sixty-fifth birthday and the fortieth anniversary of his company, Pergamon Press, in June 1988, was confidently predicted to outdo them all, in terms of both opulence and pomp.

No one, not even his many critics, could deny that Maxwell was on a colossal roll: from Oxford to Osaka, his empire was booming. As he had boasted just a few weeks earlier, 'The banks owe us money; we have so much on deposit.' At the same time, academic institutions were queuing up to bestow honours upon him: Maxwell had just been given a doctorate of law by Aberdeen University as well as honorary life membership of the University of London's Institute of Philosophy.

So many guests had been invited – around 3000 – that it had been decided to hold the party over three consecutive nights. Friday night would be white tie and 'decorations', and Saturday night black tie, while the Sunday night party would be a more informal affair for members of staff. In between, there was a lunch party on the Saturday where there would be a hot and cold buffet, Pimm's and wine to drink, as well as a coconut shy, hoopla and skittles.

In the days leading up to the first party, vast marquees were erected around the house. Two floor-to-ceiling windows were removed to improve access to the main marquee. Legions of florists came down from London to create elaborate displays in the house, the marquees and even the swimming pool – this involved them transporting the flowers out to the middle of the pool in little dinghies.

A stage had been built at one end of the main marquee and a dance floor laid so that guests could dance to the sound of the Joe Loss Orchestra and, later on, a disco. At the end of the meal, the cast of the West End musical *Me and My Girl* would perform high-lights from the show. To ensure that everyone enjoyed unimpeded views of the entertainment, the dining area had been constructed on two levels. A mobile darkroom had also been set up in the grounds. Guests who had their pictures taken during the evening by a team of six dinner-jacketed photographers would be able to collect them as they left.

To mark the fortieth anniversary of Pergamon, a special book of tributes had been compiled. Pergamon had grown into the world's largest scientific publishers, and the editors of Maxwell's scientific journals – more than 300 in all – along with various Nobel laureates extolled his virtues in extravagant terms.

The Editor of the *International Journal of Hydrogen Energy* noted that 'Everything Bob Maxwell touches turns to gold', while the director of one of his Japanese companies wrote, 'Each time I have the pleasure of meeting him, I am reminded of F. Scott Fitzgerald's words that a millionaire is no ordinary man.' Arthur Barrett, Editor of the journal *Vacuum*, recalled how his initial doubts about Maxwell had soon disappeared: 'I have to confess that, quickly realizing his predatory and entrepreneurial ambitions, I none the less took a great liking to him.'

There were also some unexpected contributions. The Editor of *Planetary and Space Science* recalled how as a favour Maxwell had once agreed to publish a book by his sister Margaret called *Talking About Cakes*. Apparently this had done so well that it had spawned a successor, *Talking About Puddings*.

Among the congratulatory telegrams was one from the US President, Ronald Reagan: 'As the Happy Birthdays ring out, Nancy and I are delighted to join in the chorus of appreciation.' The Prime Minister, Margaret Thatcher, offered a – somewhat solipsistic – contribution of her own: 'Robert Maxwell has never made any secret of the fact that officially he is politically opposed to me. But to tell the truth, I think he rather liked my approach to politics and government – a sense of direction and decision. These are the very qualities that have taken him far.' As far as the Labour leader, Neil

Kinnock, was concerned, 'If Bob Maxwell didn't exist, no one could invent him.' Kinnock went on to pay tribute to Maxwell's 'basic convictions of liberty and fairness'.

On the night of the first party, the guests passed down a receiving line where they were greeted by Maxwell, Betty and all seven of their children. Some of the guests arrived bearing birthday presents. The broadcaster David Frost turned up with a £500 bottle of wine. Unaware of how much it had cost, Maxwell's chef later tipped it into a beef stew.

As they sipped their drinks, the band of the Coldstream Guards marched back and forth across the lawn. Before dinner started, Robert and Betty Maxwell made their formal entrance into the marquee to an announcement from the Master of Ceremonies – 'Ladies and Gentlemen, would you please welcome your host and hostess, Robert and Elisabeth Maxwell' – and a fanfare of herald trumpeters.

Everyone stood up to applaud. Along with a row of medals pinned to his black tail coat, Maxwell was wearing a large white enamel cross on a chain around his neck. This was the Order of the White Rose of Finland, a decoration normally only given to foreign heads of state in recognition of 'outstanding civilian or military conduct'. Betty Maxwell wore a dress made of gold-embroidered tulle over yellow taffeta silk.

At one of their earlier parties – in 1986 – the speech had been given by a former Prime Minister, Harold Wilson. Suffering from the early stages of Alzheimer's, Wilson had begun his speech brightly enough, but then clearly forgot who he was supposed to be talking about. This time nothing had been left to chance. The main speech was given by Maxwell's banker, Sir Michael Richardson, Managing Director of Rothschild's bank and an economic adviser to Mrs Thatcher.

'Betty and Bob, this must be the Party of the Decade!' Richardson declared to shouts of 'Hear Hear!' and another round of applause. 'All of us are delighted to be here because we believe you have made a major contribution to all our lives.'

But, as she sat beaming away by Maxwell's side, Betty found herself wondering if the party might not be too puffed up with self-importance. If something vital might not have been lost along the way. In particular, she had major doubts about the herald trumpeters. 'I thought it was really over the top, but I managed to play my part . . . For all its success, for me, it had lost the intimate quality that our previous parties had had. It was just too vast.'

While the Friday night party passed off without incident, at the Saturday lunch party an uninvited guest appeared: Eleanor Berry. Although Berry hadn't been invited to the party – possibly Maxwell thought she might make a scene – she decided to turn up anyway. Unsure of the appropriate dress code, she plumped for 'white, tight-fitting, leather trousers, a white V-necked sweater and RM's [Robert Maxwell's] favourite red snake-skin, stiletto-heeled boots'. To steady her nerves beforehand, she fortified herself with some amphetamines.

Claiming to have mislaid her invitation card, Berry managed to persuade the security guards she was an old friend of the family's. Inside the marquee Berry saw that a film was being shown about Maxwell's many achievements, but there was no sign of Maxwell himself.

Eventually she found him in the house.

'RM was standing in an inner chamber. I didn't know which room it was because its ceiling and walls were draped with white cloth like an Arab's tent.

'"Hello Bob. Happy birthday," I said and kissed him. As always, he was pleased to see me.'

Maxwell introduced her to the people he was with. '"This is Eleanor Berry and I'm one of her greatest admirers . . . she's got spunk."'

But when Berry asked for another drink, he refused. '"No, I can't give it to you as it will make you ill. You've already had several glasses of wine. Last time you got drunk here, you started talking to me about necrophilia."'

Shortly after they had sat down for lunch, Maxwell was called to the phone – 'Apparently Gorbachev was wishing him a happy birthday.' By this stage the amphetamines Berry had taken earlier were starting to wear off. 'I threw my napkin under the table to give the impression I had dropped it, and took more Speed.'

Although this pepped her up, it also left her itching for a fight. Berry took particular exception to a Polish woman who she thought had been trying to monopolize Maxwell's attention: 'She was slim, her long curly hair was dishevelled and she wore a see-through white garment descending into her cleavage. Her shirt was strategically raised and her sun-tanned legs were crossed.'

The moment Maxwell left the marquee, Berry swung into action. 'I caught her eye and said, "For Christ's sake put your legs under the table and cover them with your skirt. This is a respectable residence, not a disorderly house."'

As she drifted around the marquee after lunch, Berry noticed something about the other guests – something that seemed to confirm Betty Maxwell's suspicions that the larger their parties had grown, the less intimate they'd become. Approaching one of them, Berry asked her how she knew Maxwell.

'I don't,' the woman told her. 'I've never met him.'

'Well, what are you doing here then?'

The woman admitted she had no idea. 'My name was taken from the telephone directory, I suppose.'

That evening, Peter Jay found himself sharing Betty Maxwell's misgivings. 'It was as if people came because they wanted to see Maxwell; it was a spectacle. And although they sucked up to him and enjoyed his hospitality, you could see them raising their eyebrows at the same time.'

Maxwell's Chief Leader Writer, Joe Haines, had been hoping for a relatively quiet evening. Instead, he found himself in charge of one of the tables. His wife, Irene, was even more unlucky: she sat between 'the East German ambassador and his dour wife. You could have scoured the country to find anyone less appealing to Irene and not succeeded.'

After dinner was over and the cast of *Me and My Girl* had finished performing, guests were asked to go back outside into the garden.

There they were treated to a firework display, the culmination of which – just like Maxwell's Christmas card – was a huge flaming sign spelling out the words 'Happy Birthday Bob!' across the Oxford skyline.

But not all the guests stayed to watch. Keen to avail themselves of an unrivalled opportunity, some of them succumbed to curiosity and went snooping. Mike Molloy, by now the Editor-in-Chief of the *Mirror*, was particularly struck by the décor of Headington Hill Hall: 'All the furniture looked as if it had been bought from the sale of a second-rate country house in the 1920s. There was something oddly shabby about it. And the paintings were terrible, absolutely terrible. I've never seen a worse collection.'

Having inspected the art, Molloy peered into Maxwell's drawing room. 'There were all these bookshelves with books on them. Except when I looked more closely, I saw that they weren't real books: they were made out of cardboard. I couldn't get over it. Here was this man who had made his fortune out of publishing and yet there weren't even real books on his shelves.' In fact, not all the books were false; only those concealing Maxwell's stereo system.

Julia Langdon was equally surprised by what she saw of Headington Hill Hall. 'I went looking for a loo at one point, and on my way back I did something I don't normally do in other people's houses – I had a nose around. I opened one cupboard and found it was completely full of Heinz Salad Cream. There were bottles and bottles of it, stacked from floor to ceiling.'

Among the other guests that night were Neil Kinnock and his wife, Glenys. 'I did go on that occasion, but frankly most of the time I found good reason not to go,' Kinnock recalls. As always, whenever he had any dealings with Maxwell, he found himself in a tricky position. 'I was in this constant dilemma of not wanting to defer to him, and not wanting to lose his support either. How do you deal with this extremely capricious man with an overwhelming sense of his own power? It was very difficult.'

After the fireworks were over, the Kinnocks took to the dance floor. When Neil Kinnock decided he'd done enough dancing, another guest stepped up to partner his wife: Peter Mandelson. Although it would be another few years before Mandelson was dubbed 'The Prince of Darkness', mention of his name already prompted mingled awe and dread in Labour circles.

'Glenys, Neil, Julie Hall his press secretary and I danced for about an hour and a half,' Mandelson remembers. 'We got all hot and sweaty and it was great fun. But I never spoke to Maxwell. It was very strange because you'd simultaneously want to be at his parties and at the same time shrink away from him. Because he was such a bully and so unpredictable. To be honest, I was frightened of his company. He had that ability to make you feel completely small and inadequate, and that just scrambled my head.'

While the dancing was going on, Maxwell asked another of the guests, Gerald Ronson, if he would like to come into the house for a quiet drink. 'He waved his fat finger at me and said, "Let's go into the library because I don't want to talk to these people."'

They were, Maxwell told him, 'a bunch of arseholes' who would go anywhere if they were invited by someone important. It wasn't just that, though: Maxwell had something he wanted to show him.

'Bob said, "You always thought I was joking when I told you that I had won the Military Cross."'

He then opened a large photo album and proudly pointed to one of the photographs. Taken more than forty years earlier, it showed Field-Marshal Bernard Montgomery pinning the medal on to the uniform of a much younger, slimmer Maxwell.

Ronson laughed and held up his hands.

'I said, "I take it all back, Bob. I'm sorry if I didn't believe you, but you do tell so many stories . . . "'

21

Listening In

At a dinner for senior police officers in early 1988, John Pole, a Detective Chief Superintendent at the Metropolitan Police, was approached by a colleague who wondered if he might be interested in a new job. With retirement fast approaching, this was exactly what Pole was looking for.

He asked what sort of job it was.

Head of Security at Maxwell Communications, he was told. The man wrote down a phone number and suggested he make an appointment. A few days later, Pole went to see MCC's Managing Director and was promptly hired: as far as he could tell, there didn't appear to be any other applicants. At first, the work was straightforward enough. 'My job was to go into various buildings that Maxwell owned and decide whether the security there was adequate.'

But it wasn't long before everything changed. 'Maxwell had another police officer working for him called Les Williams. Les came to me and said, "Mr Maxwell wants to know if people are loyal to him. Is there a way of finding out what they are saying on the telephone without breaking the law?"'

If Pole thought this was unusual, he had no intention of jeopardizing his new job by saying so. He did, however, seek advice and was assured that bugging phones was perfectly legal at the time. 'The actual bugging was fairly simple. Although you had to do each phone individually, it was really just a matter of changing the wiring around – taking a plug from one socket and putting it in another one.'

As well as bugging the heads of department at the *Mirror*,

Maxwell asked Pole to bug his own office. Pole installed two concealed microphones, both of them activated by a switch concealed beneath Maxwell's desk. 'There was a microphone at each end of his office because we quickly realized that when someone was moving about, they would go out of range. So we put in a system where it was possible to follow someone around the room. Whenever they went out of range of one microphone, the other one would automatically pick them up.'

Maxwell also asked Pole to put bugs in all the meeting rooms. These soon had a dramatic effect on his negotiating techniques. 'When Maxwell held a meeting, after a while he'd say to the people there, "We'll take a little break now. Why don't you retire to this particular room and we'll meet up again in half an hour?" '

Everybody would go into one of the meeting rooms and discuss how things were going. Meanwhile Maxwell would sit in his office listening to what they were talking about. Although he'd long had a reputation as a formidable deal-maker, now it was as if Maxwell had developed psychic powers. Uncannily, he always seemed to be one step ahead of the game.

And there was something else Maxwell wanted Pole to do. 'He said to me one day, "I want you to install a system which is obedient to my voice, and my voice only." ' Like Ali Baba, Maxwell wanted to be able to say, 'Open!', and a door would open. Everything – and everyone – would jump to his command. 'I said, "Mr Maxwell, I don't think that technology is available." '

The bugged conversations were all recorded on ninety-minute cassettes – the tape recorder was hidden in a cupboard behind his desk. Maxwell would usually listen to them at night when he was alone in his penthouse apartment. Sometimes, though, he would do so in the middle of the day. 'He listened to them obsessively whenever the mood took him. They were supposed to be recordings of confidential conversations, but he used to play them at full volume.

'A couple of times I walked into his private office and he would be sitting there listening to the tapes. I would say to him, "Mr

Maxwell, people can hear the conversation all over the building."
He'd just lost it completely.'

It seemed to Pole that Maxwell had become increasingly suspicious in the time he had been working for him. 'He really didn't trust
anybody any more. He would say things like, *"They're* not telling me
the truth", or *"They're* not onside." But there was never any indication of who "they" were. Gradually, bit by bit, I got the impression he
was more and more paranoid.'

Although Maxwell didn't mention it to Pole at the time, there
was one conversation in particular that he wanted to eavesdrop on.
A conversation that would make him suffer what Eleanor Berry
called 'the torments of the damned' when he eventually heard it.
But that wouldn't be until more than a year later, and by then everything he had tried so hard to control would be slipping helplessly
from his grasp.

Maxwell being presented with the Military Cross by Field Marshal Montgomery in March 1945. The day before, he had learned that his mother and one of his sisters had been murdered by the Nazis.

Maxwell and Betty shortly after their marriage.

Maxwell with Barry in post-war Berlin.

Clash of the titans: a rare photograph of Maxwell and Rupert Murdoch in the same room, together with the Japanese businessman Yosaji Kobayashi.

A genius for hobnobbing: Maxwell
with Mrs Thatcher and Nelson
Mandela.

'That odious man': Maxwell with Princess Diana.

When the going was good: Maxwell with Andrea Martin and Peter Jay.

Up above the clouds: Maxwell stretched out on his private jet.

Headington Hill Hall: 'the best council house in the country'.

DAILY Mirror

Wednesday, November 6, 1991 **NEWSPAPER FOR THE NINETIES** Last month's daily sale: 3,684,098 (INCORPORATING THE DAILY RECORD) **25p**

MAXWELL DIES AT SEA

THE MAN WHO SAVED THE

DAILY Mirror

DEAD: Mirror Group publisher Robert Maxwell, whose body was recovered off Tenerife

By THE EDITOR

BOB MAXWELL is dead. His body was taken from the sea off Tenerife last night after he disappeared overboard from Lady Ghislaine, the yacht he loved.

In one of our many late-night conversations I asked him what he would like to be remembered for when he died.

"As the man who saved the Mirror," he said without hesitation. It's true. He did. If he hadn't taken over the Mirror group in 1984, the papers would have slid gently into terminal decline.

None of us here will ever forget the fact.

And that is why our front page headline this morning remembers just that.

LUXURIOUS: Lady Ghislaine, the yacht Robert Maxwell loved

Publisher in yacht tragedy

A GREAT BIG EXTRAORDINARY MAN

Pages 2 to 11, 18, 19, 34 to 36

The *Mirror* pulls out all the stops to report Maxwell's death.

22

A Glorious New Dawn

A dark blue sky appears on screen. Stars fly by. A triumphal blast of trumpets sounds. This is followed by a bewildering jumble of images: Robert Maxwell getting into his helicopter; Robert Maxwell shaking hands with assorted world leaders; Robert Maxwell striding off to yet another important meeting . . .

An enormous letter 'M' swims closer, with the Earth wedged between its legs. Then comes Maxwell again, staring into the camera, his pitch-black hair slicked back, his eyebrows on full alert: 'I'm very proud to say that today our group is internationally recognized as one of the world's leading ten global publishers and professional information providers.'

Just in case anyone should doubt this, a disembodied voice announces: 'The past year has seen a remarkable transition in the affairs and standing of Maxwell Communications. Information is the gold-dust of the twentieth century. Prosperity in the next century will be governed by information flow. Those who provide that flow will be at the centre of the world stage. And who will the leading players be? Maxwell Communications will be one of them.'

The trumpets fade away, replaced by a chorus of heavenly voices. A man called Kevin Gruneich, 'Publishing Analyst, First Boston', appears on screen along with a caption hanging over his head reading 'Independent Opinion' in large letters. According to Gruneich, 'The consolidation of Maxwell's businesses in the United States and in the UK has been completed with unprecedented success.' And, what's more, the vast majority of these businesses are 'largely recession-proof'.

Music swells to underline the point; the heavenly voices soar.

Kevin Gruneich gives way to another 'Independent Opinion', this one belonging to a Publishing Analyst called Kendrick Noble. 'I expect Maxwell Communications to be an excellent investment,' says Noble. Then, giving a little smirk, he adds, 'So much so that I intend to buy some shares for myself.'

A long list of Maxwell's ventures follows: academic journals, newspapers, new and exciting technological ventures such as CD-ROM, along with more traditional forms of publishing: 'The adult books have an interesting backlist which includes F. Scott Fitzgerald and Ernest Hemingway.' But the emphasis is firmly on the future – on businesses like the Berlitz language school. 'We've seen a lot of occurrences over the past year such as the fall of the Berlin Wall and the emergence of freedom in Eastern Europe that are going to cause a need for Berlitz's services.'

The world stands on the brink of a new era – an era of greater tolerance and internationalism. Already the American political scientist Francis Fukuyama has declared that history as we knew it has ceased to exist. In the great ideological battle of the twentieth century, liberal democracies have triumphed, and no one – at least no one in their right mind – could ever again embrace any other form of government.

'Everything has changed more in the last year than anybody dared hope. The Berlin Wall has fallen. The Iron Curtain has been replaced by open doors and windows. Market forces are winning over military force.'

Who could possibly have foreseen such upheavals? Only one person, it seems. 'Robert Maxwell, a statesman as much as a businessman, committed his life to providing greater openness, particularly in Eastern Europe. Tireless political efforts are now opening major new business opportunities. Maxwell Communications is today a sharply-focused major player in international communications.'

Maxwell's two sons Kevin and Ian then appear. 'We recognize that the largest single market which will give immediate opportunity to our group is Europe,' says Ian. 'We look forward to 1992 when the removal of trade barriers, followed by the opening of the Channel

Tunnel in 1993, will facilitate far closer integration of our publishing, communications and distribution operations in the UK and on the Continent.'

By now the choir has given way to Elgar's 'Nimrod' from the *Enigma Variations*, guaranteed to stir the flintiest of hearts. The enormous M swims back into view, straddling the Earth. All around are clusters of stars, twinkling in the darkness. The message is unmistakable: this is a company whose ambitions cannot be confined within a single planet, but which stretch out deep into space:

Maxwell Communications
One World
One Vision

Maxwell Communications corporate video. 1990.

Shortly after buying the *Mirror* in 1984, Maxwell told one of his new employees, 'I own the pension fund.' Strictly speaking, he was right. As he controlled the *Mirror*, he also controlled the pension fund. At the time this arrangement didn't cause anyone any disquiet – least of all the *Mirror* pensioners who were reaping the benefits of some shrewd investments over the past few years. But what none of them realized was how literally Maxwell meant what he said.

Two years later, in 1986, he borrowed £1,500,000 from the fund to tide him over a temporary shortfall. A few weeks later, the money was repaid. The next year – 1987 – he borrowed considerably more: £9,000,000. This too was repaid. What Maxwell was doing wasn't exactly illegal, but nor was it exactly legal either. The pension fund's deed of trust stated that trustees could only 'lend money on such security as the Trustees think fit to any person except an Employer'.

Maxwell, of course, was an employer – their employer.

But as far as he was concerned the pension funds were another of his personal fiefdoms; his to do whatever he wanted with. At a meeting with the Polish Head of State, General Jaruzelski, in July 1985, Maxwell told him proudly that 'apart from being a journalist and politician, I also manage a pension fund to the tune of five hundred million pounds'.

Plainly intended to impress Jaruzelski, this statement failed to have the desired effect. The Polish leader turned out to be far more interested in Maxwell's personal contradictions: 'I had the impression that he had two, and maybe four souls,' Jaruzelski recalled. 'On the one hand, he had been a young boy from a very poor and backward part of Europe . . . And on the other hand, he was a man who had climbed Mount Olympus.'

However many souls Maxwell possessed, Jaruzelski suspected that he'd failed to bridge the gap between any of them. Such fluffy theorizing would have meant nothing to Maxwell himself, of course; he was far more concerned with unifying the different parts of his empire. Bringing them all together under his centralized control.

In March 1988, he decided to combine Mirror Group Newspapers' four pension funds into one – to be known as the Common Investment Fund (CIF). By now, the combined assets of the CIF amounted to more than £300,000,000. Day-to-day running of the fund would be in the hands of another new company, Bishopsgate Investment Management (BIM). In turn, ownership of BIM would be transferred to a charitable body – the Maxwell Charitable Trust – based in Liechtenstein.

Despite being the smallest, least visited country in Europe, Liechtenstein has the highest gross domestic product per person in the world. This is entirely due to the fact that anyone with a large enough pot of money can – for a fee – deposit it there, ensuring it stays both free of tax and safe from scrutiny. As far as Maxwell was concerned, there were a number of advantages to such an arrangement. Anyone asking to see BIM's accounts would be told that as the company was registered in Liechtenstein, they were unable to do so. In effect, it provided him with a smokescreen behind which he could do whatever he wanted.

To celebrate Maxwell's purchase of Macmillan in October 1988, a lunch was held at Claridge's hotel – the same hotel where four years earlier the manager had run after him insisting he settle his bill before he left. Among those raising their champagne glasses to toast him now was a former US Vice-President, Walter Mondale. But even as Maxwell soaked up the plaudits, he must have known that the smokescreen was wearing thin. Far from facing a glorious new dawn, Maxwell Communication Corporation, his publicly owned parent company, was crippled by debt and facing sharply rising interest rates.

In an attempt to prop up MCC's share price, Maxwell had started paying shareholders absurdly high dividends. At the same time he had been secretly buying up shares in MCC, spending £100,000,000 in an attempt to make them appear more desirable. To raise the money, he had to borrow even more heavily from the banks. Once again, they were happy to oblige. If the banks had any qualms about extending him another raft of loans, one thing above all set their minds at rest.

As he had repeatedly told them, Maxwell possessed billions of pounds in cash – which he had prudently salted away in Liechtenstein. It was true that no one knew just how much money he actually had in Liechtenstein. Nor had anybody seen any evidence of its existence. None the less, the banks readily believed him when he assured them the money was there. After all, the *Sunday Times* Rich List for 1989–90 had estimated Maxwell's fortune at between 1.2 billion and 1.5 billion pounds. What's more, he'd done something that counted just as much as any number of bank statements, accounts or written guarantees.

He had given them his word.

23

Crossing the Line

In the summer of 1990, eight months after the fall of the Berlin Wall, Maxwell flew to the city in his private jet for a series of meetings. As far as he was concerned, the fall of the Wall had all sorts of implications, personal and professional. More than forty years earlier, post-war Berlin had been the making of him; he'd emerged from the ruins of the city bearing the building blocks of what would become his publishing empire. Now he was back – bigger, infinitely richer, but as keen as ever to capitalize on the opportunities offered by political upheaval.

Travelling with him was his 'Personal Photographer', Mike Maloney; his 'Head of International Affairs', a former British ambassador to Poland called Sir John Morgan; his valet, Simon Grigg, and his PA, Andrea Martin. At the time Andrea Martin was twenty-six years old. She had started working for Maxwell two years earlier as a secretary in his 'outer office'. Learning that she had a degree in Modern Languages, Maxwell asked if she spoke French.

Martin said that she did.

'Fluently?'

'Yes.'

He then fired a series of questions at her in French. Martin answered them all.

'You'll do,' said Maxwell, and walked away.

Just a few weeks after she started work, Maxwell began phoning through to the outer office asking for Martin by name. He then promoted her to become his Personal Assistant, or 'Programme Manager', as he insisted on calling it. While Maxwell had detested

Peter Jay's attempts to put his life in order, he soon grew to depend on Andrea to organize his schedule and keep everything on track.

The *Mirror's* Foreign Editor, Nick Davies, was among those who noticed how important Martin had become to him: 'She had the run of the place and in Maxwell's eyes could do no wrong. He came to rely on her to run his diary, his business life, his office and his office staff. And he in turn became attentive to her needs. He would make sure Andrea had what she wanted, and the butlers were instructed to provide her with whatever she wanted to eat.'

Davies, popularly known as 'Sneaky' because of his furtive manner, also ran a company specializing in manufacturing underwater television sets. Although undeniably a niche market, this was less bizarre than it might sound: at the time underwater televisions were much in demand in the oil industry. A man of expensive tastes – he'd once owned a string of polo ponies – Davies had recently gone through a messy divorce. As his second wife, a former *Dr Who* actress called Janet Fielding, soon learned, Davies had been serially unfaithful, once inadvertently murmuring 'Oh Susan' into her ear while they were making love. Newly single, he was once again looking for love.

With her pencil skirts, her clipped manner and her Princess Diana pageboy haircut, Andrea Martin also made a big impression on Roy Greenslade. Recently appointed Editor of the *Mirror* after Richard Stott had returned to the *People*, Greenslade was struck by how adroitly Andrea managed Maxwell: 'She was a good-looking blonde, well-dressed, cool, efficient and apparently unflappable. She also had a well-developed but understated sense of humour that probably helped her cope with Maxwell's temper and his sudden changes of mood.' As a bonus in Greenslade's eyes, 'she had this slight injury to her lip which helped make her very fanciable'.

It wasn't long before Maxwell had given Andrea his personal American Express card to use 'whenever she saw fit'. When she bought a flat, he offered to act as guarantor for the mortgage and, for her twenty-sixth birthday, presented her with a new black BMW.

At the same time, Maxwell's long-serving PA, Jean Baddeley, was none too gently eased aside: she would end up in charge of corporate entertaining.

Yet even Andrea didn't escape his anger. One day Nick Davies found her in tears after Maxwell had been particularly demanding. The solicitous Davies did his best to console her – 'instinctively I put my hand on her knee' – and said that if she was ever feeling disheartened, she should give him a call.

'Don't let him get you down,' he told her. 'Don't let him push you too hard.'

Martin nodded and said, 'Thanks, but I'll be all right.'

Maxwell also insisted that Andrea accompany him on all his foreign trips. Immediately after finishing his meetings in Berlin, he was due to fly to London to see the Prime Minister, Margaret Thatcher. A landing slot had been booked several days earlier to ensure his plane arrived in time for him to reach Downing Street. Maxwell told Grigg he would collect Andrea Martin from the hotel where they had all been staying and bring her himself.

'I remember asking him if he was sure. He said, "Yes, yes," in his big bass voice. "You go ahead and I will collect Andrea."'

Grigg, Maloney and Sir John Morgan headed off to the airport. As usual Maxwell was late; by the time he arrived it was almost time for the plane to leave. But when he got out of the back of the car, Grigg saw that Maxwell was alone. 'I thought, bloody hell, where's Andrea? What's happened?'

As tactfully as he could, Grigg told him that he must have forgotten to collect her – that if he was to get back to London in time for his meeting with Mrs Thatcher, there was no alternative but to leave her behind.

Maxwell was livid. 'One by one he started berating us – me, John Morgan, Mike Maloney, the pilot . . . "Why is Andrea not here? Why didn't you think of it?" The ridiculous thing was we were completely innocent. I think he knew it too, except he couldn't afford to admit it to himself; it was just easier to blame others. Being the object of Maxwell's wrath was a very daunting experience. Although you knew you hadn't done anything wrong, you still felt completely stripped; it was as if you were standing there naked in front of him.'

Meanwhile the clock was ticking away. However, Maxwell refused to budge without Andrea – 'he made it perfectly obvious he wasn't going anywhere'. Eventually Sir John Morgan was dispatched to call Downing Street, offer profuse apologies and explain that Maxwell had been unavoidably detained in Berlin. A car was sent to pick up Andrea from the hotel and, more than an hour later than planned, the plane took off.

Afterwards, everyone who had been waiting on the tarmac that day found themselves asking the same question: why was Maxwell so determined to travel with his PA that he was prepared to stand up the Prime Minister in order to do so?

It was a question Betty Maxwell had also been asking herself. Although Maxwell seldom went to Headington Hill Hall any more, Betty would often come up to London to check he was looking after himself. Increasingly, she felt that her husband had gone through some fundamental change. A line had been crossed. Maxwell had always worked hard, but now his life had become even more frenetic than before. Everything was in a constant state of flux, as if he couldn't stand to be in the same place for long. Always he had to be jetting off to yet more countries, meeting more important people, buying more companies . . .

In the same way that he tried to satisfy his hunger by wolfing down food with his hands, Maxwell seemed to be gorging himself on activity. By now he was moving so fast it was difficult for anybody else to keep up. Behind him, he left a trail of chaos. 'The truth was that by the late 1980s, Bob's office was in an appalling state . . . It was impossible to believe that anyone could operate in such disorder.' While the outer office was bad enough, Betty found that Maxwell's own office was even worse. The heaps of paper on his desk may have looked reasonably tidy, but, when she examined them more closely, she saw that some of the letters he hadn't replied to were several years old.

Increasingly, Maxwell expected Betty and their son Ian to stand in for him at engagements he was either too busy, or too disorganized, to attend. At a reception at 10 Downing Street, Mrs Thatcher asked, 'Where's Robert?' in a puzzled voice – hardly surprising in view of what had happened not long before. Much to Betty's embarrassment, he twice failed to show up for dinners at the French embassy: 'The ambassador was furious – and rightly so.'

Sometimes she would find she was supposed to attend a function on the day it was happening. When she called to complain, she was no longer put through to her husband; instead, she would be fobbed off with a secretary. After this had happened several times Betty wrote him a curt letter: 'You must give orders to your secretaries that no invitations should be accepted on my behalf without having had the courtesy to send or fax me the invitation. I no longer want to stand in for you unless you deem my presence imperative.'

Betty had no doubt where the blame lay. Unlike Roy Greenslade, she was not at all impressed by the way in which Andrea ran Maxwell's affairs. 'It was ludicrous to expect a girl in her mid-twenties and with her lack of experience to be able to assume responsibility almost single-handedly for an office as busy as Bob's, but he liked her partly because she followed his instructions, didn't answer back, didn't nag him and had an even temper.'

Maxwell, Betty clearly saw, had become 'besotted' with Andrea, 'his infatuation blinding him as to her suitability for the job'. He would call her last thing at night to wish her good night and first thing in the morning to check she had slept well. He even told her she was welcome to come and live in his apartment.

Several years later, after reading that Andrea had complained about Maxwell's attentions, Betty was not inclined to be sympathetic. 'If this were true and her complaints serious, she could easily have walked out, she obviously enjoyed the high salary and perks of the job – travelling in private jets, staying in *de luxe* hotels, or on the *Lady Ghislaine*.' As for Maxwell himself, plainly he should have known better – 'but in the end the infatuation of an ageing man for a young girl appeared to take precedence over his duties as chairman of a vast empire'.

Ever since Nick Davies had found Andrea crying, he had felt there was 'an unspoken bond' between them. As always, Davies was on hand to offer a comforting shoulder and words of advice: 'I warned her to be careful.' It was advice that, for the time being at least, would go unheeded.

Ian Maxwell had recently been appointed joint Managing Director of Maxwell Communication Corporation along with his younger brother, Kevin – Ian looked after the publishing side and Kevin the financial. He too had noticed how different his father was when he was around Andrea. 'He was much more childlike. He also calmed down; he never swore or flew off the handle when she was there. I never saw him being physically affectionate to her, but I could see how important Andrea was. Although she was very guarded and never said much, you got a sense that nothing escaped her. I was also conscious of the fact that it was important to keep on Andrea's right side. She basically controlled access to him; she was the gate-keeper.'

In December 1988, leaders of all the member countries of the European Economic Community met in Rhodes to discuss the future direction of the EEC. Afterwards everyone who'd been present agreed the meeting had been a great success. As the official report declared proudly, 'The European Council notes with particular satisfaction that the decisions adopted with a view to making a success of the Single European Act have already contributed to the creation of favourable conditions for the smooth, steady and dynamic development of the Community as it moves towards 1992.'

The conference was a great success for Maxwell too – though not necessarily for the same reasons. As the *Lady Ghislaine* was being chartered out in the Caribbean, he hired another, equally large, yacht to take him to Rhodes. All the senior editorial staff on the *Mirror* were instructed to accompany him. So too was Andrea. Throughout their stay, Maxwell insisted she remained by his side.

According to Mike Molloy, 'It was obvious that he wouldn't let her out of his sight.'

Every evening, after the conference had finished for the day, the journalists adjourned to a local restaurant, where they drank lavish quantities of wine, smashed plates and generally engaged in traditional forms of Greek revelry. 'I remember Andrea asking me what we got up to in the evenings. Normally, she was very cool and collected, but on this occasion she was practically whispering. I explained about the restaurant we all went to, and she said she would like to come along. But she never did. She had to dine on the yacht with Maxwell – he wouldn't allow her to go anywhere else.'

One of the *Mirror* journalists found a shop on the island selling cut-price leather jackets – whereupon everyone went along looking for a bargain. Once again Andrea wanted to go, but again Maxwell forbade it. Instead, he called up the shop owner and told him to bring a large selection of his stock out to the yacht. 'The entire deck of the yacht was covered in leather jackets so she could make her choice.'

As well as being more than forty years younger than Maxwell, Andrea was a fraction of his size. On their last day in Rhodes, he called a breakfast press conference. Molloy could see that Maxwell was in a particularly foul mood: 'He sat at the head of the table seeking victims to bully while he crammed astonishingly large amounts of food into himself.'

This was to have unexpected consequences. 'The table at which we ate was equipped with wrought-iron chairs and, as he raved, his vast weight began to buckle his chair legs. Gradually, he sank lower and lower, until his chin was almost level with the table. He tried to get up, but it proved impossible to manage, so he ordered us all on deck. We never did find out how he extricated himself.'

Despite his ballooning size, Maxwell's obsession with Andrea made him even fussier than usual about his appearance. For some years now, the chief barber at the Savoy Hotel, George Wheeler, had been coming to Maxwell House every week to dye Maxwell's hair and eyebrows with L'Oréal CreScendo – 'imparts thickness, body, shine and long-lasting colour to even resistant grey'.

Maxwell's corporate lawyer, Deborah Maxwell – no relation – became used to walking into Maxwell's apartment and finding him sitting in the kitchen with a towel round his shoulders and a freshly blackened head. 'I would have to walk by and pretend that nothing unusual was going on.' Maxwell's increasing pickiness took even George Wheeler aback. 'Even if he saw a grey eyebrow, he would go berserk.'

Any qualms Andrea may have had about being on the receiving end of Maxwell's attentions seemed to have disappeared – for the time being at least. When the two of them travelled together on his new Gulfstream G4 private jet, she would sit opposite him with her feet tucked beneath his thighs. On transatlantic flights, they would even lie down together on the plane's divan bed. As far as Simon Grigg was concerned, 'it was clear that he was in love with her, and she was in love with him. Although Andrea had this cool exterior, there was an insecurity to her; she was a very private girl. I think perhaps Maxwell saw this and related to it.'

There were those who couldn't – or wouldn't – believe that their relationship was ever consummated. Others, however, were less sure. Deborah Maxwell was with them both on a trip to Lisbon when she walked into what turned out to be Maxwell's hotel suite. 'I thought I was going into the lounge part of his suite, but by mistake I went into the bedroom. There were two double beds in there and I could see they had both been used. Andrea was in the room in her dressing gown. I remember thinking, "Oh my God", and quickly withdrawing. However young she may have been, I think she was a woman for whom the power was clearly intoxicating.'

On one of her periodic visits to Maxwell House, Eleanor Berry also suspected that something was going on – this despite swallowing 'two or three happy pills' beforehand. While she waited for Maxwell, Berry went to have a cigarette in his private lavatory. When she came out, she found Andrea waiting.

'You had a cigarette in Mr Maxwell's lavatory,' Andrea said accusingly.

Berry too was not impressed – either by Andrea's attitude or by her appearance. 'I couldn't understand what Bob saw in her. She was wearing awfully naff green eye shadow and a ridiculously short mini-skirt which left nothing to the imagination. In fact, it was so bloody short that it was just about possible to see her cervix.'

Berry was in no mood to be conciliatory. 'You are a shorthand typist,' she told her, 'and I am a distinguished woman of letters. When I die, my profile will be engraved on the coins. When your time comes up, no one will know or care that you'd ever existed.'

There was a long pause.

'Do you have psychiatric problems, Miss Berry?' Andrea asked.

There was another pause.

'Oh piss off, you silly little nit,' said Berry.

Seeing how besotted Maxwell had become with Andrea, Peter Jay felt that he should do whatever he could to steer her away from danger. 'It was all rather like King Lear, in terms of an old man becoming extremely foolish and making himself look ridiculous. It was obviously a very sensitive situation, but I considered that I had some responsibility for this junior member of staff. I did try to talk to her, to give her an opportunity to say, "Please help," but she never took me up on it. Through thick and thin, she stoutly maintained that nothing was going on.'

24.

Obsessed

As he watched Andrea's growing closeness to Maxwell, Nick Davies found his own feelings becoming more and more torn. Like many others, Richard Stott felt that Davies's nickname of 'Sneaky' had been aptly chosen: 'He had this habit of talking behind his hand' – something Stott put down to the fact Davies was also running his underwater television business from his office phone.

Every so often Stott liked to have black-tie dinners for the senior staff. At one of them, Davies astonished everyone by launching into a lengthy speech in which he denounced Maxwell as a hopelessly incompetent proprietor. A watching Joe Haines couldn't understand what was happening. 'He went on and on. People were getting embarrassed. When he eventually finished, I said, "That's the longest suicide speech I have ever heard."'

What Haines didn't know was that Nick Davies had also fallen for Andrea Martin. Nor at this stage did Maxwell have any idea about Davies's feelings for Andrea – or her growing feelings for him. But all that was about to change. In early 1990, Maxwell and Davies flew to Bulgaria, where they had a number of meetings with the new Prime Minister, Andrei Lukanov. Maxwell got off to a flying start by announcing at their first meeting that he was prepared to take on responsibility for Bulgaria's entire foreign debt – then running at around 11 billion dollars.

'You have my word that you can trust me,' he told Lukanov. 'Remember, I have been a friend to your country for many years now and we can trust each other.'

Typically, this was only half the story. The former President Todor Zhivkov was one of the Soviet bloc leaders whom Maxwell had buttered up by featuring in a series of biographies he published in the 1970s and 1980s entitled *Leaders of the World*. In his 1977 book on the Soviet Premier, Leonid Brezhnev, he had piled on the flattery with possibly the world's largest shovel, referring to him as 'This outstanding personality in the international communist and working class movement whose versatile, tireless and productive work is an inspiring example of utter devotion to the socialist homeland.'

In his meeting with Zhivkov, Maxwell sought to go one better, offering operatically protracted condolences on the recent death of the President's daughter: 'Hundreds of state and government leaders, leaders of Communist and workers' parties, politicians and cultural figures the world over expressed their condolences to the Bulgarian people, to the Central Committee of the Bulgarian Communist Party and personally to you for this great loss . . . I would like to ask you in connection with this how does the project of Mrs Zhivkova on aesthetic education, defined as realization of the vital necessity to live according to the supreme laws of truth and beauty, fit into, if I may express myself so, the more orthodox targets of the Communist education?'

But even the supreme laws of truth and beauty weren't enough to save Zhivkov's skin. After he was toppled in November 1989, Maxwell quickly set about ingratiating himself with his successor. He told Lukanov that he liked Bulgaria so much he was thinking of settling there. 'I would like to buy a country estate and have it as my summer residence,' he said. 'Somewhere I could station my helicopter and work from.'

'Why don't you view one of the former President's palaces?' Lukanov suggested. 'They are all available for rent to people such as yourself.'

Maxwell agreed this was a splendid idea. Zhivkov, it turned out, had had a grand total of thirty-two separate lodges and palaces, dotted all over the country. Maxwell expressed an interest in six of them. He was particularly taken with Zhivkov's former summer palace on the shores of the Black Sea. After he and Nick Davies had inspected it, and Maxwell had bounced up and down on Zhivkov's old double bed, they sat out on the balcony gazing at the view.

'Are you going to take it?' Davies asked.

Maxwell did not reply – not directly. Instead he said, 'Do you think Andrea would like it here?'

'I don't know,' Davies replied cautiously. 'It's a little remote for her, I would imagine.'

'It would be very peaceful for her,' Maxwell insisted. 'I could see her working out here on the balcony in the sunshine.'

Nothing more was said, but back in London Davies noticed that Maxwell's attitude towards him had gone through a dramatic change. The easy conviviality of before had disappeared; now there were surliness and suspicion. Clearly something had happened, but what? Davies thought he knew the answer. Like others at the *Mirror*, he had heard rumours that the phones were bugged. He told Andrea to check her office phone for anything unusual, and, sure enough, 'She found what looked like a microphone attached to a tiny camera, hidden in the high ceiling above her desk.'

There was worse to come. One of the *Mirror*'s security officers tipped Davies off that he was now a 'marked man'. Apparently Maxwell had ordered that he should be followed around the clock by a team of private detectives. Another team had been instructed to follow Andrea. 'Every detail of our movements and any possible meetings had to be reported back to Maxwell within twenty-four hours.' Maxwell had also asked the same man to see if he could buy the flat next door to Andrea Martin's in Docklands. 'If that was possible, the security staff were ordered to purchase it immediately, drill holes in the wall and install cameras to spy on her.'

Ever since Maxwell had asked John Pole to bug the office phones, he would sit in his apartment when he was unable to sleep, listening to the tapes. Pole too had seen how obsessed he had become with Andrea. 'Occasionally, I would ask myself, how are you going to get out of this one, Andrea? I remember one day she went out to lunch with Nick Davies and Maxwell kept asking me, "Where did she go? Who was she with?"'

Shortly afterwards, Andrea went away for a fortnight's holiday. When she returned, Maxwell was beside himself. All he could do was go round saying, 'Andrea's back! Andrea's back!'

Pole soon had the evidence to prove that she and Nick Davies were very much in touch with one another. Like many others, he had assumed that Maxwell's relationship with Andrea was simply a fling. It was only now that he realized his mistake. 'It wasn't a game; it was extremely serious.'

In one taped conversation, Andrea and Nick Davies could be heard discussing her underwear. As he watched Maxwell listening to the tape, Pole could see how badly affected he was. 'I got the impression he was a broken man.' Soon afterwards, Pole went to see him and was told he was up on the roof of Maxwell House. 'I stepped out of the lift and Maxwell was sitting in a chair on his own. Here was one of the richest men in the world, and yet he seemed completely isolated, completely alone. I thought as one human being to another that I would say to him, "Do you want me to sit with you?" I didn't though; I told myself it was nothing to do with me. Besides, I suspect he would have thrown me off the roof if I had. Instead I just went back in the lift and came down again, but the memory has stayed with me ever since.'

In January 1990, Maxwell and Andrea travelled to Moscow on a business trip. As Nick Davies recalled, twenty-fours later, he received a phone call. 'He knows,' a panic-stricken Andrea told him. 'He knows everything about us.'

From the moment they had left Heathrow, Maxwell had repeatedly bombarded her with the same question. 'Have you anything to tell me?' To begin with, Andrea didn't know what he was talking about. Then Maxwell blurted out that he knew she was having an affair with Davies.

As Davies later described, 'He began a long, obviously well-rehearsed speech, which basically amounted to a tirade against me; informing her that he was only bringing up the matter for her own good because I was no good for her: a twice-married man with teenage children who was old enough to be her father.'

While there may have been something in this, what Maxwell omitted to mention was that while Davies was old enough to be Andrea's father, he was old enough to be her grandfather. Apparently Maxwell had then quietened down, but not for long. Forty-eight hours later, Davies received another call – from Jerusalem this time. 'She was in tears, obviously distraught and sounded frightened.' Maxwell, Andrea said, had walked unannounced into her bedroom that morning and forced himself on her, 'trying to kiss her as she fought him off, shouting at him to stop, hitting out at him as she struggled to escape his bear-like arms'.

In the end, she had persuaded him to leave, locked the door and phoned Davies. Subsequently Maxwell had apologized and reiterated that he was merely concerned for her welfare. That she was in danger of throwing her life away on a wastrel. The rest of the trip passed without incident, but back in London Maxwell soon started up again. Unable to bring himself to say Davies's name, he referred to him simply as 'that dreadful man'. One evening he asked Andrea to marry him.

'Andrea was dumbstruck, just shaking her head and saying, "No."'

As both Davies and Andrea were worried about losing their jobs if this carried on, they decided to separate for a while – 'to take the heat out of the situation'. But for Maxwell the damage had already been done. Like John Pole, Simon Grigg could see how crestfallen, how broken-hearted, he was.

'The wind had been completely knocked out of his sails.'

25

Three Departures

At the end of 1989, Maxwell walked into Peter Jay's office and suddenly announced that he wanted him to leave – he had decided that he no longer needed a Chief-of-Staff.

Having spent the last three years being belittled, ridiculed and telephoned in the middle of the night, Jay was not unduly downhearted. Apart from anything else, he'd just been sounded out by the BBC, who wondered if he would be interested in becoming their Economics Editor – an offer he later accepted. He had also realized long ago that it was impossible to bring order to anyone's life when they were hell-bent on creating as much chaos as possible.

The two of them agreed that Jay would carry on working at the *Mirror* for the next three months. In those three months, Maxwell's behaviour changed markedly. 'He became much nicer to me,' Jay recalls. 'Almost fatherly. I don't think he exactly wanted me as his friend because he didn't have any capacity for friendship. To be friends with someone you need to have a mutual regard which he wasn't capable of. But I do think he wanted someone to be close to.'

And there was something else that Jay noticed. 'Once or twice I had the sense Maxwell was deliberately excluding me from things. Things I would have expected to have been involved with. Subsequently, I found myself wondering if there was a kind of affection at work in Maxwell's mind. Somehow he seemed to be shielding me from those parts of his activities which might have been damaging to my reputation. As if in some strange way he was trying to protect me from what was to come.'

*

After four years working as Maxwell's valet, Simon Grigg was exhausted. 'I had been very happy there, but I felt I had gone as far as I could go. I'd basically lived and breathed the guy; it had been my entire life. I had even got to the stage where I could second-guess him. If Maxwell wanted a cup of coffee, he didn't have to say anything. I could practically feel it.'

Grigg decided to hand in his notice. However, this proved easier said than done. It wasn't until he was staying with Maxwell in the Helmsley Palace Hotel in New York in November 1990 that the opportunity finally arose. 'Maxwell came back one night at around midnight and I had my resignation letter ready. I remember I was feeling quite nervous.

'I walked into his bedroom and he was lying on the bed leafing through a newspaper.' Having handed Maxwell his letter, Grigg stood at the foot of the bed, waiting. 'When he'd read it, he put it down and said, "What's the problem, Simon?" I could see how upset he was; there was a tear in his eye. But then I was welling up myself.'

Grigg explained there wasn't a problem – he just felt like a change. 'Maxwell seemed quite taken aback by that, but it was true. In all the time I'd spent there, I'd never had a problem with him.' After four years, Grigg reckoned that nothing Maxwell did could surprise him any more. But here he turned out to be mistaken. Early the next morning, he was lying in bed when he heard a knock on his door.

'Come in,' Grigg called.

Maxwell entered, carrying a tray.

'I have brought your breakfast, Simon,' he announced.

Before that there had been another departure. Andrea Martin's and Nick Davies's resolve to see less of one another didn't last long. Nor did it take long before Maxwell found out – this time Davies had no idea how. One afternoon in the spring of 1990, he summoned Davies to his office, shut all the doors and instructed his secretaries that under no circumstances was he to be disturbed.

Sitting slumped in his chair, Maxwell didn't say anything at first. It was only after several minutes had passed that Davies realized he was so upset he was physically incapable of talking – 'emotion was running so high through his body, constricting his throat'. Eventually, Maxwell managed to call for water. Once he'd drunk it, he said hoarsely, 'I have to talk to you about Andrea. We must have an agreement.'

Davies asked what he had in mind.

'I don't know,' Maxwell told him, 'but something must be done. I can't go on like this.'

If Davies and Andrea continued to see one another, he said, he would be forced to sack her. The editors of his various papers wouldn't want a senior member of staff having an affair with his PA – apart from anything else, it would be bad for business.

Although there wasn't a great deal of evidence to support the idea, Davies had always liked to think of himself as a gentleman. He decided to do the gentlemanly thing and fall on his sword. 'That being the case, I shall resign,' he declared. 'Andrea is far more vital to you as your PA than ever I am as Foreign Editor. You're always describing her as your right arm. You can easily go and find someone else to do my job.'

'I'll be in touch,' Maxwell told Davies. 'This is strictly between you and me. No one must know of our conversation.' By way of a send-off, he said plaintively, 'You are my friend.'

For the next few weeks an uneasy calm prevailed. Despite their conversation, Davies carried on working as Foreign Editor and Maxwell made no move to replace him. Then, in May 1990, Maxwell finally snapped. For no apparent reason he starting shouting at Andrea, telling her she was fired. She was ordered to hand over her keys and her security pass, and leave the building. A few days later he called her, saying that he'd made a terrible mistake and imploring her to come back.

With considerable reservations, Andrea agreed. To begin with Maxwell could not have been more solicitous, but, just as she had suspected, the black mist soon descended. This time she'd had enough.

Maxwell told her that if she left, he wouldn't give her a penny. That she would be left impoverished and unemployable. 'Every time she tried to talk sensibly to him Maxwell would go wild, tearing into her, shouting at her until she was reduced to tears.'

Once again, Nick Davies felt compelled to intervene. Only now he decided to be more forceful than before. Maxwell, he said, was acting outrageously, even by his standards. How could he claim that he cared about Andrea when he treated her so badly? Why was he bullying someone who couldn't possibly answer back? He should be thoroughly ashamed of himself.

Maxwell sat in silence throughout.

'What are we going to do?' he asked when Davies had finished.

There was nothing more to be done, Davies told him. Whatever happened, Andrea was leaving. Before he left, he offered a parting shot:

'You've blown it.'

Another fortnight went by. One Sunday afternoon, Davies was at work when Maxwell phoned and asked if he would come up to his apartment. Shown into his bedroom by one of the Filipina maids, he found Maxwell lying on his bed in a white towelling dressing gown, watching television.

First, Maxwell complained of having a cold which he couldn't shake off. Then, according to Davies, he stood up and walked over to the window. As he stared out of the window, Maxwell started talking – more to himself than to Davies, or so it seemed: ' "Sometimes I don't know why I go on," he muttered. "Everything I try, people turn against me . . . I've got no friends, no one I can turn to . . . no one to share my life with . . . Sometimes I think I should just end it all, throw myself out of the window . . . I sometimes feel I can't go on." '

26.

What Have I Done to Deserve That?

One evening in June 1990, Betty Maxwell was preparing to go to a party that she and her husband had been invited to a few miles away from their home in Oxford. Although Maxwell now hardly spent any time at Headington Hill Hall, on this occasion he'd agreed to accompany her. But while Betty was dressing, the phone rang. It was Maxwell. He had decided not to come, he told her. He didn't offer any apology or explanation, merely that she should take their son Ian instead.

Just as Betty and Ian were about to leave, they were surprised to hear the thump of rotor blades overhead – Maxwell had arrived back in his helicopter. Walking into the house, he announced that he had a splitting headache and was going straight to bed. Ever attentive, Betty went upstairs with him to turn the bed down and close the shutters. Maxwell didn't say anything; he just stood there glowering.

'He then abruptly dismissed me and asked me to leave him alone.'

Before Betty went, she asked if there was anything else she could do – whereupon Maxwell began to shout at her. 'He accused me of callously leaving him in the hands of servants when he was ill. I was outraged . . . I couldn't take any more of his ranting.' Even so, she was still sufficiently concerned about his welfare to ask the kitchen to prepare hot soup and a light meal for his supper before she and Ian left in a chauffeur-driven Rolls-Royce.

They were only ten minutes away from the house when the car phone rang.

Once again it was Maxwell.

'This time you've really gone too far,' he said. 'You're heartless and stupid and I'm leaving you.'

Betty asked the driver to take them back to Headington Hill Hall. The chauffeur dropped her off, then took Ian on to the party, where he had to apologize for the fact that both his parents had been unavoidably detained.

Going back upstairs, Betty found Maxwell propped up in bed. She asked what on earth was going on.

'I've come to the conclusion that you're absolutely raving mad,' Maxwell told her. 'After all I've done for you, you don't even have the decency to stay with me when I come home sick and tired. You prefer to go out dancing. I've decided irrevocably to leave you.'

Betty tried to reason with him, but it was hopeless; he refused to listen. In all the time they'd been together – almost fifty years – she had never seen him so angry.

The next morning, at around eleven o'clock, Maxwell asked her to go to his study. There, he repeated what he had said the night before – that she was mad and he wanted nothing more to do with her. He then said that he wanted an immediate legal separation which would be announced in *The Times* on 1 July. 'I was stunned. I didn't argue with him, but just said, "Why do you want to make it such a public affair? What have I done to deserve that? If you want me to leave, I'll go. I've no wish to hurt you in any way."'

But Maxwell was adamant he wanted a public announcement. '"I don't want to see you again," he said. "I don't want you to phone me. I don't want to talk to you any more. I no longer love you. This is the end and I really mean THE END."'

Before Betty left his study, Maxwell asked her if she wished to be involved in the wording of the announcement.

'No,' she told him, 'You are the communications man. You must do as you think best.'

'All right,' said Maxwell gloomily. 'People will say it was all my fault anyway.'

'Yes, they're sure to say that,' Betty agreed. 'And they'll be right too,' she added.

After she left she telephoned her son Kevin to ask if he had any idea why his father was behaving like this. She also wanted his help in trying to work out a financial settlement. Kevin advised her not to ask for too much – 'Mother, don't do an Ivana Trump on him. Just ask him for what will amply cover your present and future needs.'

A week later, Betty was in Headington Hill Hall when once again she heard the thump of rotor blades overhead. This time Maxwell had come to ask if she'd given any further thought to what they had discussed. By way of a reply, she handed him a piece of paper.

On it she had written a list of conditions for her agreeing to their separation. The first was that she wished to spend eight days with Maxwell on board the *Lady Ghislaine*, 'So that we can discuss the various aspects of our separation in a civilized manner, as two people who have loved each other very much and spent forty-seven years together. Specifically, I need sufficient money to:

- Complete the building of Fraytet [the house in France that Betty had bought].
- Buy myself a *pied à terre* in London.
- Pay for the removal of all my personal furniture and chattels from Headington and their installation in my new London base and in Fraytet.
- Settle such debts as I may have in England.'

The second condition said simply, 'I wish to leave Headington Hill Hall soon after March 11th 1991, my seventieth birthday.'

In the third and final condition, she asked to be given a lump sum on her birthday 'to ensure an adequate income for me for life'.

Maxwell read over the list, grunted and put it in his pocket.

'My answer is yes for the eight days on the boat,' he told her. 'When would you like it to be?'

Betty said that any time in August would be fine for her. Maxwell then went back out to the helicopter, leaving her feeling more confused than ever. 'I found myself alone, reflecting on what a ridiculous way this was to part and wondering what on earth had happened to the man I had loved so dearly, protected and slaved for all my life.'

On the morning of 1 July 1990, Betty opened *The Times* and scanned the Personal columns. There was no announcement of their separation. Nor was there any word from Maxwell. For the next month, they neither met, nor spoke on the phone. But in August they agreed – by memo – to meet in Turkey in order to spend their final eight days together on the *Lady Ghislaine*.

When Betty arrived, she discovered that Maxwell had left an hour earlier on his private plane. Unsure what to do, she called his office. 'I plucked up my courage and phoned Bob.'

He said she should head for the island of Samos and he would meet her there. But when she reached Samos there was no sign of him. Again Betty phoned. This time Maxwell told her to meet him in Lesbos – a day's sail away. Off she went once more, but he never showed up there either.

For a fourth time she tried. He would definitely be waiting for her in Ephesus on the Turkish coast, Maxwell said. The yacht duly set sail.

He never appeared.

27.

Intangible Assets

Maxwell Communications Press Information.
4 June 1990.

MAXWELL INSTITUTE TO BOOST PEACE

The Gorbachev–Maxwell Institute of Technology was launched in America yesterday by Soviet President Mikhail Gorbachev. The Institute of Global Technology will be an international centre for American, Soviet and European scientists and engineers to conduct research into problems ranging from food and health to global warming and communication.

With President Gorbachev at his side during the launch ceremony in the Minnesota Governor's mansion, *Mirror* publisher Robert Maxwell said the Institute will honour the Soviet leader and he praised him for the 'great service' he had rendered in ending the Cold War.

Mr Maxwell said he would contribute $50,000,000 to be matched dollar for dollar by Governor Perpich and a committee of Minnesotans. The new Institute of Global Technology, he said, 'will conduct truly international research, for science cannot be restrained by national boundaries. The world stands on the threshold of its greatest leap forward since the invention of the wheel.'

Minnesota Governor Rudy Perpich campaigned for years to bring the Institute to Minneapolis. The Governor said, 'Mr Maxwell, through his great generosity, will unite scientists in a great human endeavour.'

President Gorbachev, who spent seven hours in Minnesota after ending his Washington Summit talks, said, 'This institute is another element of common co-operation. We join our efforts to come to grips with the problems that are of concern to us all.'

A month earlier, in May 1990, Rupert Murdoch's *Sun* announced that the paper was offering a £5,000,000 first prize in a game called Spot-the-Ball. One of British tabloid newspapers' oldest and most hallowed competitions, Spot-the-Ball consists of a photograph of a football match which has been divided into a grid. The ball, however, is missing.

Anyone taking part has to guess which numbered square on the grid the ball belongs in. This involves a certain amount of skill. Clues as to its whereabouts can be gleaned from the positions of the players, the direction of their gaze, and so on – but the ball is seldom, if ever, where you might expect to find it.

All too predictably, Maxwell announced that he also wanted to run a Spot-the-Ball competition. But he baulked at matching the £5,000,000 first prize, and settled instead for £1,000,000. Calling the *Mirror*'s Editor, Roy Greenslade, into his office, Maxwell told him, 'I have decided to be the chairman of judges of the first Spot-the-Ball thing. You will chair them from then on.'

Before Greenslade left, Maxwell had one last thing to say. 'Make sure this doesn't cost me a million.' Just in case Greenslade was in any doubt, he repeated it: 'I don't want to pay out one million pounds.'

It soon became clear what Maxwell meant. Rather than correctly identifying the position of the ball on one occasion, the winner of the *Mirror*'s competition had to do so on five consecutive days. A panel of adjudicators would then decide if anyone had guessed correctly on all five occasions. But Maxwell also introduced another innovation. He told the adjudicators to wait until all the entries were in. Having done so, they were to select a combination of squares that nobody had chosen.

This put an entirely new spin on the idea that the ball was never where you expected to find it. In Maxwell's version of the game, its position either defied the laws of physics, or else involved superhuman feats of contortion from the players. These, though, were trifling concerns as far as he was concerned. Played by Maxwell's rules, there need never be a winner unless he decided to create one.

Forced to run a game that he knew no one could win, a disconsolate Greenslade wrote in his diary: 'Tonight I spoke of resignation. The sure knowledge that I must carry out RM's Spot the Ball commands now haunts me.' What, he wondered, had made Maxwell rig the competition? Was it simply meanness? Or could there be another explanation? Could the reason that Maxwell didn't want to give anyone the million-pound prize because he no longer had the money to spare?

Later that month Maxwell went to a reception at 10 Downing Street. Despite their political differences, Maxwell and Mrs Thatcher had always got on well, and on this occasion his appearance brought out the warmer, nursier side of the Prime Minister's character. To begin with, they discussed a visit she was hoping to make to Russia to see President Gorbachev. Mrs Thatcher told Maxwell that she regarded him as one of her main links to the Soviet premier. Then, gazing at him more closely, she said, 'Robert, you look tired. I do hope you're not overdoing things.'

At the end of July 1990, a short paragraph appeared in the 'Lex' column of the *Financial Times* – so short that anyone who wasn't a careful reader might easily have missed it. The day before, MCC had published its annual report. On the surface, it appeared to offer yet more good news to shareholders. But the author of the 'Lex' column wasn't convinced. What the report failed to take into account was that interest payments on the company's debts were continuing to rise far more quickly than MCC's profits.

Nor were the profits all they seemed. In an attempt to nudge the figures as far as possible into the black, properties worth £41,000,000 had been sold off. If you took the debts and the property sales into account, the company barely had enough money to cover their dividend payments. MCC's shares, the column concluded, were basically worthless. Far from being in profit, the company was running at a considerable loss.

The moment he read this, Maxwell sprang into action, complaining the article was 'irresponsible and impermissible'. For a start, it made no mention of MCC's numerous 'intangible assets'. As their name suggests, intangible assets – things like brand value or intellectual property – have no physical substance. Although you may not be able to see or feel them, they can greatly affect a company's fortunes. But, because of their nature, putting a value on intangibles is a notoriously subjective business.

Maxwell persuaded the paper to publish a letter in which he raged against the 'scribblers' who were trying to do him down. However, throughout July the share price continued to fall, and by the end of the month it had dropped to 142p – a loss of almost 30 per cent in three years. In an attempt to stop the price from falling further, Maxwell began to buy even more MCC shares – in July 1990 alone, he spent more than £75,000,000.

On 23 August, one of his private companies, Bishopsgate Investment Trust, bought 15.65 million shares. Six days later, the same company bought another 10 million shares. Maxwell also entered into an arrangement with Goldman Sachs whereby he sold 15.65 million MCC shares to the bank on the understanding that he'd buy them back at the end of November for a set price – £1.85 each.

But still the share price kept falling. On 23 October, Maxwell was due to repay loans worth more than £200,000,000. If he defaulted on his repayment, the true scale of his problems would become clear to everyone. In an attempt to raise more money, he embarked on a giant sale of assets – a sale he announced would bring him £600,000,000. Among them were his encyclopedia business, his 22 per cent stake in the banknote printers De La Rue, and 51 per cent of the satellite rock channel MTV.

This announcement caused considerable surprise – MTV in particular was widely reckoned to be a business whose profits were about to go through the roof. As for Maxwell's share in De La Rue, he sold it at a £50,000,000 loss. However, nothing he did made any difference: the sale failed to raise anything like the £600,000,000 he'd been hoping for. Meanwhile the shares continued to fall.

By November 1990, MCC's total debt had risen to 2.4 billion pounds.

The more desperate Maxwell's finances became, the more he tried to throw himself about on the international stage, as if this might take his mind off all his difficulties. A few weeks before, he had asked Mrs Thatcher for an urgent appointment: 'He says that he has important information for you on Gorbachev,' the Prime Minister's Private Secretary, Charles Powell, wrote in a memo.

Mrs Thatcher agreed to squeeze him in the following afternoon. When they met, Maxwell told her that Gorbachev's plan to reform the USSR's political and economic systems – *perestroika* – was in grave danger. Unless the Soviets received 20 billion dollars to buy food and consumer goods, it wasn't only *perestroika* that might collapse, but the whole Soviet Union. In return for the 20 billion dollars, Gorbachev could supply the UK with chemicals, fertilizers and coal.

Was Mrs Thatcher willing to help? If so, Maxwell was prepared to try to broker a deal.

While she may have valued him as an intermediary, on this occasion Mrs Thatcher decided to keep her distance. Perhaps she had no desire to help out, or perhaps she felt that in presenting himself as the potential saviour of the entire Soviet Union, Maxwell was going too far, even for him. Rather than deal directly with his proposal, she passed it on to her Secretary of State for Trade and Industry, Nicholas Ridley.

As far as Ridley was concerned, it was an offer he could happily refuse. A fortnight later, his Private Secretary wrote to Powell: 'Dear Charles, My Secretary of State was interested, but far from persuaded by the points that Mr Maxwell made to the Prime Minister.'

However, Maxwell had better luck with the Israeli Prime Minister, Yitzhak Shamir. In November 1990, Shamir asked him to pass on a letter to Gorbachev in which he expressed his hope that diplomatic relations between the two countries might be restored – enabling flights from Russia to Israel to start up again 'with no restrictions on Jewish emigrants flying on them'.

Maxwell promised to pass the letter on, but when he got to Moscow he realized he'd left it behind in London. One of the Filipina maids was detailed to rummage through the drawers of his bedside table. Eventually she found the letter, which was then dictated to Maxwell's secretary in Moscow. Eight months later, a flight packed with Jewish emigrants left Moscow bound for Tel Aviv.

Despite the setback with Mrs Thatcher, Gorbachev and Maxwell continued to enjoy close relations – relations that were about to be enshrined in the Gorbachev–Maxwell Institute of Technology. Having spent so long trying to bring the institute to Minneapolis, Governor Perpich was understandably keen to get everything moving.

After much discussion, it had been decided that the name 'The Gorbachev–Maxwell Institute for Technology' didn't adequately reflect what was described as the 'thrust' and 'synergies' of the enterprise. In future it would be known as 'The Gorbachev–Maxwell Institute for Technological Change'. By October 1990, Perpich was close to raising the $50,000,000 he had promised back in June. All that remained was for Maxwell to contribute his $50,000,000 and then the 'great human endeavour' could get under-way. But when the Governor tried to get in touch with him, he found that Maxwell was peculiarly elusive. His calls were never put through, his letters went unanswered. Mikhail Gorbachev seemed just as puzzled as Perpich by Maxwell's behaviour.

It would take a while longer before the truth finally dawned on them: the money was never coming. Maxwell had reneged on the deal. Quite possibly he'd never had any intention of donating $50,000,000; instead he was milking his pledge for as much publicity as he could – just as he had done with the 1986 Commonwealth Games. But even if he had originally planned to hand over the money, those days were long gone. While the world may indeed have been on the brink of its greatest leap forward since the invention of the wheel, the Gorbachev–Maxwell Institute for Technological Change wouldn't be playing any part in it.

28.

Légumes du Maurier

Midway through the negotiations to buy the *New York Daily News*, in March 1991, Maxwell suddenly announced that he was flying back to London. He had an important function to attend, he told union representatives: a dinner to celebrate his wife Betty's seventieth birthday.

The dinner was a typically lavish affair – the final bill was estimated to be around £250,000. One hundred and fifty guests had been invited to the Orchid Room at the Dorchester Hotel. They included assorted peers and business leaders, as well as the Soviet ambassador to Czechoslovakia. The menu had been chosen to reflect different aspects of the Maxwells' life together. The main course was Lamb Meynard – Meynard had been Betty's maiden name – which came accompanied by Légumes du Maurier – du Maurier being the name Maxwell was going under when they first met.

Beside each place setting was a Birthday Book which had been specially compiled by the Maxwells' twin daughters, Isabel and Christine. In the preface Maxwell himself paid a warm if somewhat stiff tribute to his wife. 'You have been an outstanding mother to all our children,' he wrote, before switching to Betty's native French: 'Nous avons eu neuf enfants ensemble et j'ai une femme que j'aime tendrement' – we have had nine children together and I have a wife who I love dearly.

The book included photographs from their family album – Maxwell in Berlin; Maxwell being presented with his Military Cross by Field-Marshal Montgomery; Maxwell with Barry the German shepherd; Maxwell and Betty on their wedding day, as well as photos of the two of them alongside some familiar faces: Prince Charles, Nelson and Winnie Mandela, Ronald and Nancy Reagan, Mrs Thatcher and the President of Israel, Chaim Herzog.

There were also tributes from more than 200 friends. The former Prime Minister, Harold Wilson, and his wife, Mary, wrote that 'Elisabeth is a delightful person – talented and capable, yet modest about all her achievements; so supportive of Robert, yet maintaining her own work in different directions. We are devoted to her.'

The broadcaster David Frost described how Betty had always endeavoured to 'make a difference', while the property developer Gerald Ronson noted that in the years he and his wife, Gail, had known the Maxwells, 'life has had its ups as well as its downs'. At the time, Ronson's own life was going through one of its down phases: he'd just been released from Ford open prison after serving six months of a one-year sentence for conspiracy, false accounting and theft. Nine years later, the European Court of Human Rights ruled that his conviction had been unfair. For her part, Eleanor Berry thanked Betty for all the support she had given her – including 'helping me with my thesis on the Marquis de Sade'.

Amid all the eulogies, only one sounded a less than laudatory note. The journalist William Davis, Editor of *Punch* magazine, wrote, 'As we all know, Bob can be a bit of a monster. He often alienates people who thought they were close to him . . . Betty usually manages to smooth ruffled feathers with a kindly phone call or a charming letter. I have, more than once, decided to forgive him for some particular example of outrageous behaviour after her diplomatic intervention. He never knew about it, or if he did he probably took it for granted.'

Two months earlier, Betty had made a last attempt at a reconciliation, writing Maxwell an eighteen-page letter. Rather than send the letter – she suspected he would never bother to open it – she went to his office and asked him to read it aloud in front of her. Grudgingly, Maxwell did so, making annotations in the margins as he went along. In essence, she was proposing that they should try again. Maxwell agreed with some of her practical suggestions, but carefully steered clear of any emotional issues. When he had finished reading, he told her that he couldn't spare her any more time; he had important business to attend to.

The next time she saw him was the night of her birthday party. The 150 guests who turned up that evening had no inkling that anything was amiss. They had come, principally, to celebrate Betty's birthday, but also to mark what appeared to be a long and happy marriage. However, it can't have been long before it became plain to the most unobservant guest that something odd was going on. For a start, Maxwell was late – so late there was some discussion about starting the meal without him.

When he did finally arrive, he gave Betty a peck on the cheek, but otherwise ignored her. Unusually for him, he hardly ate anything and kept glancing at his watch. Then, when the guests were still halfway through their desserts, he suddenly rose to his feet. Caught by surprise, several diners carried on talking. It took a few moments for the room to fall silent. By then Maxwell had already begun his speech. While his timing may have been a little off, there was nothing particularly unusual about this. It was what he said – or didn't say – that took everyone by surprise.

Barely mentioning Betty, Maxwell chose instead to tell the guests how his plans to buy the *New York Daily News* were going. Negotiations were proving tougher than expected, he said, but he was cautiously optimistic of a positive outcome. Although the guests listened politely, this was not what they had come to hear. Finishing as abruptly as he had started, Maxwell looked at his watch again before announcing that he had to be going – 'I've got to leave for New York now.'

Amid a ripple of puzzled murmurs, he headed for the exit, leaving Betty to listen to the toasts and cut her birthday cake on her own. As she recalled in typically stoic fashion: 'I was embarrassed by his perfunctory appearance, but I was surrounded by all those dearest to me who helped me forget my sadness.'

Outside on Park Lane, Maxwell's claret-coloured Rolls-Royce was waiting to take him to Battersea Heliport. From there his helicopter would fly to Farnborough airport to catch the Gulfstream back to New York. Maxwell reckoned he had just enough time to make it before the heliport closed at ten o'clock. But, instead of his usual chauffeur, there was a man behind the wheel he had never seen before. This put him in an even fouler mood.

The moment Maxwell was in the car, he began bellowing orders, telling the chauffeur to weave in and out of the traffic, ignore the speed limit and drive straight through red lights. When the man protested that he'd risk losing his licence, Maxwell's patience snapped. Telling him to pull over, he half dragged the man out of the car, then managed to squeeze behind the wheel himself. Standing on the pavement with his cap in his hand, the chauffeur watched in astonishment as Maxwell sped off into the night.

Back in the USA, Maxwell had another important social event to attend. Just as he'd predicted, his purchase of the *New York Daily News* had been finalized shortly after he returned to New York. Nine days later the annual Gridiron Dinner was being held in Washington. With the President as the Guest of Honor, the Gridiron Dinner was one of the most coveted invitations in the Washington social calendar. Its guests are made up of the cream of the nation's journalists and media proprietors. While the mood is traditionally light-hearted – the President is expected to crack jokes at his own expense – the trappings are anything but informal. Women wear ballgowns and men white tie and tails, along with any medals they might have been awarded.

An invitation to the dinner would be the official anointing of Maxwell's new ranking among the elite. However, there was a problem: the guest list had already been finalized. After frantic lobbying by the paper's Publisher, Jim Hoge, last-minute invitations were secured for Maxwell, along with senior members of his staff, including Richard Stott.

The day before the dinner took place, they all flew down to Washington and checked into the Capital Hilton Hotel. But then came another problem: it turned out that Maxwell had left his tail-coat, trousers and medals behind in London. Given his size, no tailor was likely to be able to run up a replacement before the dinner started twenty-four hours later. Besides, Maxwell was adamant that he wanted to wear his medals.

He therefore decided to send his general factotum, a man called Bob Cole, back to London on Concorde to pick up his outfit, then come straight back – a round trip that would cost in excess of £8000. But with three hours to go before guests were due to arrive, there was still no sign of Cole.

Maxwell was growing testy. What was going on? It turned out the return flight had been delayed due to fog and nobody could be sure when Cole would arrive.

By now Richard Stott had problems of his own: he realized he had no black socks to go with his dress trousers. All the shops were shut so he went in search of Maxwell's butler, Josef Perera.

' "Josef," I said, "I need a pair of black socks."'

' "But Mr Stott," ' Josef told him, ' "I only have the pair I'm wearing." '

' "I'll swop you," ' Stott said, and handed over a blue pair of his own, dark enough for Maxwell not to notice. 'The deal was done.'

With only an hour to go before the dinner was due to start, an exhausted Bob Cole finally appeared with Maxwell's outfit. Fifteen minutes later Stott went to Maxwell's suite for a pre-dinner drink only to be met by Cole running down the corridor in tears. ' "He definitely told me white tie and tails," he wailed. "But when I get here, he shouts and screams at me saying, You've brought the wrong fucking suit, you idiot – it's dinner jacket. Go and get me one. But where do I get a dinner jacket his size at this time of night?" '

Stott reassured Cole that he had brought the right outfit; Maxwell had just made a mistake. That appeared to be the end of the matter, except it wasn't – not quite. When Maxwell put on his white tie and tails, complete with his extensive array of medals, he realized that he too didn't have any black socks.

'That fucker Cole didn't bring any,' he complained.

'Oh you've got to wear black socks, Bob,' Stott told him. 'It's part of the uniform.'

Maxwell looked at Stott and asked him where he'd got his socks from.

'Your butler,' Stott said. 'It was his only pair.'

At this point Josef, who was pouring the drinks, hitched up his trouser leg to show Maxwell that he was now wearing Stott's blue ones. Maxwell looked from Stott to Josef and back again.

'He's my fucking butler,' he said. 'I should have those socks.'

But Stott refused to budge. 'Well, I'm not taking them off, Bob. I've done a deal and Josef has got my socks.'

An impasse threatened. It was finally resolved by Maxwell pulling out his wallet and giving Josef a $100 bill. 'Josef went off in search of the most expensive pair of socks in newspaper history, leaving one Capital Hotel waiter very happy, even if he did have cold feet for the rest of the night.'

However thrilled Maxwell was to attend the Gridiron Dinner, he was over the moon when he learned that Jim Hoge had fixed up a small lunch party the next day at a friend's house in Georgetown. Once again, the President, George Bush Snr, would be attending, along with the two men who had masterminded the recent victory in the Gulf War: Colin Powell, Commander of the US Army, and General 'Stormin'' Norman Schwarzkopf, leader of the coalition forces.

This time Hoge had gone one better – he'd arranged for Maxwell to sit next to the President. Beaming with pleasure, Maxwell took his seat at the table. But the lunch failed to go as well as Hoge had hoped. As he soon realized, the reserved, patrician Bush and the extravagantly egocentric Maxwell did not make a natural pairing. 'At the start of the meal, Bush talked to Bob for about three minutes,' Hoge remembers. 'That was fine, but then Bob went off and talked non-stop at the President for what seemed like a very long time.'

Although he was sitting at the other end of the table and couldn't hear what Maxwell was saying, Hoge could see it was impossible for Bush to get a word in edgeways. 'After a while he gave up and just sat there nodding. Then, the moment Bob paused for breath, the President stood up saying that he had to be somewhere else.' As he was escorted back to his motorcade, a dazed-looking Bush was seen mouthing to an aide, 'Who Was That Guy?'

29.

Selling the Crown Jewels

As Betty Maxwell knew only too well, the bond that existed between her husband and Pergamon Press was as strong as – perhaps stronger than – anything else in his life. It was as if their fates were fused together; when Pergamon was doing well, Maxwell's spirits rose; when it was doing badly, they sank back down again.

At the end of March 1991, Maxwell asked Anna Moon, the General Manager of Pergamon's Publishing Services, to come up to London to see him. 'I had no idea what he wanted. When I walked into his office, he just looked at me and said, "I'm selling Pergamon tomorrow."'

Moon was so stunned it took her a few moments to recover.

'I said, "Why didn't you tell me before?" After all, I'd worked for the company for more than twenty years. But Maxwell just said, very brusquely, "You didn't need to know."'

However dismissive he may have been, Moon was in no doubt what this meant: 'He was essentially selling the crown jewels.' As well as making Maxwell's initial fortune, Pergamon had transformed scientific research and earned him the admiration of people that he himself admired.

His children were equally astonished. All of them, with the exception of Isabel, who became a documentary film maker, had worked for their father at some stage: Christine was now running Pergamon's editorial operations on the US West Coast, while Ghislaine had been in charge of Maxwell's corporate gift business.

Twenty-two years earlier, the previous sale of Pergamon had brought Maxwell to the edge of ruin. Now the stakes were far higher. 'For me, it was an extraordinary development,' Ian Maxwell recalls. 'That was when it dawned on me that nothing was sacred any more.' Nor was Ian in any doubt about what an emotional wrench this was for his father. 'I remember Kevin did the actual deal because Dad couldn't bring himself to do it.' Christine was equally shocked. 'It killed us, frankly. We were all very upset. Very sad.'

On 28 March Maxwell announced that Pergamon had been sold to the Dutch scientific publishers Elsevier, for £440,000,000. At the same time, he decided to step down as Chairman and Chief Executive of MCC. It was possible, Maxwell conceded, that the 'Max Factor' was having an adverse effect on the company's share price. A former Conservative Cabinet minister called Peter Walker would be taking over as Chairman, while Maxwell's son Kevin became MCC's Chief Executive.

News of the Pergamon sale didn't simply stun Maxwell's family; it spread far wider than that. The publisher Anthony Cheetham had worked for Maxwell during the 1980s. One day when Cheetham was in Headington Hill Hall, Maxwell had proudly shown him some of the original scientific papers he'd brought out of Berlin after the War.

'It was like being taken down to Valhalla. They were kept locked up and only he knew the combinations to the locks. Here were the foundation stones of his empire, the original texts that had come down from the mountain. He showed them to me and said, "This is where we make the money that you spend."'

For Cheetham, Maxwell's decision to sell Pergamon could only mean one thing: 'The moment I heard about it I had no doubt he knew the end was coming.'

Two weeks later Maxwell came to the *Mirror*'s Finance Director with a proposal. Lawrence – Lawrie – Guest was a mild, affable man who was a keen sailor and a stalwart of his local golf club. As conscientious as he was self-effacing, he had served the company uncomplainingly for the last twenty years. Although no one would ever have guessed it from his manner, he was possessed of considerable courage: he'd once run into a burning building and saved the lives of two young boys trapped inside.

Normally Maxwell treated Guest with ill-concealed impatience, but on this occasion he couldn't have been more friendly. His proposal was very simple: the Mirror Group's financial year ended in December, but the pension funds' financial year ended in March. Wouldn't it make more sense to bring them both into line? Guest considered the proposal and saw no reason for concern. As Maxwell had said, it was purely a tidying-up exercise.

However, there was one – apparently irrelevant – consequence of this new arrangement: it meant there was no need to audit the pension funds' accounts for another six months. And since there was no pressing need to audit the accounts, there was no need for anyone to look too closely at the share certificates. If they had, they would have seen that in April alone Maxwell had sold £96,000,000 of the pension funds' assets. Rather than transferring the money back to the funds once he'd done so, he had used it to prop up other parts of his now-teetering empire.

The announcement that Maxwell was selling off Pergamon and stepping down as Chairman of MCC galvanized the City. Not only did the company's shares stop sliding – they did an immediate about-turn. In the first three weeks of April 1991, they rose by 60 per cent. Disaster had been averted – or so it seemed. Yet inevitably there was more to it than that. Once again Maxwell had been buying shares in MCC, frantically trying to drive the price up in a bid to keep the company afloat.

This involved him churning his money around in ever more hectic circles.

First Maxwell, or people acting on his behalf, would take funds out of MCC, including the pension funds, and transfer them to one of his private companies. The private company would then pass them on to an offshore trust, which bought up the shares – thereby ensuring the paper trail never led directly back to Maxwell's door.

However mad this seemed, it was underpinned by grim logic. Maxwell's loans now totalled more than £300,000,000. If MCC's stock market value fell below 145 per cent of the value of these loans, the banks would demand more security. All Maxwell could offer them was another block of MCC shares. But in order to make sure the price of his shares stayed as high as possible, he had to keep on buying them.

At the beginning of April 1991, Maxwell made another unexpected decision: he was going to float Mirror Group Newspapers on the Stock Exchange. Again not everyone was convinced that buying MGN shares was a wise, or even a sane, move. Among the doubters was the author of the *Financial Times*'s 'Lex' column, who noted that 'Past experience might suggest that no investor in his sober senses would bother.' One analyst headlined his piece 'Can't Recommend A Purchase'. The acrostic didn't escape anyone's notice, least of all Maxwell, who complained it was 'totally unprofessional and extremely rude'.

He had hoped to raise £500,000,000 by selling 49 per cent of MGN, but this, he was told, was impossible – he'd be lucky to get half that. None the less, Maxwell insisted on running a huge campaign to launch the flotation. As well as lavish coverage in the *Mirror* itself, there would be TV advertising, advertising hoardings and a press conference.

The press conference took place on the morning of 17 April 1991. Wearing an enormous red bow-tie, Maxwell appeared to be in an extravagantly good mood. It didn't last long. 'Why would you trust a man who had been condemned by government inspectors more than twenty years earlier?' he was asked shortly after the press conference had begun.

Topped by a jet-black widow's peak, Maxwell's brow darkened.

'My record since then, as Chairman of many public companies, I hope will satisfy even you, sir,' he said.

'May I ask another question?' the reporter asked.

Maxwell gave a sideways chop of his hand.

'No, you cannot.'

Meanwhile his life continued at the same frenetic pace. He met the new Prime Minister, John Major – who'd succeeded Mrs

Thatcher five months earlier; he had lunch with the German Foreign Minister; he flew back to Sofia, where he dined with the Bulgarian Prime Minister and reiterated his plan to launch a new bank. As an initial deposit, he promised to transfer $20,000,000.

'It will be the beginning of a new era!' he proclaimed.

On the rare occasions when Maxwell sat still for long enough, his stockbroker, Sir Michael Richardson, tried to warn him that preparations for the flotation were not going as promisingly as they might. It seemed that hardly any British institutions had expressed interest in buying MGN shares.

Maxwell ignored him.

A month after the press conference – on 17 May 1991 – Maxwell arrived at Michael Richardson's office in the City to watch the Mirror Group being launched on the Stock Exchange. Richardson offered him champagne to celebrate, but unusually for him Maxwell stuck to coffee. The two of them watched the dealers' screens as the shares were launched at 125p. To begin with, they rose briefly, as if trying to take to the air, but then began to fall back. More people, it seemed, wanted to sell *Mirror* shares than buy them.

By the end of the day the share price had gone up by just 0.5 pence. Maxwell wasn't around to see it: he had stormed off earlier in a huff. 'He was surprised,' Richardson recalled. 'I don't think he understood the Max Factor; he had the ability to blank that out of his mind.' Maxwell had also blanked out any idea that he might be responsible for what had happened. Casting around for someone to blame, he settled on Richardson.

The next evening – 18 May – Maxwell hosted a dinner-dance at Headington Hill Hall that had been arranged several weeks earlier in confident expectation that the flotation would prove to be a triumph. All the traditional trappings were there: the marquees, the dance floor, the magnums of champagne, the huge photographs of Maxwell grinning away . . . But something was different. Although Maxwell's parties could be peculiarly stiff affairs, now the atmosphere seemed positively joyless.

Some of the guests also noticed that Michael Richardson wasn't seated at Maxwell's table at dinner. Just three years earlier, at Maxwell's sixty-fifth-birthday celebrations, Richardson had not only sat at top table – he'd proposed the toast. Now he'd been banished to the most distant reaches of the marquee. After dinner Maxwell stood up to give a speech. He proceeded to thank everyone who had helped with the flotation – with one conspicuous exception. When he sat down Kevin Maxwell was seen whispering in his father's ear.

Maxwell stood up again.

'Oh, I do apologize,' he said. 'I unintentionally omitted my thanks to Sir Michael Richardson for all his help. Thank you, Michael.'

On 15 July, Peter Walker resigned as the Chairman of MCC. Walker had become increasingly concerned that Maxwell was artificially inflating his profits. In a letter to MCC's Company Secretary, he wrote, 'I do wonder what the hell is going on in this company.'

A few weeks after the *Mirror* flotation, a friend of Rupert Murdoch's who also knew Maxwell phoned him to offer some advice. 'This friend of mine told me, "I thought I should tell you that 'our acquaintance' seems to be getting desperate,"' Murdoch recalls.

Although Murdoch had nothing to fear from Maxwell, his friend felt it was prudent to warn him that he was now in such a state that he might say, or do, anything. 'He wasn't worried about my personal safety or anything like that. It was just that he thought Maxwell was acting completely irrationally. That he was under enormous pressure and drinking very heavily. So it was just, "Watch out, be careful."'

30.

Don't You Worry About a Thing

Wherever he was in the world, Maxwell always travelled with at least two fax machines. All through the night they would whir away. A ceaseless churn of deals and transactions; records of money moving from account to account, from country to country, from behind one curtain to another. By morning the floor would be covered in a sea of rustling white fax paper. 'You'd go into his hotel suite and it would literally be six inches deep,' remembers his son Ian.

When he was in London, Maxwell spent most of time alone in his apartment in Maxwell House. Unable to sleep for more than two hours at a time, he would while away the hours by watching old James Bond movies and gorging himself on Chinese takeaways. Before he was dressed, two Filipina maids would come in and tidy up. As well as clearing away the empty takeaway containers, they would have to pick up towels that had been left lying about – towels that Maxwell now sometimes used instead of toilet paper, then tossed on to the floor.

It's tempting to regard this as an extreme example of his lack of consideration for others. Yet there are other ways of seeing it too: as a reversion to the helplessness of babyhood; or the behaviour of someone who has abandoned any pretence of being civilized and given in to self-disgust.

Every weekday morning at seven o'clock sharp, Ian and Kevin Maxwell would go to their father's office to discuss the day's programme. And every morning they would brace themselves for what lay ahead.

'Increasingly, he would be in a foul mood, partly because he'd hardly slept,' Ian recalls. 'The meetings were always pretty hellish;

to be shouted at by him was no fun at all. He had this ability to look straight through you and know exactly what you were thinking. You had to be very well prepared, or he'd just tear into you.'

Along with his ever-shortening temper, Ian noticed that his father was falling asleep more often, sometimes in the middle of meetings. 'It was quite obvious to me that something was going to happen to Dad physically sooner or later; I just couldn't see how he could possibly sustain this lifestyle.'

Occasionally Maxwell would call up MCC's former corporate lawyer, Deborah Maxwell, who had now left the company and moved to Paris. 'He would just phone for a chat from time to time. I could tell from his voice that he was depressed. Actually, he sounded like a completely different person. But at the time I just thought it was because he was on the phone and I wasn't physically in his presence.'

Flying into New York for a few days from her home in California in June 1991, Maxwell's daughter Christine went round to her father's hotel, the Helmsley Palace. It had been several months since they'd last seen one another and she was looking forward to spending time with him. But when she arrived at the hotel, she received some bad news.

'Apparently he was too busy to see me.'

It was possible Maxwell might be able to spare some time in a couple of hours, she was told, but no one could make any promises. 'I was so mad I said, "I'm not going to sit here for two hours under any circumstances. I'm out of here."' It would be the last occasion that Christine and her father were in the same building, albeit on different floors. 'It was the last time I tried to see him, and I couldn't.'

By then Christine too had realized how much he had changed. How estranged he had become, from his family and everyone else. 'Physically, Dad wasn't in good shape. He only had one lung that worked properly so his brain wasn't getting enough oxygen. Also there was a lot going on psychologically which was not good. I definitely think he had megalomania at that stage; for him it was a real disease. Nothing was ever enough any more, and at the same time he just couldn't stop. He'd boxed himself into a corner that he couldn't get out of.'

The consequences were to be as drastic as they were inevitable: 'In the end, he pushed us all away.'

Of all his children, Maxwell remained closest to his youngest daughter, Ghislaine. Yet even here his devotion was starting to fray. Maxwell's PA on the *New York Daily News* was a woman called Carolyn Hinsey whom he insisted on calling 'Tiny' – she was six feet tall – and liked referring to as his 'Cultural Ambassador'. 'I would say that by this stage he tolerated Ghislaine rather than anything else,' Hinsey recalls. 'He used to take her calls, but grudgingly. It also drove him mad when she took his chauffeur-driven car without telling him.'

In public he continued to behave as if he didn't have a care in the world. At New York's annual Israel Day Parade, Maxwell, proudly wearing the white sash of a Grand Marshal, stood alongside the Mayor, David Dinkins, and the Governor of New York State, Mario Cuomo. A few days later he was at another parade – the ticker-tape celebrations to welcome home servicemen and servicewomen from the Gulf War. This time Maxwell stood beside General Colin Powell, Chairman of the Joint Chiefs of Staff.

To celebrate his sixty-eighth birthday on 10 June, 200 guests were invited to a party held on board a tall ship – the *Peking* – at the South Street Seaport. But even in New York Maxwell no longer had much to cheer about. The *New York Daily News* continued to lag far behind its 1.2 million pre-strike circulation – it was now selling fewer than 750,000 copies a day. The projected annual revenue was $100,000,000 less than Maxwell had predicted.

Having agreed to stay on to ensure the transition from one proprietor to another ran smoothly, the paper's Publisher, Jim Hoge, decided he'd had enough: 'My conviction that he had bought a death-knell was stronger than ever.' Maxwell accepted Hoge's resignation, but persuaded him to embark on a whirlwind tour of his various publications, then write a report on what sort of shape they were in. Hoge duly set off around the world and two weeks later reported back: 'Basically, I told him that he had major problems at every one of them.'

Not surprisingly, this news went down badly. 'Maxwell got very upset and kept saying, "What do you know?" He was no longer puffed up and full of himself like he'd been before. Instead, it was as if someone had taken the putty of his false personality and just ripped it off.'

However estranged he had become from his family, Maxwell did fly to Wyoming for the wedding of his son Ian, to a television producer called Laura Plumb. This was the first time Betty had seen her husband in more than two months and she was apprehensive about how he might behave. But Maxwell couldn't have been more charming. He greeted her warmly and after the wedding service insisted on shaking hands with the pastor, telling him, 'You are the first priest I have ever heard who has moved me.'

For Ian, relief that his father was behaving himself was tempered by concern for his appearance. 'I remember thinking he looked like hell. He was sweating profusely for a start. I also remember that at the reception Dad and Kevin were together a lot talking. I'm assuming they weren't talking about my wedding; I think they were trying to protect me from what was going on.

'At one point the three of us were standing next to this white paling fence looking out over the mountains. I said, "Dad, I'm really grateful that you could make it." And he said, "You have no idea."'

That night Ian and his new bride left on their honeymoon and the next day the rest of the family went on a picnic to Yellowstone Park. Maxwell was particularly keen to see the park's famous geyser, Old Faithful, which promptly erupted as soon as he arrived.

'Look,' he exclaimed. 'It's come to greet me!'

'It was one of my last really happy memories of Bob, joking, relaxed and good company,' Betty recalled. 'I had almost forgotten how nice he could be. That day we probably all had our last glimpse of the Bob of old.'

Back in London, Maxwell asked Lawrie Guest to come and see him. He had decided to shake things up a bit, he said. Although Guest would retain the title of Finance Director of MCC, a man called Michael Stoney, formerly Finance Director at Pergamon, would become Commercial Director. This meant that in future Stoney, not Guest, would be in control of the Mirror Group finances. It would be a mutually beneficial arrangement for the pair of them, Maxwell insisted – 'I want you both to live in one another's pockets.'

Inevitably, he had an ulterior motive: the *Mirror* was the only part of Maxwell's empire he hadn't yet plundered for cash. As diligent as he was diffident, Guest was bound to object if everything wasn't done by the book. Stoney, a Maxwell loyalist through and through, might be less of a stickler for convention. Shortly afterwards, £38,000,000 was moved out of the Mirror Group's bank account and into Maxwell's private company accounts. From there, the money went to pay off his most pressing debts.

Maxwell had always been a heavy gambler. His son Ian had seen him win £750,000 on one occasion, and lose £400,000 on another. A croupier told Mike Maloney that Maxwell had once won £1,500,000 in a single session. Now he took to spending his nights in London casinos, often playing three roulette wheels simultaneously. But the big win he was clearly hoping for eluded him. The columnist – and fellow gambler – Taki Theodoracopulos saw him at the White Elephant on Curzon Street. 'The table had a rope round it so that no one else could gamble there. I could see that Maxwell was playing enormous amounts – £20,000 to £30,000 on each spin of the roulette wheel – and completely absorbed. He was obviously trying to recover something.'

That summer Maxwell also made what would be a final attempt to reconnect with his past. At the end of July he went to Jerusalem, where he was filmed visiting the Yad Vashem Holocaust memorial. With his head lowered and his hands plunged into his jacket pockets, he walked through canyons of stone blocks bearing the names of communities that had been wiped out.

Stopping in front of one of the blocks, he pointed at the lettering. 'At the bottom is the *shtetl* Solotvino where I come from,' he said. 'It is no more. It was poor, it was Orthodox and it was Jewish. We were very poor. We didn't have things that other people had. They had shoes and they had food and we didn't. At the end of the War, I discovered the fate of my parents and my sisters and brothers, relatives and neighbours. I don't know what went through their minds as they realized they had been tricked into a gas chamber. But one thing they hoped is that they will not be forgotten . . .'

Tears welled up in Maxwell's eyes as he glanced towards the sky. Barely able to speak, he managed to add: 'And this memorial in Jerusalem proves that.'

Overcome, he walked away.

A month later, Maxwell appeared unexpectedly at Betty's house in south-west France, where Ian and Laura Maxwell were having a party for friends and family who had been unable to make it to their wedding. Betty was stunned by the deterioration in his appearance. 'All of a sudden, he looked very old; he was gasping for air and sweating profusely,' she recalled. 'At first I took it to be the heat, but I couldn't get over how much weight he had put on since I had last seen him barely two months previously. Bob was far from his usual exuberant self.'

However unwell her father was looking, Isabel Maxwell saw a side of him that she hadn't seen in years. 'He played pick-a-stick with me and my five-year-old son. As we were playing, he looked at me and said, "Izzy, you're a very nice person." I was flabbergasted; it was the first and only time he ever said that.'

After Maxwell had left, Betty discussed his health with another of the guests – a nephew of hers who was a heart and lung specialist. 'He told me that unless he went in for serious treatment, he was courting disaster.'

It wasn't just Maxwell's finances that were spinning out of his control. So too was the world he had known, and whose fortunes he'd once helped shape. A series of revolutions in the winter of 1989 had toppled Communist leaders across Eastern Europe. In Romania Nicolae Ceauşescu and his wife, Elena, had been executed by firing squad. Like President Zhivkov of Bulgaria, Ceauşescu had been the subject of one of Maxwell's *Leaders of the World* series, lauded for his 'constant tireless activity for the good of the country'.

On 18 August 1991, a group of senior army officers went to see the President of the Soviet Union, Mikhail Gorbachev, at his dacha in the Crimea. There, they presented him with an ultimatum: he must either declare a state of emergency or resign.

Gorbachev refused.

The next day Boris Yeltsin, President of the Russian Soviet Federative Socialist Republic – the largest republic in the Soviet Union – clambered on to a tank outside the Russian parliament building in Moscow and called on the rebel soldiers to lay down their guns. They promptly obliged. The collapse of the attempted coup set off a political earthquake whose effects were felt around the world. Four months later Gorbachev resigned. A month afterwards the Soviet Union officially ceased to exist.

Less than a year earlier, Maxwell had warned Mrs Thatcher that this might happen. Now his prediction had come true – but, far from feeling vindicated, he couldn't accept that it had taken place without his involvement. Ken Lennox was covering the story for the *Mirror*: 'I phoned up the news desk to tell them what I had seen. Maxwell happened to be standing there at the time, so the News Editor said, "Why don't you tell him yourself?" When I'd finished there was a long pause, and then Maxwell said to me, "Don't be a cunt. Don't you think Yeltsin would have called me before making a speech like that?"'

Maxwell had underestimated Lawrie Guest's conscientiousness. Although Guest had been sidelined, he still noticed that something was amiss. At the beginning of August 1991, he went to see Maxwell to ask about the £38,000,000 that had gone missing from MGN's accounts.

'Don't you worry,' Maxwell told him. 'I've deposited it with American banks.'

Four weeks later, Guest told the Managing Director of MCC that he was having what he described as 'problems'. Specifically, there was some money missing – £38,000,000. Once again Maxwell was asked for an explanation. This time he gave more details.

Apparently the money had been deposited with Goldman Sachs in New York – 'to improve our credit rating'. It was only a temporary arrangement, he said, the money would be returned shortly.

Guest waited.

Nothing happened. Ten days later, he went back to see Maxwell. When was the money going to be returned? Just as he'd done before, Maxwell told him not to worry. Only this time he showed an unexpected concern for Guest's welfare. 'You really need a holiday,' he told him. 'Take three weeks immediately. Everything will be sorted out by the time you return.'

Guest agreed that he could use a break. But before he left he wrote a memo to Michael Stoney outlining his concerns. Stoney wrote back: 'I've spoken to Bob. The money is coming back within one week. You've nothing to worry about. But please don't shake the tree. You must be loyal to the company.'

As soon as Guest returned three weeks later, he checked the Mirror Group accounts. Just as he had feared, the £38,000,000 was still missing. People in the office noticed that Guest, always a heavy smoker, now seemed to be smoking more than ever.

On one of Maxwell's now rare visits to Headington Hill Hall, he was alone in his bedroom late one night when his son Ian walked in. To Ian's surprise, he saw his father bending down with his nose almost touching the glass of his enormous television. On the television was a documentary showing newsreel footage of Jews arriving at Auschwitz, being unloaded from the cattle cars and divided into two groups – those deemed fit for work and those who were to be sent straight to the gas chamber.

'What are you doing?' Ian asked.

Slowly Maxwell straightened up, and then turned around.

'I'm looking to see if I can spot my parents,' he told him.

31

Hurricane Bob

Ever since Andrea Martin's departure from the *Mirror*, Maxwell and Nick Davies had trodden warily around one another. Davies knew that Maxwell was still seething with jealousy and apt to explode at any moment. The best way to ensure this didn't happen, he decided, was to stay as far away from him as possible. In theory, that shouldn't have been too difficult. As the *Mirror's* Foreign Editor, Davies inevitably spent a good deal of time abroad. The trouble was that circumstances kept pushing them together.

In October 1991, Davies flew to Zimbabwe to attend the Commonwealth Conference. It wasn't expected to be a taxing assignment – a few days in a smart hotel with no need to file more than the occasional paragraph. But while he was there Davies had some unwelcome news. He learned that the American investigative writer Seymour Hersh was about to publish a book called *The Samson Option*, in which he claimed that both Maxwell and Davies were international gunrunners.

The following day, as Davies put it, 'all hell broke loose'. The allegations centred on his friendship with a man called Ari Ben-Menashe. A former government official in Tel Aviv, Ben-Menashe had met Davies in the early 1980s, when he passed on a number of stories about his time as a Mossad spy. As Davies put it, 'He would feed me titbits which turned out to be true, but I was never totally satisfied that his information was always on the level.' None the less, they got on sufficiently well for Davies to invite Ben-Menashe to stay with him and his then wife, Janet Fielding, whenever he was in London, much to Fielding's annoyance – 'I thought he was a creep.'

Ben-Menashe was also responsible for Davies's becoming involved in arms-dealing, she believed. Shortly before their marriage broke down, Fielding had come across a letter from a company called Armter in Ohio. Addressed to Davies, it confirmed his order for 155 guns and 30,000 rounds of ammunition, as well as the hire of a five-ton truck to transport them. When she tackled him, Davies admitted that in addition to working at the *Mirror* and running his underwater television business, he'd recently added a third string to his bow.

For Fielding, it was the final straw: 'How can you respect someone who's an arms-dealer? The odd thing is that I think part of Nick really wanted to be an old-fashioned man of honour; it was just that the need for cash got in the way.'

Arrested in 1989 for trying to sell three military cargo planes to Iran, Ben-Menashe spent a year in jail in California before the charges were dropped. By the time he emerged, he and Davies had fallen out; Davies claimed to have realized – belatedly – that Ben-Menashe was not on the level, or anywhere near it.

In *The Samson Option*, Seymour Hersh wrote that the two of them, together with Maxwell, had been involved in a company which sold arms – principally to Iran. Three years earlier, Davies had apparently gone to Cleveland, Ohio, where he had met up with another arms-dealer, called Ben Kaufman, to broker a sale.

At first, no newspaper would touch the story for fear of being sued for libel. But after two MPs, protected by parliamentary privilege, had raised the matter in the House of Commons, the *Daily Mail* decided to run extracts from Hersh's book. When the allegations were put to Nick Davies in Harare, he dismissed them as nonsense. Apart from anything else, he'd never been to Ohio, he insisted.

But there was more to the story than that; Hersh also claimed that Davies – acting on Maxwell's orders – had betrayed the whereabouts of the nuclear spy, Mordechai Vanunu, to Mossad. In 1986, Vanunu, a technician at a nuclear base in the Negev desert, had secretly taken photographs of Israel's nuclear weapons programme which he passed on to the *Sunday Times*. After an anonymous tip-off, he'd been snatched off a street in Rome by Mossad agents, injected with a paralysing drug, smuggled on board a ship and taken back to an Israeli prison.

Previously divided by their respective feelings for Andrea Martin, Maxwell and Davies now found themselves on the same side. As soon as the extracts appeared, Maxwell sued Hersh's publishers and the *Daily Mail* for defamation. The claims, he declared, 'were ludicrous'. As for Davies, Maxwell said he was 'innocent of whatever the allegations are'.

In Harare, Davies found that his colleagues were no longer paying much attention to the Commonwealth Conference; instead, they were far more interested in him. Two days after he had denied ever having been to Ohio, Rupert Murdoch's *Sun* published a front-page photograph of Davies and 'notorious arms-dealer' Ben Kaufman at Kaufman's house in Cleveland drinking cups of ice-tea.

The *Sun*'s headline read: 'YOU LIAR'.

Besieged in his hotel room, Davies recited Rudyard Kipling's poem 'If' to himself to keep his spirits up. He found the opening two lines especially comforting:

> If you can keep your head when all about you
> Are losing theirs and blaming it on you . . .

But on the flight back to London he appears to have forgotten all about Kipling's counsel. Davies found himself sitting next to Simon Walters, a political journalist on the *Sun*. Like many others, Walters felt that Davies's nickname of Sneaky suited him down to the ground: 'He loved to talk in whispers and to give the impression he knew about top-secret matters.'

Maybe Davies was more stressed than he let on, or maybe he was more tempted by the free alcohol than was entirely wise, but he proceeded to unburden himself. Walters listened with growing fascination. 'What struck me most was how extraordinarily confident he was – and how slick. It seemed to me that he was in big trouble, but he just acted as if nothing odd was going on.'

Walters's account in the following morning's *Sun* made gripping reading. Headlined 'I Only Use A Third Of My Talent', it went on, 'Lying Nick Davies has opened his heart about his life on the *Daily Mirror*, his eye for the ladies and his secret assignment for publisher Robert Maxwell.' Davies's comments about 'the ladies' are unlikely to have gone down well with Andrea Martin: 'I can't stop myself,' he was quoted as saying. 'I would go to work on Monday and say to myself I must stop, but by Tuesday I had gone off with another one.'

As well as being sexually rapacious, Davies, by his own account, was a man of enormous, largely untapped, abilities. 'I'm good at my job but I only use 30 per cent of my potential; it bores me at times,' he had told Walters. 'Really, I am very frustrated. There is an anger inside me.' Again he emphasized that he'd never been an arms-dealer, and nor had he ever been to Ohio. He also took a passing swipe at Janet Fielding: 'I married her simply so she could stay in Britain.'

During the flight, Davies had been making vigorous efforts to chat up the stewardesses, but as soon as their plane landed in London, Walters noticed that he was a lot less confident than he had been before: 'He completely panicked and this cocky façade just evaporated.' Picked up by *Mirror* representatives, he was bundled into the back of a car and driven off, leaving his last words to Walters hanging unconvincingly in the air: 'I am not a Walter Mitty character.'

Taken to the *Mirror* offices, Davies was interviewed by Richard Stott, now reinstalled as Editor of the *Mirror* after the dismissal of Roy Greenslade, and Joe Haines, the paper's Political Editor. In his defence Davies said that he had happened to visit Ben Kaufman when he was on a trip to America, not having any idea he was an arms-dealer. He also claimed to be unaware that Cleveland was in Ohio.

Haines was not impressed. 'I said to him, "For Christ's sake, Nick, you're the bloody Foreign Editor."'

They both recommended that Davies should be fired for gross misconduct. Then came an unexpected turn. Maxwell pleaded with Stott and Haines to give him another chance. At first, neither of them could work out what was going on. Finally, the truth dawned on them – even now, Maxwell was trying to curry favour with Andrea Martin by preventing her boyfriend from being sacked. But, Stott and Haines stood their ground: Davies had to go.

The next day the *Mirror* announced his departure on its front page under the headline 'A Matter Of Trust'. 'The truth,' it declared with feverish piety, 'is our only currency. We cannot duck and dive around it, play fast and loose with it, or regard it as an occasional companion.'

Although Maxwell had reluctantly accepted that Davies couldn't stay, he continued to phone him at home to reassure him it would all be fine in the end.

'I will work everything out,' he said.

The allegations against Maxwell may have been flimsy – there is no convincing evidence he was involved in arms-dealing – but they reinforced his increasing sense that everyone was out to get him. They rattled the City too. The slump in MCC shares now began to accelerate. On the day the story broke, they lost another 6 pence to finish at just 80 pence each. Having spent millions of pounds buying his own shares to try to prop the price up, Maxwell effectively had no more money left to spend.

It wasn't just the City that had sniffed Maxwell's demise. For months he had known that the BBC current-affairs flagship, *Panorama*, was preparing a programme about his business activities. Worried what they might have unearthed, Maxwell threatened to obtain an injunction to stop the programme from going out. He also took to phoning *Panorama*'s Editor, Mark Thompson, with a familiar mix of threats and bluster. Thinking it might be useful if any attempt to stop the programme came to court, Thompson decided to record Maxwell's calls.

One conversation in particular stuck in his mind. As they were talking, Maxwell suddenly announced, 'The pension funds are completely safe with me!'

Thompson was baffled. What was he talking about? There'd been no mention of pension funds before. Why on earth was Maxwell bringing it up now?

Despite Maxwell's fears, there was no mention of pension funds in the BBC *Panorama* programme. Instead, it concentrated on his efforts to rig various *Mirror* competitions, including Spot-the-Ball, to make sure there was never a winner. But the programme did note that MCC's shares had lost a third of their value in the last four months, and that Maxwell – 'a man of influence who moves on the world stage' – had been inflating his pre-tax profits to make MCC appear in better shape than it was.

On the evening it was due to be transmitted, *Panorama*'s Deputy Editor, David Jordan, took the tape to BBC TV Centre. 'As a precaution, I did something I'd never done before: I took an alternative programme with me, so we could put that on in case Maxwell issued a last-minute injunction. I can remember sitting there watching the clock as the time got nearer and nearer, waiting for the phone to ring. We didn't know we were safe until the titles rolled.'

Maxwell seems to have decided that he would draw more attention to himself by trying to stop the programme than if he let it go ahead. For once in his life, he kept his head down. But if *Panorama* wasn't the body blow he had been dreading, it still landed enough punches to make the City take further fright.

Meanwhile Lawrie Guest was getting more and more anxious. Privately, he wrote down his suspicions. 'I am now convinced that MGN resources have been used to support other parts of the group. But I have no proof. I think I have frightened the Chairman, but my main concern must be to get the money back.' As he knew by now, any attempts to do so were likely to come at a heavy cost. In August, one of the directors of MGN had warned him, 'Don't forget that you have a wife and a mortgage to pay.'

Guest was even told that his life might be in danger if he carried on digging. None the less, he confided to a banker friend that he was determined to slug it out. 'He said he would see it through even if he ended up in a one-bedroom flat.' According to his wife, Beverley, 'He was extremely concerned and frustrated, but he wouldn't give up; he was like a dog with a bone.'

On 21 October, Guest ordered an internal investigation into the missing funds. Later that day, Maxwell took another £50,000,000 from the Mirror Group. A few days later Guest went to see him again to ask for an explanation of what had happened to the missing £38,000,000. He was so concerned, he admitted, that he couldn't sleep.

'Don't worry,' Maxwell told him again. 'You are losing sleep and that's not right. You will receive everything. Don't worry . . .'

However, Guest had long passed the point where he could stop fretting. Richard Stott noticed he was 'in an appalling state; his hands were shaking and he was chain-smoking'. At home, Beverley Guest did her best to relieve the tension: 'He never shouted, not once, but I used to shout on his behalf and that seemed to make him calmer.' Convinced after a series of apparently inexplicable coincidences that his phone was being bugged, he started using public phone boxes to alert the other directors of MGN to what was going on.

Even now Maxwell couldn't stop spending money, as if one new deal, one new venture, might magically put everything right. In New York, he launched an American edition of his latest newspaper, *The European*, with a party at the United Nations building. Six hundred guests drank champagne, listened to Frank Sinatra Jnr belting out his father's old hits, and discussed the prospects for closer European integration with varying degrees of enthusiasm.

Midway through the party Maxwell disappeared. *The European's* Editor, Ian Watson, went to try and find him. 'Eventually I came across him sitting on his own in a room. I said, "Bob, I really think you ought to come back to the party."' By way of a reply, Maxwell pulled up the legs of his trousers. Watson was appalled. 'His legs were all black and swollen and his ankles were literally hanging over his shoes.'

A doctor was called who recommended an X-ray. The next day Maxwell went to see Dr Alfred Rosenbaum, a radiologist suggested by Dr Henry Kissinger. 'He had chest pain and I understood he had coronary artery problems,' Rosenbaum recalled. 'This might have been a sign of an angina attack.' Although X-rays revealed that Maxwell's heart wasn't swollen, as Rosenbaum had suspected, he might have a blood clot, or even pneumonia. To make sure, further tests would need to be carried out.

It wasn't only Maxwell's physical state that was causing concern. While he was in New York, Maxwell asked Jules Kroll, the head of Kroll Associates, America's best-known firm of private investigators, to come and see him in the Helmsley Palace Hotel. During a two-hour meeting – which Maxwell insisted took place on the patio as he was convinced his suite was bugged – he repeatedly told Kroll that people were trying to destroy both his business and his life. 'It's one thing for people to speculate whether I'm over-leveraged financially,' Maxwell told Kroll, 'but this is going far beyond that.' The meeting ended with Kroll asking him to compile a list of people who might want to ruin him. Maxwell warned it was likely to be a long list, but promised to let him have it within a fortnight.

Before Dr Rosenbaum could conduct any more medical tests, Maxwell flew back to London. There, he learned that the Finance Director of MCC, Basil Brookes, was threatening to resign after discovering that £255,000,000 had disappeared from MCC accounts. Despite being given repeated assurances that the money would be returned, Brookes had lost all faith this was ever going to happen.

When George Wheeler came for his fortnightly appointment to dye Maxwell's hair, he found him in a maudlin mood and drinking from a bottle of port.

'He looked me straight in the eyes and said, "You know, Mr Wheeler, you are my oldest friend."'

Wheeler was in no mood to be sentimental.

'I replied, "Mr Maxwell, I am your *only* friend."'

Glumly, Maxwell agreed he was right. Before he left, Wheeler told him that he had decided to sell all his MCC shares. By then the bottle of port was empty.

Maxwell now owed more than one billion pounds. Between them, Lehman Brothers and Goldman Sachs were owed £250,000,000. Swiss Bank – owed £57,000,000 – was threatening to summon the Fraud Squad. Maxwell was caught in a trap from which there was no escape; the more he took from one part of his empire to prop up another part, the more he was hacking the ground from under his own feet. The foundations had been removed, the cracks were widening.

The whole edifice was starting to fall.

At the beginning of September 1991, Carolyn Hinsey, Maxwell's 'Cultural Ambassador' in New York, asked him if she could take the evening off. She wanted to attend the memorial service of a friend of hers who had died recently in tragic circumstances. Maxwell said he wanted to know all the details before he would decide whether to let her go.

'I told him that my friend, Helen O'Connor Tracy, had been on board a sailing boat with her husband, Tom, when they had become caught in a hurricane – Hurricane Bob.'

At this point Maxwell accused Hinsey of making this up. 'I promised him that I wasn't. The hurricane really was called Bob.'

Hinsey went on to tell him that the Tracys had set off early one morning from Jupiter Point in Connecticut intending to sail to another port further up the coast – a journey they had assumed would take around four hours. Although weather reports had said that Hurricane Bob wasn't due to hit the area until later, they soon got into difficulties. One of the waves was so big it knocked them both overboard. As well as wearing life jackets, they were carrying flares and mini-strobe lights.

By now it was one o'clock in the afternoon. The couple decided they would be safer if they tied their life jackets together. As Tom Tracey later recalled, 'I swam for a couple of hours and we got within a mile of Horton Point. I could see houses. We had whistles and we blew in unison.' No one heard them. 'We had six pocket flares. They were sealed, but only two worked. We set them off.'

There was no response.

When night fell, they turned on the strobe lights. 'As it got late, about 10 p.m., Helen got a little panicky. She worried that it was the end. She asked me for a sweater. I tried to explain to her that I couldn't get her a sweater.' Tom told Helen to put her arms around his shoulders and he would try to swim towards the lights in the distance.

'In the hours before dawn, Helen succumbed to delirium. She said, "Let me go. I want to die." I said, "No, you can't die. Lots of people love you." But, by morning, you could tell she was in distress. She was breathing, but humming as she breathed. Her head was supported by the life jacket. I was trying to tow her.' At around nine o'clock a wave washed over her. A few minutes later, Tom Tracy realized that his wife had drowned. More than twenty-fours after they had been swept overboard, the couple were spotted by a cabin cruiser, their life jackets still tied together.

When Hinsey had finished telling Maxwell what had happened, he carried on staring at her for some time. Then he shook his head and said, 'That will never happen to us, will it, Tiny?'

32.

A Long Way Down

There were few events in Maxwell's calendar that he enjoyed as much as the annual Labour Party Conference. It was an opportunity for him to talk political turkey, press some important flesh and generally make his presence felt. But not everyone found it so pleasurable. The Labour leader, Neil Kinnock, always regarded the prospect of spending time with Maxwell with a mixture of gloom and apprehension.

'While I knew I couldn't afford to lose his support, I knew too that he could change in an instant; it was like walking on eggshells. His skin was awful bloody thin for a big guy like that. I once asked Maxwell why he had to prove how important he was the whole time. Why couldn't he be a bit more humble? I remember he wouldn't answer the question; he just ignored me.'

But the Robert Maxwell who arrived at the Metropole Hotel in Brighton at the beginning of October 1991 was a changed man from the Maxwell of old – sickly, despondent and under siege. Two weeks earlier he'd met up with the most famous lawyer in the country, George Carman. Over the years Maxwell and Carman had seen a lot of one another. Whenever Maxwell issued a libel writ – something he did on an almost weekly basis – he would turn to Carman to represent him. In the past Carman always came to Maxwell's office if they needed to talk. This time round, though, Maxwell went to see Carman in his chambers. As far as Carman was concerned, it was a hugely symbolic moment.

'I know my father was very flattered,' his son Dominic recalls. 'He felt it was a sign of respect on Maxwell's part. But I strongly suspect there was another motive – Maxwell knew he was likely to face criminal charges and he wanted to talk to my father about it away from his office. I know there were discussions about strategy – about what Maxwell should say if the police asked him such-and-such a question.' Their meeting ended on a defiant note. 'One of the last things Maxwell said to my father was, "You and I, George, we'll nail those fucking bastards."'

On the second day of the Labour Party Conference Maxwell asked Joe Haines – now retired as the *Mirror*'s Political Editor, but still writing leaders for the paper – to come to his suite at the Metropole.

'I went to see him and straightaway he asked me if I was loyal to him.'

Something made Haines hesitate.

He replied that he was loyal to the *Mirror* – but this wasn't what Maxwell wanted to hear. 'He said again, very insistently, "Are you loyal to me personally, Joe?"'

Again Haines hesitated.

'I wasn't prepared to give him my word because I feared by the nature of the request that something illegal was afoot. So again I said, "I'm always loyal to the *Mirror*, Bob."'

Maxwell didn't take this at all well, Haines remembers. 'He was very crestfallen. I felt that he had something weighing on his mind that he wanted to share. He needed a confidant, someone he could lean on.' Although Haines couldn't possibly have known it, it would be the last time he saw him. 'Ever since then I've looked back with some sorrow because he was clearly hurt, but I don't see what else I could have done.'

The same day there was a buffet lunch for senior *Mirror* staff at the hotel. Among the guests was the paper's new Political Editor, Alastair Campbell. It was soon clear to Campbell that something was wrong. 'At one point Maxwell asked me to walk out on to the balcony with him because he didn't want anyone to overhear what he was going to say. That struck me as odd because I must have been the most junior person there. It was an extremely small balcony up on the top floor and we barely fitted on to it. He started to tell me how everyone was out to get him. How I had to understand that if these people destroyed him, they would also destroy the Labour Party.

'He was really ranting. He kept saying that it was vitally important that I made sure that Neil Kinnock understood that. I remember there was a very narrow balustrade on the balcony and I had this feeling that Maxwell sort of wanted to tip over. It even half crossed my mind that I was going to have to reach out and grab him.'

That evening there was a large party at the hotel hosted by Maxwell. Alastair Campbell invited a friend of his to come along – a man who happened to suffer from bipolar disorder. 'My friend was going through a particularly manic phase at the time. He ended up having a chat with Maxwell at the party and I remember afterwards he said to me, "My God, that guy is off his fucking head."'

A week later, Maxwell asked John Pole to give him a transcript of any phone calls Lawrie Guest had made from his office phone. Among them was one in which Guest said simply, 'It's all going up.'

The next evening – Saturday, 12 October – Maxwell called Guest at home.

'I hear you're not happy,' he said. 'We'd better meet.'

In the morning, Maxwell told Guest that all the missing money had been returned, and reinvested in gilts. 'You'll get the contract notes for the gilt deals soon,' he said. 'The money will be back within two weeks.' Worn out with worry, Guest, against his better judgement, allowed himself to believe him.

Physically, Maxwell was in a worse shape than ever. Breathless and still dogged by pains in his chest, he'd been unable to shake off a persistent cold. 'He couldn't breathe,' recalled his chauffeur, John Featley. 'He couldn't talk properly. He had a sore throat. If he'd been a horse, you would have put him down.'

In New York, Carolyn Hinsey could see how much strain Maxwell was under. On Saturday, 26 October, they spent the day together at his suite at the Helmsley Palace. 'He was in the worst mood I have ever seen. All day he screamed at me, "Get that dickhead on the phone", and I would say, "Which dickhead?" ' At one point Maxwell told Hinsey she was a 'fucking idiot' and threw a telephone at her head.

Three days later, on Tuesday, 29 October, one of MGN's non-executive directors, Sir Robert Clark, informed Maxwell that there were grave concerns about unauthorized investments. 'It's all a mistake,' Maxwell said airily. 'I'm going away for a few days to get rid of this cold. I'll explain everything when I return.' Clark told him that the MGN board wanted to convene an audit committee as soon as possible to investigate. Maxwell seemed unperturbed, although he must have known that any investigation would reveal that he'd drained the pension funds dry.

'Go ahead,' he said.

All the time the blows kept raining down. Deciding that they had waited long enough for the $60,000,000 they were owed, Goldman Sachs quietly sold off 25 million MCC shares. Citibank was also about to sell shares in an attempt to recover its $40,000,000 loan. Meanwhile in New York, Lehman Brothers were threatening to sell their shares unless their loan – $100,000,000 – was repaid in full.

And so it went on. Five other UK banks demanded that the £60,000,000 they were owed between them be repaid immediately. Although Maxwell managed to raise £80,000,000 by mortgaging various London properties, it was too little, too late. Still waiting for their £57,000,000, the head of Swiss Bank felt he had no alternative but to alert the relevant authorities to 'suspected breaches of the law'.

The next day – Wednesday, 30 October – at around 7.45 in the evening, Maxwell asked his press officer/general factotum, Bob Cole, to come and see him. Over the years Cole had soaked up more punishment from Maxwell than anyone, with the possible exception of Peter Jay. Now, to his astonishment, Maxwell embraced him warmly, kissed him on the cheek and thanked him for everything he'd done. 'That was the last I ever saw of him,' Cole recalled. 'And looking back on that meeting now, I can't help feeling that somehow he knew it was to be our last.'

33.

Lost

On the night of Thursday, 31 October 1991, Gus Rankin, captain of the *Lady Ghislaine*, was eating a curry at an Indian restaurant in Gibraltar when one of the yacht's stewardesses ran in. She had just heard some very alarming news: Robert Maxwell was flying out to Gibraltar early the next morning. Apparently he intended joining the *Lady Ghislaine* for what were described as 'a few days' rest and recreation'.

Normally an unexcitable man, Rankin was just as shocked. His first reaction was to assume it must be a practical joke. Leaving his meal, he rushed back to the yacht and called Maxwell's home number in London. There was no reply. He then called one of his secretaries on her home number.

When at last she picked up the phone – she had already gone to bed – Rankin learned that Maxwell would indeed be arriving at 9.30 the following morning. There was nowhere near enough time to make everything ready, he protested. No food had been laid in and the yacht had just been prepared for a transatlantic crossing. In anticipation of rough weather, the portholes had been covered and anything breakable stowed away.

To make matters worse, the chief stewardess was on leave, so there were only ten crew on board instead of the usual eleven. As Rankin knew only too well, the smallest thing was likely to set Maxwell off and this seemed sure to spark a major conflagration. But, even as he was talking, he realized he was wasting his time. If Maxwell had made up his mind to come, there was nothing he, or anyone else, could do about it.

The next morning, Rankin was waiting at the airport to meet

Maxwell's private Gulfstream jet. The first thing he noticed as Maxwell came down the steps was that he was travelling alone – normally he was accompanied by several staff, including his butler. Eankin was also surprised by how little luggage he had with him – just one suitcase along with five large boxes of files. He was, however, relieved to see that Maxwell appeared to be in uncharacteristically good spirits. Not only that, he was plainly making an effort to be on his best behaviour.

After apologizing for giving him so little notice, Maxwell said he would fit in with any plans Rankin might have. He explained that he'd been suffering from a heavy cold and was taking a short break to try to shake it off. Previously, Maxwell had asked him to sail to New York, where he intended spending Christmas. When Rankin said that he'd been planning to stop off in Madeira, Maxwell told him that was fine. As for the food, he would eat anything the staff could rustle up. Then Maxwell repeated that he had no wish to cause any fuss – 'I'm just here for the ride.'

Later that morning, the *Lady Ghislaine* set sail. Over the next two days Maxwell remained in the same relaxed, jolly mood as he'd been in when he arrived. 'I would say he was very happy,' Rankin recalled. 'He seemed healthy. He ate and drank well.'

In retrospect, the only thing that struck him as odd was that Maxwell did almost no work while he was on board. Usually, he spent several hours a day poring over papers. But now 'it was if he had decided to drift, to just let everyone else get on with it'. Instead he passed the time by listening to his favourite Mozart operas, watching old James Bond videos and sitting on deck gazing out to sea.

As the *Lady Ghislaine* sailed towards Madeira, back in London Maxwell's son Kevin had some unscheduled visitors. A group of lawyers acting for the Swiss Bank Corporation told him they had passed on to the City of London police details of MCC's refusal – or inability – to repay Swiss Bank's £57,000,000. The lawyers made it clear they were offering MCC one last chance. If the money wasn't repaid by Tuesday, 5 November – the same day as the scheduled meeting between Maxwell and the audit committee – then they would go public with the story.

Soon after 8.30 on the morning of 2 November the *Lady Ghislaine* sailed into Funchal harbour in Madeira. Two hours later Maxwell went ashore. After buying some British newspapers, he tried, unsuccessfully, to find a history of the island to read. According to Rankin, his mood hadn't changed. This, however, would be contradicted later by a Funchal shipping agent who said he saw Maxwell sitting on his own in a café looking morose and preoccupied.

In the afternoon he decided he wanted to go swimming, so Rankin sailed to a group of uninhabited islands nearby called Las Desertas. With some difficulty, Maxwell climbed down the hydraulically operated 'swim-stair' at the back of the yacht and lowered himself into the water. While he wasn't a strong swimmer, he was fond of floating about in a giant rubber ring the size of a tractor tyre which was tethered to the side of the boat. Not that he had any need of buoyancy aids. According to the first mate, Nigel Hodson, 'He couldn't sink anyway. He floated so well that he didn't need to make a stroke.'

Returning to Funchal, Maxwell dined by himself in his stateroom before going to a local bar with the second mate, Mark Atkins. While they were having a drink together, he noticed a building nearby bathed in blue and pink light – the Ta-Madeira casino. Maxwell told Atkins to go back to the yacht and return with his passport and $3000 in cash from the safe. He spent the next twenty-five minutes in the casino playing roulette before calling on his walkie-talkie and asking to be picked up.

That night, he informed Rankin that he intended leaving the following morning and flying back to London. But by breakfast Maxwell had changed his mind. Was there was an airport anywhere between Madeira and the Caribbean, where his private jet could land? When Rankin told him there was nothing but open ocean for the next 3500 miles, Maxwell seemed surprised. He then changed his mind again. Now he instructed Rankin to sail in the opposite direction, to the Canary Islands, 250 miles away. The Gulf-stream could follow and pick him up from Tenerife.

The next night – Sunday, 3 November – Ian Maxwell called the yacht to remind his father he was supposed to be speaking at the annual Anglo-Israeli Association dinner in London the next day. Before he had left London, Maxwell had told Ian how keen he was to attend. But now he said he wasn't feeling at all well and didn't know if he would be up to it. They agreed to talk again in the morning and see how he was.

By this point the *Lady Ghislaine* had left Madeira and was on its way to the Canary Islands. After another sleepless night, Maxwell said he was still feeling poorly and that Ian should go to the dinner in his place. That evening, Maxwell had what was later described as 'a shouting match' with his son Kevin on the phone.

On the Tuesday – 5 November – Maxwell and Kevin were due to go for a meeting with the Governor of the Bank of England, Eddie George, where they were bound to face awkward questions about their solvency. November the 5th was set to be a day of reckoning on almost every front. Swiss Bank were about to go public if their £57,000,000 was not repaid, Goldman Sachs were going to announce they had been selling MCC shares after repeated delays to the repayment of their loans, while Maxwell was scheduled to meet MGN's audit committee to explain the £38,000,000 hole in the pension funds.

Kevin Maxwell was also going to be interviewed by the *Financial Times* about the state of his father's businesses. But when he told his father that he would like him to come back to London as soon as possible, Maxwell refused. 'We needed to prepare for that meeting [at the Bank of England] and I was a bit hacked off that he was going to leave it until the last minute,' Kevin recalled.

The next morning, 4 November, Maxwell struck Rankin as being more irritable – more like his usual self – than he had done before. But as the day went on his mood improved. He was particularly taken with Rankin's suggestion that the Gulfstream should stage a fly-past on its way to Tenerife, passing directly above the boat at low altitude. As the plane went by, Maxwell threw his head back and waved at the pilot.

'He seemed in very good spirits watching the aircraft fly over the boat.'

At four in the afternoon, the *Lady Ghislaine* reached the port of Santa Cruz in northern Tenerife. At 8.15 that evening, Maxwell went ashore, wearing check trousers, an open-necked shirt, a light summer jacket and one of his trademark baseball caps. A taxi driver called Arturo Hernandez Trujillo drove him to the Hotel Mencey, the only five-star hotel in town. Maxwell got into the front of the Toyota Camry and pushed his seat back as far as it would go, but his knees were still wedged against the dashboard, Trujillo noticed.

When they arrived at the hotel, Maxwell was shown to the best table in the dining room – Table One – overlooking the gardens. Although the Hotel Mencey can't have seen many 22-stone men wearing baseball caps having dinner on their own, Maxwell doesn't seem to have attracted much attention – at least from the other diners. He made more impression on the staff, several of whom claimed later that he had appeared out of breath when he arrived and had spent some time jabbing impatiently at the buttons of his walkie-talkie.

After glancing at the menu, Maxwell asked the head waiter, Sergio Rodriguez, for his recommendations. Taking Rodriguez's advice, he started with a spinach and asparagus mousse, before moving on to hake with clams in a mushroom and parsley sauce. To drink, he ordered a beer. As he was so large, Rodriguez decided that one beer would never be enough, and brought him two.

Maxwell did not object, later ordering a third.

For dessert, he had a single pear. Before leaving, Maxwell complimented Rodriguez on the food – everything had been 'very good' – and paid the 3000 peseta bill (around $25) in cash, leaving a 20 per cent tip. On the way out his mind must have been elsewhere because he forgot his jacket, which he had hung over the back of his chair. Rodriguez had to run after him and give it back. Outside the hotel, Maxwell caught a taxi, returning to the *Lady Ghislaine* shortly after 10 p.m.

Immediately, he told Rankin to set sail: 'Mr Maxwell wanted to cruise all night out at sea.'

Maxwell went straight to his stateroom, where he made a number of calls on the yacht's satellite phone. Shortly afterwards he complained that he could smell exhaust fumes. To try to clear the air, two stewardesses turned on a portable fan. At around 10.45 one of the stewardesses, Liza Kordalski, checked to see if there was anything else that he wanted. Maxwell told her he was fine. As Kordalski was on her way out, he asked her to lock the sliding door to his stateroom from the inside, then leave through the bathroom – this in turn led through Maxwell's study into the dining room.

At 11.15 p.m., Ian called the yacht on the satellite phone to let his father know how his speech to the Anglo-Israeli Association had gone. 'He was in a good mood. I told him that the speech had been very well received. He wanted to know how a particular joke we had discussed had gone down.' During their conversation, Ian referred to the fact that the next day was going to be a 'big day' with 'important meetings'.

The call ended with him saying, 'See you tomorrow then.'

'You bet,' said Maxwell.

Afterwards he told the bridge that he didn't want to take any more calls. But five minutes later the phone in his suite rang again. This time it was Rabbi Feivish Vogel from the Jewish Orthodox Lubavitch movement. Vogel was calling from Moscow and insisted on being put through. He wanted to discuss a campaign that he and Maxwell were involved in to secure the release of an archive of Jewish manuscripts from the Lenin Library.

'He sounded completely fine,' Vogel remembers. 'He was as robust and as helpful and positive in his last call as in all our other calls. I had no inkling that anything was wrong.'

After receiving another couple of phone calls, Maxwell retired to bed. But he can't have slept for that long because when one of the crew, Graham Leonard, came on watch at 4.10 a.m, he saw him standing by the stern rail. He was wearing a white dressing gown over his nightshirt and looking at the lights of Gran Canaria on the horizon. By now the wind had got up and there was a light easterly breeze. This time Maxwell complained that his bedroom was too hot. Leonard turned on the air conditioning. Having done so, he went back to the bridge, leaving Maxwell standing on deck gazing out over the stern rail.

It was now 4.15.

Half an hour later, at 4.45, Maxwell called and said that his bedroom was now too cold. The air conditioning was turned off. The *Lady Ghislaine* continued to sail on though the night.

At around six o'clock the next morning Kevin Maxwell phoned his father. There was no reply. At 9.45 Gus Rankin docked in Los Cristianos in southern Tenerife. At 10.30, a banker from Rothschild's in New York called and asked to be put through to Maxwell's stateroom.

Again there was no reply.

'Mr Maxwell is still asleep,' he was told. Could he try again later?

Half an hour later John Bender, senior Vice Chairman of Maxwell Macmillan in America, telephoned. Bender had urgent business to discuss, he said. After Rankin had tried putting the call through to Maxwell's stateroom, he tried other internal phones around the boat.

Still there was no answer.

Puzzled but not especially concerned, the crew went looking for him. 'I was surprised,' Rankin recalled later. 'Where was he? We went and looked in all the usual places.' There was no sign of Maxwell in the dining room, or the kitchen, or on any of the decks. Next, Rankin and the chef, Robert Keating, tried the main door to the stateroom. It was locked. Trying the other door that led from Maxwell's stateroom on to the rear deck, they found that this too had been locked.

Repeated knocking failed to get any response. Going back to the bridge, Rankin fetched his pass key. Although Liza Kordalski was sure she had left the key in the other side of the lock the night before, Rankin found he was able to insert his pass-key and slide the door open.

'Mr Maxwell?' he called out.

Again there was no reply.

'Mr Maxwell? Are you all right?'

When Rankin walked into the stateroom, the first thing he saw was Maxwell's dressing gown, lying crumpled on the floor. Next, he looked in the bedroom. By now, Rankin was half anticipating what he might find: Maxwell lying in bed having suffered a seizure of some kind. But the bed was empty. So was Maxwell's dressing room, as well as both bathrooms.

At this point the whole crew, led by Rankin, searched the yacht from top to bottom. They conducted the search three times, looking in the staff quarters below decks, as well as in the inflatable dinghy that was suspended alongside. As soon as they had finished one search, they started all over again. 'We were even opening drawers, we were so confused.'

They found nothing.

Even then, the truth was so hard to comprehend, so appalling in its implications, that they couldn't quite believe it. 'At some point it sunk in that he was not on the boat,' Rankin recalled.

Running back to the bridge, he telephoned the local SOS station, Gomera Radio. It turned out that no one there spoke English. He then told a local shipping agent, John Hamilton, to alert the authorities in Los Cristianos. At 12.02 p.m., Rankin called Brian Hull, the Gulfstream operations manager at Farnborough airport.

'How are things?' Hull asked.

'We're not doing very well,' Rankin admitted. 'We've lost Mr Maxwell.'

34.

Found

Shortly before six o'clock that afternoon, Captain Jesús Fernández Vaca of the Spanish National Rescue Service was about to abandon his search for the day. The sun was already slipping beneath the horizon and the light starting to fade. Within a few minutes it would disappear completely. Just as Vaca was about to turn his helicopter around and fly back to Gran Canaria, he spotted a dark shape in the sea below.

Unsure just what he had seen, Vaca descended for a closer look. Directly beneath the helicopter was the naked body of a man. It was lying on its back with its legs spread-eagled and its arms stretched out on either side. A rescue diver, José Francisco Perdoma, was lowered into the water. First of all, he checked for a pulse: nothing. He then tried to roll the body into a special basket that had been lowered with him. But it was too big to fit in, and so a large nylon harness normally used to rescue cattle and horses from flood zones was lowered instead. Even this proved difficult.

In the gloom it eventually took five men to attach the harness and winch the body up into the helicopter. By the time it landed at Gando airfield in Las Palmas twenty miles away, Betty Maxwell was already on a plane out to the Canaries. Immediately after Gus Rankin had alerted the Gulfstream operations manager at Farnborough airport, Kevin Maxwell had called the *Lady Ghislaine*. Rankin explained that his father had gone missing during the night. Kevin then went to see his brother Ian.

'My initial reaction was utter disbelief,' Ian remembers. 'It just seemed too far-fetched to be true. I remember standing up and having a thirty-second cry and it was accompanied by the most bizarre feeling, a combination of exhilaration and being scared. In a sense, exhilarated to be free of this extraordinary alpha male presence in my life and at the same time incredibly scared as to what the future would look like without him.'

While Kevin and Ian remained in London, Betty Maxwell flew out to Gran Canaria with her oldest son, Philip. Travelling with them in a private jet were the *Mirror* photographer Ken Lennox and John Jackson, a *Mirror* reporter. 'Betty was dressed in black, even though at this stage Maxwell was still missing,' Jackson remembers. During the flight, the co-pilot asked Lennox if he could have a word in the cockpit. 'He told me that they'd just heard that a body had been found, but they didn't know if it was Maxwell or not. They wanted someone who knew him well to make sure it was him before they showed the body to Betty.

'I then went and told her. There were no tears or anything; she was quite composed.' Almost immediately afterwards, Betty Maxwell said to Jackson, ' "I'll tell you one thing. He would never kill himself. It's not suicide." She was very clear about that.'

When they arrived at La Palmas, a reception party was waiting to greet them, including the British vice-consul. While the vice-consul stayed with Betty Maxwell and John Jackson, Ken Lennox accompanied one of the officials to the pilots' mess. 'I went in and there was Robert lying naked on a table. I was asked how I could recognize him and I said that he had two black moles behind his left ear. I then walked around the body and had a good look. There was one mark on his body, on his upper arm. It looked like a scrape mark, greenish-blue in colour. Otherwise, there was nothing unusual.'

After Lennox had signed a statement formally identifying Maxwell, a photograph was taken of him holding up the statement with the body in the background. 'Once that was done, I went outside and said, "Betty, it's Robert." '

In the meantime Betty and John Jackson had been talking to Captain Vaca. He gave her as much information as he could about recovering the body: about where it had been found and its exact condition. In Vaca's opinion, the body had been in the water for about twelve hours. He also told Jackson that when the body was winched up into the helicopter no water came out of its lungs. 'He said, "I have taken many, many bodies out of the sea and I can tell you for certain that he didn't drown." '

A few minutes later, Betty Maxwell and John Jackson were taken into the room where the body was now lying beneath an orange rubber sheet. 'Two doctors, a man and a woman wearing white coats, were in attendance,' Betty recalled. There was also an audience of sorts. 'The vice-consul, a police officer and other officials were seated on chairs lined up along one side of the room. I braced myself, fearing from all I had heard about drowning that the body would look bloated or mauled by sharks. I walked slowly towards the head of the stretcher. The lady doctor lifted the sheet, uncovering Bob's face and torso.'

Betty's fears that the body might be disfigured proved groundless. 'Even in death he looked a most impressive figure. He seemed taller, his body was completely straight and his whole bearing was one of extreme dignity, even defiance . . . There he was lying dead and yet his imposing attitude moved everyone in the room into silence. We were all stunned, and I felt intimidated: the combined emotions of grief, shock, fear, sadness, awe and perplexity that overshadowed us were almost too much to bear.'

She asked the doctor to remove the sheet completely so she could see Maxwell naked. 'Although I felt embarrassed, I needed to be sure that his body was whole and intact. I noticed nothing abnormal, except for slight bleeding from the nose, which I was told was usual in such circumstances in death.' When she touched Maxwell's hand and his forehead, she was surprised to find that his skin was soft. 'It seemed strange that rigor mortis had not set in.'

Jackson noted that Maxwell's skin hadn't discoloured or wrinkled at all, despite being immersed in the sea for twelve hours. Nor had his hair dye run. But it wasn't this that made the most impression on him. 'Maxwell was lying with arms up either side of his head.

Both his hands were clenched together as if he was trying to hold on to something. I remember looking down at him and thinking that he looked just like a baby who had fallen asleep.'

From Las Palmas, Betty Maxwell was driven to the *Lady Ghislaine* in Los Cristianos harbour, along with John Jackson and Ken Lennox. A Spanish police officer was also there to offer his condolences. When Betty asked how long the police would need to conduct their investigations, she was astonished to learn that they had already done so.

'You've completely finished?'

'Yes,' the policeman told her.

'What, you've seen all you wish to see?'

'Yes.'

What puzzled her even more was that the main cabin hadn't been sealed by the police. Nothing had been taken away for analysis. Nor did anything appear to have been given more than the most cursory examination. As she looked around, Betty had a sense which she couldn't define, but which would never leave her: a nagging suspicion that something wasn't right.

'I had not met Captain Rankin before. He was tall and rather stout, in uniform, but casually so, not giving the spruce naval appearance of previous captains, as one would expect on a luxury yacht like the *Lady Ghislaine*. Some of the crew gave me the same impression. The boat did not seem quite shipshape to me.'

Her sense of disquiet deepened when she spoke to Rankin. She didn't care for the familiar way in which he talked about Maxwell, almost as if the two of them had been best friends. It didn't ring true, she felt, 'familiar as I was with Bob's loathing for intimate conversation'.

'What do you think happened?' she asked him.

Caught offguard, Rankin said that his immediate assumption was that Maxwell had committed suicide.

Going into the main cabin, Betty saw that it was exactly as Maxwell had left it. His swimming trucks – still damp – were lying on the bathroom floor. On a table by the telephone, labelled 'Strictly Confidential', was a copy of 'The Maxwell House Contact System', a bound alphabetical directory of important phone numbers. In the bedroom, sweatshirts were strewn over the sofa, there were pieces of orange peel on the carpet and an empty glass on the bedside table.

Intending to sleep there that night, Betty asked the stewardesses to change the bedding, clear up the mess and 'follow normal procedure, just as if Mr Maxwell were still alive'. By now Maxwell's youngest daughter, Ghislaine, about to turn thirty, had flown in. 'She was really, really upset,' Lennox recalls. 'You could tell this was Daddy's girl. Even as an adult, she would refer to him as "My Daddy" all the time. She was inconsolable; she could hardly speak. When she saw her mother, her knees just buckled.'

To try to stop the yacht from being besieged by paparazzi, Betty told Rankin to set sail once more – to a small fishing village north of Santa Cruz. At around ten o'clock that night the five of them – Betty, Philip and Ghislaine, John Jackson and Ken Lennox – sat down to a makeshift supper in the yacht's dining room. Throughout the meal, there was a stream of calls on the satellite phone. One was from Maxwell's lawyer in France, a man called Sam Pisar. Had Betty noticed anything about her husband's body, Pisar wondered. Or the behaviour of the crew?

Then he asked a question that was currently being asked in newsrooms all over the world: was it possible Maxwell had been murdered?

The question was so unexpected it left Betty feeling as if she'd been winded: 'My whole world was shaken to its core.' Two hours later Pisar's words were still going round and round in her head. Lying in the same bed where Maxwell had been lying less than twenty-four hours earlier, she tried to put her thoughts into some sort of order:

'The more I thought about the mystery of his death, the less I could comprehend it. How could it have happened? I must admit that the idea that he might have committed suicide did cross my mind, but I could not take it seriously. It was just not in character.'

However much Betty tried to dismiss the idea, the more it preoccupied her. If Maxwell had committed suicide, surely he would have left her a note? Unable to sleep, she got up and decided to search the cabin. 'I knew Bob's habits very well. All his life he had had special places where he would keep his money or an important letter.'

She began by looking through all the pockets of his clothes. Then she searched the drawers, the shelves, inside the pillowcases and even under the mattress.

She found nothing.

Next, she went through the five black-leather pilot cases in which Maxwell kept important papers. Just as Rankin had searched the yacht three times over for Maxwell earlier that day, so Betty also searched everything three times, 'bent only on discovering a note in Bob's hand that might give me a clue'.

Again there was nothing.

At five o'clock, exhausted and more puzzled than ever, she finally fell asleep. Five hours later, she woke up: 'My first full day as Bob Maxwell's widow had begun.'

She soon discovered just how many hurdles would have to be cleared before her husband could be buried. Three years earlier, Maxwell had bought himself a burial plot on the Mount of Olives in Jerusalem. According to Jewish lore, this was where the Messiah will arrive on the Day of Judgement, thus putting anyone interred there first in the queue for resurrection.

But Jewish lore also dictated that he would have to be buried within five days – by the following Sunday, 10 November. No funeral could take place on the Sabbath – Saturday. Similarly, no body could be admitted into Israel after sunset on Friday. That meant that Maxwell's body would have to be on a plane by Thursday evening at the latest, just thirty-six hours away.

Before then, an autopsy would have to be carried out by the Spanish authorities, and the necessary paperwork completed to transport a body to another country. That could take up to a week, Betty was told. She begged her Spanish lawyer, Julio Claverie, to hurry things along.

'Mrs Maxwell, this is just impossible,' Claverie told her, 'but I shall try.'

To complicate matters further, Maxwell's insurance brokers wanted to do their own autopsy in case there was any dispute about the cause of death. Meanwhile the phone continued to ring. To allow Betty some time to herself, John Jackson volunteered to field calls. Remarkably, given how badly their lunch had gone eight months earlier, one of the first callers was President George Bush. Margaret Thatcher also rang, as did Lord Goodman, former solicitor and adviser to Harold Wilson. Goodman wondered how such a distinguished figure as Maxwell should be commemorated, and suggested that a memorial service in Westminster Abbey might be appropriate.

After a meeting with a judge to try to arrange a death certificate, Betty returned to the *Lady Ghislaine*. That afternoon, she had another meeting with Captain Rankin. There were a number of questions she wanted answering. She asked him about Maxwell's mood during his time on the yacht, what he had said, where they had sailed to, who first discovered he was missing and why it had taken so long to raise the alarm.

None of Rankin's answers struck Betty as being peculiar, or suspicious. And yet after their conversation was over she had the same feeling she had had when she stepped on board the yacht the day before. A nagging sense of unease. Of 'malaise that is difficult to describe or explain'.

35

The First Autopsy

The day after Maxwell's body had been found, John Jackson spent the morning writing a speech for Maxwell's daughter Ghislaine to give to the world's press. Throughout the night, a stream of journalists, photographers and TV crews had descended on Las Palmas. Now they were ranged along the quayside, long lenses pointing at the yacht. Once Jackson had written the speech, Ken Lennox coached Ghislaine on how to deliver it. He made her repeat it over and again until she could reach the end without bursting into tears.

Meanwhile, Jackson looked after Maxwell's oldest son, Philip. If anything, Philip was even more distraught than his sister. 'He was a very nice, very quiet man, and at one point he asked if he could have a word. I could see how upset he was and I knew I had to keep him away from the cameras, so we went behind the funnel of the *Lady Ghislaine.*'

Of the seven surviving Maxwell children, Philip was by far the most scarred by his upbringing, and by the loss of his brother Michael in particular. Michael's death had meant that the burden of being Maxwell's male heir passed to him – a burden Philip had neither the desire nor the temperament to shoulder. After working for Pergamon as Managing Director of Encyclopedias, he had resigned because of ill-health. 'The moment we went behind the funnel, Philip became very upset. The saddest thing was that he said that his father had always hated him and that he didn't particularly like his father, but now he no longer had a chance to make up with him.'

Like Betty, Philip had a nagging sense of unease about Maxwell's death. But while she had only talked to the *Lady Ghislaine*'s captain,

Gus Rankin, Philip decided to question each member of the crew individually. None of them appeared at all evasive or shifty, and yet nothing he heard put his mind at rest.

Whenever she left the yacht to attend the coroner's office, Betty tried to make herself look as impassive as possible. 'Cameras whirred into action, flashes exploded and the journalists closed in on me . . . I just walked past them, erect, my eyes fixed slightly above the horizon, a wan smile on my face, just as I had been taught to do so long ago, when my mother made me take a course in deportment in Paris. I never said a word.'

At midday on Wednesday, 6 November, in a small, poorly ventilated room next to the undertaker's where Maxwell's body had been stored, three inexperienced Spanish pathologists began what was known as 'the opening of the cavities'. They found a small amount of water in the respiratory tracts leading to Maxwell's lungs, along with traces of vomit and a seasickness medicine. Samples were taken from his brain, his one lung, his kidneys, pancreas and stomach, and sent to Madrid for further tests.

Amid mounting speculation that he might have been murdered, the National Institute of Toxicology in Madrid was told to check specifically for substances that might have attacked Maxwell's central nervous system. This theory was lent further weight by Julio Claverie, who issued a statement saying that 'Mr Maxwell was a man who had many enemies, powerful enemies. There has to be a possibility that he was murdered.'

On the Thursday morning, Betty woke up in a panic. 'Two days had already slipped by and I realized it was going to be touch and go to get Bob's body out of Spain in time to fly it to Israel to comply with all the strictures of Jewish Orthodoxy.' There was still a mass of things to attend to. A death certificate had to be issued, along with an exit permit allowing the body to leave the Canaries. Hotel rooms had to be booked in Jerusalem, vehicles hired, a funeral service organized, security arranged . . .

The undertakers asked what sort of coffin she wanted. Betty said it should be as simple and plain as possible. Then it turned out that

Maxwell's private jet was almost certainly too small to transport any sort of coffin. Could the undertakers lend the family an empty casket so they could make sure? Alas, this was impossible, she was told. Another larger plane, specially converted into a flying hearse, was located in Switzerland.

By now the pathologists had reached their preliminary findings. Maxwell, they concluded, had died of a 'cardiovascular attack'. The absence of water in his lungs was taken as evidence that he couldn't have drowned. Either he had suffered a heart attack on deck and fallen into the water, or else he had fallen, then had a heart attack in the water.

Far from banishing Betty's disquiet, this only increased it. Something, she still felt, wasn't right – 'but who was I, at this stage, to contradict the experts?' Maxwell's insurers – Lloyds – were also unhappy about the autopsy, principally about the way it had been conducted. Not only did the Spanish pathologists lack experience; it seemed they also lacked the right instruments. With disarming frankness, the pathologist in charge of the autopsy, Dr Carlos Lemela, later conceded that it might have been less thorough than it should. 'We are not the world's best,' he said. 'I think we carried out the initial autopsy correctly and professionally, but we are open to criticism. I must admit one can be mistaken.'

Lloyds insisted there should be a second autopsy, this time conducted by Dr Iain West, a man frequently referred to, not least by himself, as 'Britain's leading forensic pathologist'. But if Maxwell was going to be buried on Sunday, there was no time to conduct a second autopsy in Tenerife. Instead, it would have to be done in Israel on Saturday night, just a few hours before the funeral started.

That afternoon Betty heard that a death certificate had at last been issued, along with an exit visa for the body. It had already been decided that she and Ken Lennox would accompany the body, while the others would come later on another plane. If they left that night, they ought to be able to make it to Israel by sundown on Friday.

But the undertakers were still refusing to release the body.

Because of the heat and the risk of decomposition, it was having to be embalmed. Unfortunately, the embalmer still hadn't finished his work.

And there was a further problem. Clearly embarrassed, the undertakers told Betty that Maxwell wouldn't fit into a normal-sized coffin and they were having problems finding a larger one.

On Thursday evening, Betty had what would be her last meal on the *Lady Ghislaine*. Although she couldn't explain why, she had a suspicion that she would never set foot on the yacht again, and she wanted to fix as many details as possible in her memory. 'I stood at the place where Bob's life was thought to have ended, gazing at the open sea, questioning, wondering, perturbed.'

In the observation lounge, Betty touched the fabric of the upholstered sofas where Maxwell had liked to entertain his guests. 'From there I went down to the great formal dining room, with its shimmering memories of stately dinners, then up an internal staircase to the study and finally back to Bob's cabin, where his last hours had been spent, and I tried to fathom the mystery of his death.'

When they had finished supper, Betty, John Jackson, Ken Lennox, Ghislaine and Philip sat around waiting. It was now after eleven o'clock. The pilot's deadline for making it to Israel had long since passed and Betty was getting desperate. All at once Julio Claverie appeared with the news that the coffin had finally been released and would be taken to the plane at Las Palmas at two o'clock in the morning. If Betty and Ken Lennox left immediately, they should be able to make it in time.

With a procession of press cars in hot pursuit, a police escort accompanied them to the local airport. After Ghislaine had said goodbye to her mother, John Jackson heard her tell the crew that there was one last thing she wanted done – and done immediately:

'Shred everything on this boat!'

36.

A Hero of Our Time

In the days following Maxwell's death, tributes poured in from all around the world. Mrs Thatcher sent Betty a handwritten three-page letter. 'No one will ever replace the energy, vision and resolve personified in Mr Maxwell,' she wrote. 'He was and will remain unique. Above all, Mr Maxwell showed the whole world that one person can move and influence events by using his own God-given talents and abilities.'

According to Neil Kinnock, Maxwell had been a 'true day star of his age'. No one was quite sure what a day star was, but it was clearly intended as a compliment. 'Many like me valued Bob's friendship and loyalty and admired his remarkable tenacity, intelligence and insights,' Kinnock went on. 'We will all miss the infectious vitality of one of the few people I have known who deserved to be called irreplaceable.'

The Prime Minister, John Major, was believed to have delayed his weekly audience with the Queen so that he could write his tribute: 'No one should doubt his interest in peace and his loyalty to friends,' Major wrote. 'During the attempted Soviet coup this August, he was able to give me valuable insights into the situation in the Soviet Union because of his many contacts . . . His was an extraordinary life, lived to the full.'

Chancellor Helmut Kohl was 'very sad', President Gorbachev was 'deeply grieved', while President Bush extolled Maxwell's 'humanitarian endeavours and his unwavering fight against bigotry and oppression'. According to the former Israeli Prime Minister Shimon Peres, 'Mr Maxwell was not a man, but an empire in his power, thought and deeds.'

Amid all this effusiveness, one tribute was brief to the point of terseness. 'Mr Maxwell was a remarkable man,' said Rupert Murdoch. 'My wife and I send our personal condolences to Mrs Maxwell and her family.'

At the same as extolling Maxwell's achievements, the *Sun*'s headline managed to get in a dig about his origins. According to the paper, he had been 'THE RICHEST PEASANT IN THE WORLD'. For its part, the *Mirror* marked his passing with the newsprint version of a twenty-one-gun salute. 'The body of Robert Maxwell, publishing giant and world statesman, was found in the Atlantic today . . .' the paper's front page announced. Readers who wanted to know more about this 'Great Big Extraordinary Man' were invited to turn to pages 2, 3, 4, 5, 6, 7, 8, 9, 11, 18, 19, 34, 35 and 36.

Joe Haines wrote that 'His death removed a colossus from the scene . . . Love him or hate him, his like will never be seen again.' Facing the television cameras outside the *Mirror* building, Charlie Wilson, the Editor of the *Sporting Life,* declared in a voice appropriately thickened with solemnity that Maxwell had been nothing less than a hero of our time. Wilson had just been appointed official spokesman for the Maxwell family – not because he knew them particularly well, but just because they needed someone at short notice.

Other newspapers took a less adulatory yet generally respectful tone. While acknowledging that Maxwell could be a terrible bully, the *Guardian* conceded that he had been an 'effective bully'. He will be 'much missed as a public figure', the obituary concluded. The *New York Times* noted admiringly that he had 'borrowed money on a heroic scale'. Lord Goodman told Betty Maxwell that he'd given a lot of thought to his earlier suggestion that there should be a memorial service at Westminster Abbey and had come up with what he felt was a more appropriate venue: St Paul's Cathedral.

Meanwhile, speculation about the cause of Maxwell's death continued to run amok. To begin with there appeared to be three possible explanations: accident, suicide or murder. Supporters of the last theory eagerly lit on reports that the *Lady Ghislaine* had apparently been shadowed by another ship as it sailed down the coast of Tenerife. Could a crack team of assassins have been aboard? Had they managed to board the *Lady Ghislaine* in the middle of the night, murder Maxwell, then slip away unnoticed?

The captain, Gus Rankin, gave this idea short shrift. 'I would say not possible, because even if there isn't someone on the aft deck, we do have equipment for detecting other boats . . . The instructions to the crew were: any vessel that comes within five miles of this boat I am to be called. I, the Captain, am to be called. Nobody called me.'

Although there was no evidence of this second ship's existence, this did nothing to quell the speculation. Or perhaps some, even all, of the crew had been responsible? As Betty wrote, they were all strangers to her and this in itself was inclined to make her suspicious: 'We had certainly never had a completely new team like this before.'

Then, out of left field, came an entirely new possibility. Could the body that had been pulled from the ocean not have been Maxwell at all? It was a theory that the *Guardian* was willing to entertain, albeit cautiously: 'In none of the documents they prepared do either the Civil Guard doctor or the autopsy doctors commit themselves to saying that the body they examined was that of Robert Maxwell. The Civil Guard report describes the cadaver as that of a "white male, with athletic build and prominent belly, chestnut hair – possibly dyed – with a slight widow's peak, 1 metre and 90 centimetres tall and weighing 130–40 kilos." The forensic experts use similar wording.

'Mr Maxwell's hair, though, was black. Most of his friends and associates suspected it was dyed and it may be that the action of the sea turned it light brown. However, according to an official in the Canaries whose job has led him to see numerous bodies pulled out of the water, the long-term effect of salt water on hair dye is usually to "burn" the hair, but not change its colour.'

The *Guardian*'s correspondent wasn't the only one entertaining the possibility that Maxwell might have faked his own death. Writing in the *Daily Telegraph*, a former MI6 officer called James Rusbridger compared the case with an ingenious Second World War plan to fool German Intelligence: the corpse of a 45-year-old Welsh tramp dressed in Royal Marine uniform and clutching a briefcase full of bogus Allied invasion plans had been secretly planted off the Spanish coast.

Rusbridger had even gone so far as to contact the eminent pathologist Sir Bernard Spilsbury to discuss his theory. Spilsbury, he claimed, had told him that substituting a dummy corpse was perfectly possible: 'You have nothing to fear from a Spanish post-mortem; to detect this man had not drowned at sea would need a pathologist of my experience, and there aren't any in Spain.'

If Maxwell had faked his own death, this might have been the answer to some of his – or his family's – problems; at least they would be able to collect his £20,000,000 life insurance policy. According to a former stewardess on the *Lady Ghislaine* called Madeleine Hult, it was an idea that Maxwell himself had entertained. Hult came forward to tell the *New York Post* that a year earlier she had overheard him planning his disappearance with his son Kevin. 'I heard him say he had some problems with money, with some loans, and that he had just bought a very secret house in South America. He said he would just disappear, make it look like he had died, and have another body found.'

Support for the idea that Maxwell had hidden away in some remote corner of the globe came from an unlikely source. According to Nick Davies, Maxwell had often talked to Andrea Martin about 'doing a Stonehouse'. John Stonehouse was a Labour MP who faked his own death in 1974. After leaving a pile of clothes on a Florida beach to suggest that he had drowned, Stonehouse travelled to Australia to start a new life, using a passport he had obtained in the name of a dead constituent. In a particularly cruel twist of fate, he was only caught because the Australian police suspected he was the missing peer, Lord Lucan.

'I have thought it would be a wonderful way of ending one's life,' Maxwell had apparently told Andrea. 'Living in a lovely house with a swimming pool in the middle of nowhere with not a worry, not a thought for all the problems. I would have plenty of money and the telephone would never ring again. I would be at peace then and happy . . .'

37

The Second Autopsy

Shortly before three in the morning on Friday, 8 November 1991, a hearse drove slowly on to the floodlit runway at Las Palmas airport in Gran Canaria. From the back of the hearse, six pallbearers took the largest coffin Betty Maxwell had ever seen. Later she would learn that her husband's remains had been encased in two coffins. There was an inner one made of lead, hermetically sealed with a glass lid to permit identification of the body by the Spanish authorities, and an outer one made of mahogany with silver handles, which Betty suspected was the most expensive model the funeral parlour had in stock.

Just before the plane took off, a Spanish official approached Ken Lennox and asked if he could have a discreet word. 'He said, "Mr Lennox, I'm afraid there's a problem."'

It seemed the coffin was too large even to fit into the specially adapted plane. The only way to get it in was to wedge it at a 45-degree angle. Mrs Maxwell had told him she was all right with that, but how did he feel? The coffin was blocking the emergency exit and if the plane crashed on take-off it might not be possible for either of them to escape. It was fine with him too, Lennox confirmed.

When at last the plane was airborne, Betty asked him to turn out the lights. 'That's when she had a little weep – the first time I'd seen her cry. Afterwards she asked if I would get her a whisky. So I got her a whisky and put the lights back on.' The two of them sat in silence gazing out of the window with Maxwell's enormous coffin wedged behind them. Having finished her whisky, Betty turned around and stared at the coffin for a while. Then she asked Lennox an unexpected question:

'Ken, do you think Bob is standing on his head, or his feet?'

Taken by surprise, Lennox said the first thing that came into his head.

' "Well, Betty," I told her, "he always landed on his feet before, so I guess that's how he is now." '

Just before the sun went down, their plane entered Israeli airspace. As soon as they did so, Betty Maxwell and Ken Lennox saw two Israeli aircraft appear, one on either side of their plane. At first, the pilot thought they were trying to force him to land, but it turned out there was another explanation: the Israeli government had sent a guard of honour to escort Maxwell to his final resting place.

'At 10.15 p.m. on Saturday 9th November 1991 at the Institute of Forensic Medicine in Tel Aviv, I performed a second post-mortem examination on the body of Robert Maxwell, aged 68 years,' wrote Iain West in his official account.

In fact, West didn't perform the second post-mortem himself. As it was conducted in Israel, a team of Israeli pathologists was in charge. They were, however, happy for him and his wife, Vesna Djurovic, also a pathologist, to be present. 'Effectively, the tasks were shared out. An effort was made to ensure that everybody saw it all.' West was there to try to determine the physical cause of Maxwell's death – whether he'd fallen overboard, possibly as the result of a heart attack, or had jumped, or been pushed.

Walking into the mortuary room, he saw Maxwell's corpse laid out on a table encased in a coarse muslin body bag. 'Maxwell R' had been scrawled in magic marker on the material. While his head was exposed, the rest of the body was wrapped in ropes that had been tied around the ankles, thighs and chest. It was, West recalled, 'an extremely unpleasant autopsy'. When the ropes were undone, they turned out to be holding the body together. Several organs and tissues were missing, as well as most of the heart. Anything left had just been tipped back into Maxwell's chest cavity.

To make matters worse, neat formalin had been used as the embalming fluid and the fumes made it difficult to breathe. The pathologists could only work for a few minutes at a time before going out for some fresh air. When they examined his skull, they quickly found what appeared to be signs of a brain haemorrhage – a pool of clotted blood known as an 'extradural'. Hitherto there had been no suggestion that Maxwell might have died of a brain haemorrhage.

'We looked at it and said, "They couldn't have missed an extradural of that size, surely?" ' Then they realized that the embalmer must have poured so much formalin into his skull that any blood there had solidified. 'Because of gravity it had hardened into a layer which made it look like a haemorrhage.'

Although the body was covered with bruises and abrasions, these could all have come from his being immersed in the sea. It was when they examined Maxwell's left shoulder that they found the first evidence the Spanish pathologists had missed: 'Dissection of the skin of the back showed an extensive 5 by 2 inches haemorrhage along the line of the left infraspinatous muscle. Some of the fibres were torn and the haemorrhage involved most of the muscle. There was a 5 by 0.5 inch extensive haemorrhage into the paraspinal muscle on the left side extending from the twelfth thoracic vertebra to the level of the fourth and fifth lumbar vertebrae. There was a small area of haemorrhage inside the right psoas muscle.'

The muscles on the back of Maxwell's left shoulder were badly torn. In addition, there was a lot of bruising on the left-hand side of his spine. West thought it highly unlikely that these injuries could have been caused by him flailing around in the water. Instead, they appeared to support the theory that he'd fallen from the boat, and then hung on to the side of the *Lady Ghislaine* for as long as he could – until what would have been excruciating pain forced him to let go.

In her report, Vesna Djurovic wrote, 'The pattern of tearing in these muscles suggests that the deceased had at some point been hanging on to an object with his left hand and with his weight being carried by that hand. This could occur, for instance, in a person who is hanging vertically from a rail with his body freely suspended. There are a number of possible scenarios where these injuries might have been received:

(a) If he was hanging on to the rail of the boat and trying to prevent himself from falling into the water, it is possible that in such a large and unfit man the muscular effort involved in trying to hoist his body back on to the boat could cause the damage seen here.

(b) If he overbalanced and fell over the railings but managed to grab the rail as he fell, it is possible that he would have torn these muscles. One must look at this, of course, in the context of a man of his age, size and state of health being able to carry out this type of action. One must also consider the ways in which an individual could accidentally fall from this boat. It is, we think, difficult to see from the available evidence how such an accident could have occurred on a smooth sea unless the deceased had been leaning well over the rail. The arrangement of the railings suggests that if he had tripped or slipped on the deck then it is improbable that he would have fallen overboard.

(c) These injuries would not be seen if an individual allowed himself deliberately to topple over the side of the boat. If, however, the deceased had climbed over the railing so that he stood on the protrusion of the outer hull at deck level, then it is possible that he could have slipped from this while still holding on to the railing with his left hand. This could well account for him hanging for a short while by that hand and for the injuries that were found.

There was another possibility, of course – that Maxwell had been murdered. If this was the case, the most likely scenario was that he had been injected with a poison, with the elbow and the back of the ear reputedly the spots favoured by professional assassins.

West checked for any evidence of puncture marks, but found nothing: 'I never saw an injection mark either in his arm or behind his ear, though a combination of decomposition and embalming might have obliterated any evidence of such marks.'

By the time the pathologists finished the second autopsy, it was five in the morning. Dawn was already breaking. In seven hours' time, Maxwell's funeral was due to start. Thirty-five miles away in the presidential suite at the King David Hotel in Jerusalem, Betty Maxwell woke up determined that, whatever happened, she would stay as composed and dignified as possible. A hairdresser came to do her hair, while a maid pressed the black cashmere suit she was going to wear.

Various people stopped by to pay their respects. Everything seemed to be going as smoothly as it could. But when Betty caught sight of her reflection in the mirror, she could hardly believe what she was seeing. All the colour, all the signs of life, had drained from her face.

'A ghost stared back at me.'

38.

The Four Horsemen

At midday on 10 November 1991, a convoy of limousines flanked by armed motorcycle outriders left the King David Hotel in Jerusalem and drove to the Hall of the Nation two miles away. As she stepped out of her car, Betty was taken aback both by the degree of ceremony and the number of dignitaries present. 'I must admit I was astounded when I discovered that Bob was being given a hero's send-off and what amounted to a state funeral.'

After Maxwell's body – wrapped in an Israeli flag – had lain in state for an hour, the family joined 400 mourners for the funeral service. The former Archbishop of Canterbury, Lord Coggan, was there, along with the most prominent members of the Israeli parliament – President Chaim Herzog, the Leader of the Opposition, Shimon Peres, and Ariel Sharon, the former Minister of Defence – as well as a group of Chernobyl schoolchildren whom Maxwell had arranged to be flown to Israel for medical treatment.

President Herzog was the first to speak. When it came to lauding Maxwell's achievements, he did not hold back. 'He scaled the heights,' Herzog declared. 'Kings and barons besieged his doorstep. He was a figure of almost mythological stature. Few are the persons who stride across the stage of human experience and leave their mark, Robert Maxwell was one of them . . .'

Herzog was followed by Maxwell's oldest son, Philip. Before he began his speech, Philip thanked everyone for attending. 'Sadly, the Prime Minister, Yitzhak Shamir, couldn't come,' he noted.

At this point a hand shot up in the crowd and Shamir – just five foot tall – called out, 'I'm here!'

Earlier that morning, Betty, determined that her children should remain as self-composed as she intended to be, had wondered if Philip would be able to get through his speech without bursting into tears. 'We, his family, were willing him with all our hearts not to break down under the strain. Mercifully, he did not.'

'Dear Dad,' Philip concluded, 'Soldier, Publisher and Patriot, Warrior and Globetrotter; father of nine children and grandfather of eight; newspaper proprietor and football club owner; speaker of nine languages; we salute you; we love you, we need you, we miss you, we cry for your presence and our very great loss.'

Outside the Hall of the Nation, the Chief Rabbi of Haifa gave a brief address – by tradition the rabbi was not allowed to enter a building containing a corpse. After he had finished, events took an unforeseen turn: a fight broke out among the clerics. Two rabbis from the Lubavitch movement began scuffling, with each of them trying to climb on to the rostrum to speak to the crowd. As the Maxwell family looked on, one of the rabbis made it to the microphone, only for his words to be drowned out by cries of protest – and what Betty later referred to as 'more jostling amongst the younger rabbis'.

Once peace had been restored, Maxwell's body was carried into a hearse to be taken to its final resting place on the Mount of Olives. As the sun began to sink behind the gold roof of the Dome of the Rock, the Minister of Health, Ehoud Olmert, delivered the final eulogy: 'He once said to me, "After all, I have not done so badly for a young Jewish boy from the *shtetl*. Indeed, Bob Maxwell, you have not done badly at all. May your soul rest in peace in this ancient ground which finally became yours."'

Olmert had barely finished speaking when the gravediggers, anxious to complete the burial before sunset, brought a stretcher bearing Maxwell's body to the opening of the tomb. Among the onlookers was the photographer Roger Allen, who had been sent out from London to cover the story for the *Mirror*:

'One of the rabbis dispensed with his black Homburg hat and jacket and jumped in the hole, waiting to receive the body. The other rabbis were lining up the stretcher at one end of the grave, ready to tip it up and send Maxwell down the chute, a bit like a burial at sea . . .

Four rabbis heaved one end of the stretcher up to shoulder-height hoping that, as planned, the body would slide down into the waiting arms of the rabbi in the hole. But Maxwell wouldn't shift – he still lay under the shroud, refusing to budge.

'The rabbis pushed harder and suddenly his body, with the force of gravity, slid quickly forward. The rabbi below looked like a goalkeeper waiting for the ball. Maxwell's body rushed towards him. It got to a certain point in its journey and then sat upright, nutting the rabbi. The poor man eventually managed to push it down to the bottom of the grave. Having freed himself of Maxwell, the rabbi leaned against the grave wall, breathing very hard. Slowly he regained his composure and then went about his duties, dressing the body in the white and blue shroud. Moments later, in near darkness, he hopped out, grabbed a shovel and started to fill the hole.'

Richard Stott was in his office at the *Mirror* late at night on Sunday, 1 December 1991, when he received a mysterious phone call. 'The four horsemen are in the Vanway,' he was told, before the line went dead – the Vanway was where the *Mirror* vans lined up to collect their copies of the paper. As far as Stott was concerned, the message was clear: 'The agents of destruction, war, pestilence and famine were upon us.'

Two weeks earlier, on Sunday, 17 November, the *Independent on Sunday* had reported that the Serious Fraud Squad was investigating MCC's failure to repay Swiss Bank the £57,000,000 it was owed. The next day MCC shares opened at 46 pence – a fall of 17 pence from the previous Friday. Appearing on BBC Radio 4's *Today* programme that morning, Kevin Maxwell insisted that 'the public companies' finances are robust'.

Could he assure investors in MCC that their money was safe? 'Absolutely.'

But this did nothing to allay suspicions that there was something terribly wrong at the heart of Maxwell's empire. The shares continued to plummet – three days later they'd gone down to 36p.

Meanwhile, photographs of Maxwell's body, lifted from a video taken during the second autopsy, had been published in *Paris Match* magazine. The magazine sought to justify its actions by claiming that it was performing a public service by proving that Maxwell really was dead. One of the experts consulted by *Paris Match*, Professor Loïc Le Ribault, a former French police forensic specialist, claimed that 'It is highly probable that the victim was struck by a violent blow to the back of the head, no doubt with the aid of a blunt instrument.'

Thirty-six hours after Stott had received his late-night phone call, the *Guardian* reported that at least £350,000,000 appeared to be missing from the funds. 'A multi-million-pound gap in pension funds linked to the empire of the late Robert Maxwell is understood to have been uncovered by accountants investigating the private business network of the publishing tycoon who died four weeks ago.'

Trading in MCC and MGN shares had been suspended – 'pending clarification of the position of the Maxwell family companies'. That night Stott was back in his office staring gloomily at his word processor. He'd already decided on the following day's front-page headline: 'MILLIONS MISSING FROM MIRROR'. Now he wrote a suitably breast-beating editorial to go with it:

'At the moment nobody, not the board, not the bankers, not the staff, can tell you where this will take the *Daily Mirror*. However, we promise you that we will bring you the truth on this matter – as on all matters – as and when we know it, warts and all if necessary.'

The next day – Wednesday, 5 December – the Fraud Squad arrived at the offices of Mirror Group Newspapers. That evening, Richard Stott once again faced the grim task of choosing the following day's headline. This time he aimed squarely for the largest wart of all: 'MAXWELL: £526m IS MISSING FROM HIS FIRMS'. Despite that, some vestige of sympathy remained. Maxwell's actions, he wrote, had been 'the increasingly desperate actions of a desperate man'.

By now, there was no longer any doubt about what was going to happen; it was just a matter of when. Even so, the end, when it came, took almost everyone by surprise. The headline in the following afternoon's *Evening Standard* said simply, 'MAXWELL EMPIRE COLLAPSES'. Earlier that morning, Kevin and Ian Maxwell had applied to have administrators appointed to their family holding companies.

As the Maxwell family's official spokesman, Charlie Wilson found himself having to perform a very public version of a man-oeuvre popularly known on Fleet Street as a 'reverse ferret'. This consists of making a complete about-turn from a previously entrenched position, ideally without betraying any flicker of embarrassment. 'Four weeks earlier I had spent several days going from TV station to TV station telling everyone what a great man Maxwell had been,' Wilson recalls. 'Now I had to do the whole tour all over again saying what a swine and a disgrace he was.'

Every trace of sympathy now gone, Richard Stott went to see 'a clearly shell-shocked' Lawrie Guest. 'I had known him for a long time, he was a decent man and he knew he was in the firing line. I had obtained the documents showing his row with [Michael] Stoney and the damning notes of his meeting with Maxwell in which he had written: "I am convinced that MGN resources have been used to support other parts of the group" – and asked him about them . . . I think it was a relief for Lawrie to get it all off his chest.'

'THE LIE', read the headline in the next day's *Mirror*: 'Robert Maxwell was dramatically challenged about the missing *Mirror* millions just before his death – and responded with a terrible LIE. The *Mirror*'s finance director Lawrence Guest confronted the tycoon in Maxwell's ninth floor office high above Holborn Circus . . .'

Joe Haines was equally stunned. In his column, he wrote that it had been 'an awful week, the worst I can remember. Bob Maxwell, a man who once genuinely saved the *Mirror*, has through his manipulations of the pensions money now delivered us into the hands of those whom he hated, the pinstripes of the City of London.'

All the time the warts kept proliferating. Maxwell the Liar soon turned into 'Maxwell the Bugger' when it emerged that he had bugged his own offices: 'A voice-activated wire tap was found yesterday in a telephone of finance director Lawrence Guest. Wires led to a tape-recorder in an office where the Maxwell empire's security chiefs are based. The tape recorder was Maxwell's own machine which he once used to record his own business conversations. The wires – still active – were uncovered in Mr Guest's suite on the 9th floor of Mirror Group's headquarters at London's Holborn Circus . . . Security boss Mr [John] Pole last night refused to comment on the discovery of the bug.'

While the *Mirror* was decking itself out in sackcloth, Rupert Murdoch's *Sun* remained in a state of ecstatic excitement. 'MIRROR, MIRROR, WHO IS THE BIGGEST CROOK OF ALL?' ran one headline. The paper also invited readers to 'send in your cracks on the Big Max' and set up a special fax line – the Faxwell – so they could do so.

After Maxwell the Fraudster, Maxwell the Liar and Maxwell the Bugger came 'Maxwell the Shagger', when his former mistress Wendy Leigh spilled the beans to Rupert Murdoch's *News of the World* about their affair. However casual it may have been, the affair had gone on for seven years and Leigh clearly cherished fond memories. When they first met, 'I was 25 and primed for adventure,' she wrote. 'He was 57 and susceptible to romance.' Their first night together, Leigh claimed, 'had been the most romantic night of my life'. Maxwell had made her feel like 'the most glittering prize in the firmament'.

But in Maxwell's former paper, the *Sunday Mirror*, Vincenza Astone, who'd once worked for him as a secretary, told a different story. 'I don't know why I slept with him – it just happened,' said a rueful Astone. 'He started fooling around and we ended up in bed. Immediately afterwards I regretted it. I went home and didn't tell anyone. He promised to give me a car and a flat but days after seducing me he made me go home to Oxford on the bus. Days later he sacked me.'

By now the full scale of Maxwell's deceit had become apparent; it was far worse than anyone had anticipated. In all, £763,000,000 was missing, including £350,000,000 from *Mirror* pension funds and £79,000,000 from other Maxwell company pension funds. The debt was so large, according to one commentator, that it qualified for the *Guinness Book of Records*.

And then of course, there was the human cost. As the manager of one of Maxwell's companies put it, 'Throughout the length and breadth of the land, there are people going to bed at night wondering if they will wake up to any future at all.' When he was asked what he and his fellow *Mirror* pensioners would like to do to Maxwell, the man took a few moments to compose himself before saying, 'We feel like digging him up and hanging him.'

On 11 December the *New York Daily News* filed for Chapter 11 bankruptcy. The next day the *European* closed. Six months later, Macmillan would follow the *New York Daily News* into bankruptcy. As casualties continued to pile up on both sides of the Atlantic, *Newsweek* magazine was in no doubt about the scale of Maxwell's villainy. He had been, it declared starkly on its cover, 'THE CROOK OF THE CENTURY'.

39.

Everything Must Go

Conrad Black was sitting at home leafing through an auction catalogue on 14 February 1992 when the phone rang. It was Rupert Murdoch. 'It wasn't unprecedented for Rupert to call me, but it certainly wasn't a very frequent occurrence.'

When Murdoch asked what he was doing, Black told him about the catalogue he'd been sent. Later that day there was to be an auction at Sotheby's of 'The Complete Contents of the Chairman's Apartment at Maxwell House – to be sold at short notice without reserve'. The contents included 'Mr Maxwell's double bed' (estimate £1500–£2500); 'Mr Maxwell's office desk (£300–£400); 'Mr Maxwell's Office Armchair' (£100–£200); 'A wooden model of a helicopter, with gold metal blades' (£80–£100), as well as four separate lots comprising 'a quantity of white towelling' (£40–£150).

As he looked through the auction catalogue, Black had an unexpected sense of melancholy. 'I said to Rupert, "I feel badly about him being found dead, floating in the water. He was an appalling character in some ways, but I still feel bad."' Murdoch, however, didn't see it the same way. 'He said, "Oh, you're a more kind-hearted person than I am, but then you didn't have to put up with him for as long as I did. For decades I've had to listen to these comparisons between our companies and his. He was a terrible man, an absolute fraud and a charlatan."'

Eleven months after the first Sotheby's sale – on 14 January 1993 – there was another auction – this time of the contents of Headington Hill Hall. A 'Court-appointed Receiver' had been put in charge of the dispersal of Maxwell's estate, with half the proceeds from the sale going to Betty and half towards making a tiny hole in the vast mountain of debt he had left behind.

In the autumn of 1992, Harry Dalmeny from Sotheby's had gone down to Oxford to see Betty Maxwell and value the various items. 'It must have been terribly difficult for Betty – the house was literally being taken apart in front of her eyes. Yet she wasn't emotional about it; I think she'd taken the view that it was a ghastly business and she just had to get through as best she could. I remember her telling me that her husband's death must have been an accident. "I know he would never have left me to deal with this," she said. "He was not that kind of man." '

Betty had been given until the end of the year to vacate Headington Hill Hall. As the staff had all been dismissed, she asked two friends to help her clear out what little furniture was left and ensure the house was clean. 'It was a filthy job, but pride compelled me to leave everything impeccable.'

When they had finished, they sat down in the kitchen for their last meal – the three of them shared two eggs, one tomato and a tin of sardines. 'We had a laugh when we remembered all the splendid meals of the past served from that very kitchen.' Although the house may have been emptied, Betty felt that something was left behind, however indefinable. 'In spite of its emptiness, the house remains a home, still infused with the love I lavished on it, and it will remain so until I and my soul leave it.'

Elsewhere, though, it was as if every trace of Maxwell was being swept away. A year after his death, the *Mirror* offices in Holborn Circus were demolished. So too was the building next door – Maxwell House.

Among the lots at the second Sotheby's sale was 'a coloured photograph of President George Bush with Robert Maxwell, inscribed by the President to "Sir Robert Maxwell" ' (£60–£80); a black lacquer and mother-of-pearl inlaid desk sign reading, "Robert Maxwell. Chairman" ' (£40–£60); a collection of commemorative clips, brooches and buttons, including a 'Ronald Reagan' tie clip (£60–£80); 'a collection of hats comprising three baseball caps one inscribed MCC, another GUVNOR together with three Trilby hats, a tweed hat and a small quantity of wooden coathangers' (£10–£20), and a Panasonic 'cinemavision' TV (£500–£800).

And there too, jumbled together with various other medals and awards, was Maxwell's Military Cross (£1500–£2000), along with 'a framed black and white photograph of Maxwell being decorated with his MC by Field-Marshal Montgomery, signed at the bottom "Montgomery. Field-Marshal"' (£150–£200). Betty tried to buy back Maxwell's Military Cross but the receiver refused to allow it.

Soon after the sale began, there was an interruption. The *Investor's Chronicle* reported that 'A pretty blond woman brandishing a cigarette forced her way to the front barking, "Let me through! I knew the man. You did not."'

After people had reluctantly moved aside to allow her through, the sale resumed. Who was this mysterious late arrival? It turned out to be Eleanor Berry, come to pay her respects to a man that she, almost alone now, steadfastly continued to idolize.

Shortly after 7.30 a.m. on 18 June 1992, two officers from the Metropolitan Police walked up to the front door of Kevin Maxwell's house in Chelsea. Having been tipped off in advance, television crews were waiting outside to record the scene. There followed an exchange which caused great hilarity when it was shown on the evening news.

One of the police officers rang the door bell. After a while a window on the first floor was yanked open. Pandora Maxwell – Kevin's wife – appeared, clearly incensed.

'Piss off. We don't get up until half past eight,' she announced, before slamming the window shut.

The policeman rang the doorbell again, for rather longer this time. Once again the window flew open.

'I'm about to call the police!' Pandora Maxwell shouted.

'We *are* the police,' said the policeman.

Later that day, Kevin Maxwell and his brother Ian were taken to the City of London magistrates' court, where they were charged with multiple counts of conspiracy to defraud. Two other former Maxwell executives, Robert Bunn, Finance Director of Maxwell's private companies, and Larry Trachtenberg, a director of Maxwell's private Bishopsgate companies, were also arrested and charged.

It would be another three years before what was eagerly billed as the trial of the decade began in Court 22 of the Old Bailey – actually a modern annexe a mile away. By then Kevin Maxwell had been declared bankrupt with debts of £406,000,000, making him the biggest bankrupt in history.

Faced with having to help raise an interim payment to Ian's creditors of £500,000, Betty Maxwell approached several wealthy family friends on his behalf. She soon had an unpleasant surprise. 'I had naively believed that we would have no difficulty borrowing such a sum. But I was now to discover a side of man's nature which Bob had never accustomed me to: meanness and cowardice. People who had been proud to be seen with me now argued that it would prejudice them commercially or socially if it became known they had lent me money.'

To begin with, the public gallery had been crammed with onlookers. But within a few days almost all of them had melted away. For week after week proceedings dragged on. Two months after the trial started, one of the defendants, Robert Bunn, suffered a heart attack and was discharged. The jurors gazed enviously at his empty chair.

Another two and a half months went by before Kevin Maxwell took the stand. He conceded that his father would 'stretch the law as far as it would go to achieve his business ends . . . He was capable of being extremely charming to people,' Kevin went on, 'To be winning – but he was also capable of verbal brutality, public dressing-downs, not only of his children but senior managers.' After eighteen days in the witness box, he made a further admission: 'I was probably one of the most arrogant people you will ever meet. I could not imagine failure. With hindsight, bloody arrogant.' This public display of contrition was received in stony silence.

As one commentator noted tartly, there wasn't a moist eye in the house.

On Monday, 8 January 1996 – the thirty-second week of the trial – the judge finally sent the jury off to start their deliberations. Before doing so, he gave them a clear instruction. Over the last few years, there had been a number of high-profile fraud cases in which the defendants had been found guilty, only for the verdict to be overturned on appeal.

To try to ensure the same thing didn't happen again, the judge told the jury that they had to reach a unanimous verdict. The only problem with this was that it's almost unheard of to get a unanimous verdict in a fraud trial. Not only do jurors find it hard enough to understand the evidence, but defence lawyers have a vested interest in ensuring they remain as confused as possible.

For the next eleven nights the jury remained cloistered in a hotel while they continued their deliberations. Then, on 19 January, the forewoman announced that they had finally reached a verdict.

Was it unanimous, the judge asked.

It was, she assured him.

The defendants filed back into court. The forewoman proceeded to read out the verdict: 'Not guilty' to each of the charges. 'There were gasps in court,' the *Irish Times* reported. Both Kevin and Ian Maxwell had tears in their eyes. Afterwards, Kevin went over and shook hands with each of the twelve jurors.'

But far from diminishing the contempt with which Robert Maxwell was viewed, the verdict seemed only to intensify it. By now he had become fixed in the public imagination as the embodiment of corporate villainy; the man who had callously deprived thousands of his employees of their pensions.

It wasn't until 2002, more than ten years after Maxwell's death, that the Department of Trade and Industry finally published its report into Mirror Group Newspapers plc. This concluded that Maxwell 'dominated the management' of all his companies. None the less, Kevin Maxwell had given 'very substantial assistance' to his father. He had known of a number of instances where pension funds were used for the benefit of MCC, and also that this information had not been disclosed to trustees. 'In our view,' the report concluded, 'Kevin Maxwell's conduct was inexcusable.'

But other members of Robert Maxwell's management team had also known what was going on. So too had Goldman Sachs, who bore 'a substantial responsibility' for allowing Maxwell to manipulate the stock market. Goldman Sachs subsequently issued a statement claiming to have been as much in the dark as anyone else: 'We, and doubtless many other firms in the City and elsewhere, were intentionally and successfully deceived. We deeply regret this and, with the benefit of hindsight and with the information now available to us, would have acted differently.' Once again, there wasn't a moist eye in the house.

The DTI report gave Lawrence Guest what amounted to a light tap on the wrist: 'Although Mr Guest became concerned in June 1991 about the payment to the private side and the payments that had been made without documentation being provided to the finance department, and took the steps we have described in circumstances where he was in a difficult position, he should have reported the payments to the board or the non-executive directors as soon as he became aware of them.'

By then there had been relief, of sorts, for Maxwell pensioners. In the end most of them received around half of what they were owed – thanks to a combination of a government bailout, and money paid back by sheepish investment bankers who had formerly advised Maxwell and were looking to salvage their reputations.

As well as being an ogre of our time, Maxwell had turned into something even more humiliating: a figure of fun. Along with a Robert Maxwell joke book entitled *A Drop in the Ocean* – 'published on 100% recycled libel writs' – there had been a Robert Maxwell board game: 'The Game for the Nineties – be the First Player to the Pension Fund!'

In 1996, almost a decade after his single share in *Today* newspaper had netted him £250,000, Jeffrey Archer published a novel, *The Fourth Estate*, based on the rivalry between Maxwell and Rupert Murdoch. Maxwell appears as 'Lubji Hoch', who changes his name to 'Richard Armstrong', becomes a British media mogul, loots $50,000,000 from his pension funds and eventually commits suicide by jumping off his luxury yacht.

This was mild stuff compared to a novel called *Max* by the Israeli writer and former Mossad member Juval Aviv. Here Maxwell is lightly disguised as 'Max Robertson', a billionaire media tycoon, who manages to steal the entire gold reserves of the Soviet Union and squirrel them away in a nuclear bunker inside Mount Haifa.

But in terms of unfettered imagination, nothing could match *Never Alone with Rex Malone*. Written by Eleanor Beckman and published in 1986, five years before Maxwell's death, the novel is set in a post-apocalyptic Britain where almost every building has been destroyed apart from the mausoleum of the former Prime Minister – and 'demi-god' – Rex Malone. An East European immigrant who rose from nothing to become a newspaper proprietor, 'RM' appears in a flashback, in which he has a tempestuous affair with a masochistic funeral director called Natalie. Later, it turned out that Eleanor Beckman was a pseudonym; the author's real name was Eleanor Berry.

There was one fictional reincarnation that would almost certainly have delighted Maxwell. Having whiled away so many hours watching old James Bond movies, he became the model for the villain in the eighteenth Bond film, *Tomorrow Never Dies*. Released in 1997, the film starred Pierce Brosnan as Bond and Jonathan Pryce as 'Elliot Carver', the megalomaniac founder of the Carver Media Group.

Initially it was assumed that Rupert Murdoch had been the inspiration for Elliot Carver before the scriptwriter, Bruce Feirstein, admitted it was actually Maxwell. At the film's climax, shortly before being disembowelled by a razor-tipped torpedo, Carver gives one last manic burst of laughter and cries, 'Great men have always manipulated the media to save the world!'

40

The March of Time

After Betty Maxwell left Headington Hill Hall at the end of 1992, Oxford City Council, owners of the building, leased it to Oxford Brookes University, where it now houses the university's law faculty. The swimming pool in which florists once created elaborate displays to delight the Maxwells' guests has been filled in. The rolls of barbed wire that topped the perimeter fence have been removed, along with the video cameras that were mounted in the trees.

Inside the house, the chandeliers, gilt furniture and bottles of salad cream are long gone; in their place are pin boards, conference tables and piles of plastic chairs. Maxwell's old study is now a seminar room, his drawing room a lecture theatre.

Yet not everything has changed. Halfway up the main staircase is a stained-glass window which Maxwell commissioned to replace one that had been damaged in the War. It depicts Samson at the Gates of Gaza. Although this is a fairly obscure scene in the Old Testament, it's not hard to see why it appealed to him. In Samson's time, Gaza was a walled city with only one entrance, consisting of two enormous wooden gates. One night, Samson decided to leave the city, but rather than waiting around for the gatekeeper to let him out, he simply tore the gates off their hinges and carried them on his back – 'bar and all' – to Hebron, almost forty miles away.

Nowadays the name of Robert Maxwell evokes little or no reaction among the students walking through the grounds. But here too traces remain, however faint. At first, the young woman working in the Tyrolean-themed snack bar outside Pergamon Press's former headquarters looks blank when asked if she has ever heard of him. Then her expression changes. 'Actually, that does ring a bell . . .' she says. 'Didn't they used to have big parties here, a long time ago?'

Although almost thirty years have passed since Robert Maxwell's death, speculation about how he died shows no sign of waning. A number of journalists have insisted, often without a tremor of doubt, that he was murdered. When it comes to contenders, the Israelis are the clear front-runners. Maddened by Maxwell's attempt to blackmail the Israeli government over top-secret computer software he had allegedly been marketing on their behalf, Mossad sent a crack team of assassins to shadow the *Lady Ghislaine*. At dead of night they boarded the yacht, where they injected Maxwell with a lethal poison before tipping him into the water.

Or so the theory goes. Anyone pointing out that it seems odd that the Israelis should have bumped Maxwell off, then given him what amounted to a state funeral within the space of five days, invariably meets with the exasperated response: 'But that's exactly the sort of thing they would do!'

It is in the nature of conspiracy theories that they are hard to disprove. They are, of course, much harder to prove. Advocates of the Mossad-backed murder plot, or any murder plot, tend to fall at the same hurdle. Why would anybody go to the trouble of sending a boat out into the middle of the ocean to kill Maxwell when it would have been far easier – and cheaper – to do so on dry land? After all, it's not as if he was difficult to track down; if anything he was so addicted to self-publicity that he practically walked around with a target pinned to his forehead.

In the absence of any convincing evidence that Maxwell was murdered, that leaves two possibilities: either his death was an accident, or else he committed suicide. The people interviewed for this book tend to divide down the middle. Among those convinced that Maxwell killed himself is his old rival Rupert Murdoch. 'I remember I got a call one morning when I was in Los Angeles saying that he had disappeared off his boat. I said straightaway, "Ah, he jumped." He knew the banks were closing in, he knew what he'd done and he jumped. I can't give any other explanation.'

Supporters of the suicide theory also believe – along with Rupert Murdoch – that Maxwell must have known the game was up. If he went back to London, he was facing imminent ruin, public disgrace and the strong likelihood of prison. However thick-skinned he may have seemed to be, Maxwell cared deeply about his reputation. The prospect of losing everything he had spent his life creating may well have been too much to bear.

Although he had fought his way back from ignominy once, that had been twenty years earlier, and Maxwell was no longer the man he'd been then, either physically or mentally. Betty Maxwell always insisted that her husband would never have committed suicide, although privately she admitted to having her doubts: 'With hindsight you go from one end of the spectrum of speculation to the other.'

Her children also believed that their father's death was an accident, with the exception of Ghislaine Maxwell, who has always believed that he was murdered. The other Maxwells maintain that it just wasn't in his nature to kill himself. He had bounced back from adversity before and was convinced he could do so again – however colossal the odds.

Contrary to some reports, it was surprisingly easy to fall off the *Lady Ghislaine*. At the point where he is thought to have gone overboard, there was only a thin metal cable at below hip height. As well as being an extremely large man, Maxwell was increasingly top-heavy. Seeing him in his swimming trunks once, Gerald Ronson thought he looked like 'a hippopotamus on two legs.'

Suffering from chronic insomnia, Maxwell often liked to urinate over the back of the boat at night. Although the yacht had stabilizers, they wouldn't have prevented it from rocking from side to side. Yet none of this explains why, for the first and only time, Maxwell chose to go on the *Lady Ghislaine* on his own, apart from the crew. Nor does it explain why Maxwell locked both his cabin door – from the inside – as well as the main door that led out on to the deck. This door could be locked from either the inside or the outside. It seemed he had gone out on deck sometime after 4.45 a.m, then locked the door behind him and removed the key – it was never found.

For Captain Rankin, the locked door on to the rear deck was the clincher: 'There was a presence of mind. Closing the door, locking it, taking the key out and having that presence of mind at that point to do that. There'd be no reason to lock the door from the outside if he were planning to go back in. And why take the key? Was this done to maybe keep us crew members to think [sic] that he was still inside. I think so.'

While there may not have been any proof one way or the other, there were plenty of crumbs for amateur sleuths to sift through. After helping conduct the second autopsy, the pathologist Iain West concluded that although Maxwell was suffering from heart and lung disease, they were unlikely to have proved fatal. Attempts to ascertain whether he had drowned were similarly inconclusive. While there was a certain amount of liquid in Maxwell's lungs, this wasn't necessarily seawater – it might have been produced by his own body.

A sample of Maxwell's bone marrow was brought back to London to test for diatoms. The presence of diatoms – tiny organisms that live in seawater – is generally considered proof of drowning. Three litres of seawater were also taken from the spot where Maxwell's body was found and analysed. But this too was inconclusive: there were no diatoms in either the bone marrow or the seawater.

Could anything be deduced from the fact that Maxwell had been discovered floating face-up, when most people who drown are found face-down? Dr West thought not. 'He was such a large, obese man that he had enormous natural buoyancy. I would not regard him as being a typical example of how a body is going to behave after death from drowning.'

Much of the uncertainty over the cause of Maxwell's death is due to the botched first autopsy, which made it all but impossible for the second to come to any clear conclusion. However, that didn't stop West from going in for some energetic theorizing. 'Did he have to be alive when he went into the water? The answer is no.' Yet that didn't mean Maxwell was dead by the time he hit the water: he could have survived for some time afterwards. 'Could he have been killed and then thrown into the water? The answer is yes, but I think it very unlikely.'

What about suicide? 'When an individual is in serious trouble you obviously have a situation where suicide could happen,' West observed. 'He [Maxwell] was not the sort of man who would be likely to carry out such an act with a lot of premeditation. If he killed himself, it would be an impulsive act.'

Most people who drown themselves, don't do so naked – either they go into the water fully clothed, or else they leave a neat pile of clothes behind. But, as West pointed out, this situation was different: Maxwell often slept naked, so he was hardly going to have got dressed just in order to drown himself.

Then there were Maxwell's torn shoulder muscles. Surely they indicate that he accidentally fell and then grabbed at something to try to save himself? Not necessarily – West had often dealt with cases where someone toyed with the idea of killing themselves before actually doing so. 'In other scenarios I have seen, the victim has climbed out of a window and taken a few steps along a ledge, or has hung on to a windowsill for a time. They either have no real intention of killing themselves or they are carrying out the act in stages – building up to it . . .

'A younger fitter individual [than Maxwell] might stand at the top of the rail and just launch himself. But at his age he might have stepped up and over the handrail to stand on the top of the curved teak rail which is smooth and varnished. He might have slipped while trying to lower his grip to the rail below the handrail. He might even have changed his mind having got over the rail, and slipped while trying to get back.'

So which way was West inclined to go? 'There is no evidence for homicide, but it remains a possibility because I am in no position to exclude it. I don't think he died of a heart attack. Without the background of a man who was in financial trouble, I would probably say accident. As it is, there are only a few percentage points between the two options, but I favour suicide.'

West, however, wasn't quite as impartial as he liked to appear: in fact he had been employed by Maxwell's insurers. Conveniently, his suspicion that Maxwell had committed suicide was enough to convince them they didn't need to pay out £20,000,000 on his life insurance policy.

Believers in the theory of Occam's Razor tended to reach a different conclusion. Attributed to the fourteenth-century Surrey friar William of Ockham, Occam's Razor holds that the simplest explanation for anything is invariably the most plausible. In Maxwell's case, the simplest explanation is that a vastly overweight man lost his balance, possibly as a result of a sudden swell, and fell overboard.

And yet . . . Looking at the escalating mayhem of the last two years of Maxwell's life; at the way in which everything was falling apart; at his increasingly self-destructive lifestyle, and his general state of mind, there is a sense that Maxwell was killing himself whether or not he was aware of it. That he was hurtling downhill at such speed that it was only ever going to end one way.

Easy to say in retrospect, of course. But if Maxwell's death was an accident, it was an astonishingly fortuitous one, given what awaited him back in London. Had the gods, who Betty Maxwell believed controlled Maxwell's fate, really snatched him away just as he was about to get his comeuppance? Or could it be that the line between suicide and accident is even more indistinct than Iain West allowed?

Perhaps Maxwell, the inveterate risk-taker, was somehow dicing with death. Half willing something to happen, while loath to take the final step himself. Perhaps he was being deliberately careless with his safety because he didn't care any more. Perhaps he lent too far out and by the time he tried to save himself it was too late. Perhaps he stepped over the rail intending to throw himself off, then changed his mind and slipped while trying to get back.

Perhaps . . .

41.

Curtain Call

Betty Maxwell died on 7 August 2013, aged ninety-two. She's buried in the Meynard family plot in a small village near Avignon. Since Maxwell's death, she had lived first at her house in France, then – when she couldn't afford to keep it any longer – in a small rented flat in Pimlico. Much of the last twenty-five years of her life was spent pursuing her interest in Holocaust Studies, a subject in which she became a respected scholar.

Three years after Maxwell died, Betty wrote her memoir, pointedly titled *A Mind of My Own*, in which she described her marriage – and her late husband – with remarkable candour: 'He seemed cast right from the beginning in the role of the Greek tragic hero, who is inevitably defeated in the end, since in Greek mythology, man cannot avoid the gods' anger or vengeance if he rebels against them in an attempt to alter his destiny.' In the final reckoning, Betty believed, Maxwell's 'worship of power had resurrected the demon of power'. Among the acknowledgements at the start of *A Mind of My Own* was one that stood out: 'It also gives me great pleasure to thank Rupert Murdoch, who "turned the tide" for me by reading the proposal himself and recommending the book to HarperCollins.'

At Betty's memorial service in the University church of St Mary in Oxford, the eulogy was given by Sir Colin Lucas, former Vice-Chancellor of Oxford University. Departing from convention, Lucas speculated on what had made Maxwell turn against her so pointedly. Why had he disparaged her efforts to resume her education, and generally sought to humiliate her?

'Betty needed to understand why Bob so peremptorily dismissed her efforts, let alone her virtues in terms that implied failure on her part,' Lucas said. 'She came (rightly or wrongly, I do not know) to explain this in terms of his Jewishness. She felt that he was full of guilt for marrying a Christian woman, and that he had not therefore created a Jewish family such as the one he had grown up in and which had been so cruelly decimated during the War. She saw him as not reconciled to grief about his family and she saw herself as irredeemably an outsider in his terms.'

Was she right? In terms of timing, Maxwell's re-embracing of his Judaism certainly coincided with a sharp rise in his antagonism towards Betty. She herself came to believe it was the visit they both made to his home village of Solotvino that altered his feelings for ever. That was when she realized just how great a burden of guilt Maxwell carried within him. 'He was convinced that had he stayed at home, he could have saved the lives of his parents and younger siblings. Nothing he achieved in life would ever compensate for what he had not been able to accomplish – the rescue of his family.'

Years earlier, in a rare unguarded moment, Maxwell had told his son Philip, 'Unlike you, I keep the door to my haunted inner chamber firmly closed' – except that the door was a lot less tightly sealed than he liked to imagine. The older Maxwell grew, the more his ghosts started to escape. But while he clearly blamed Betty for something, there is another possibility: that increasingly haunted by the death of his family, above all by the death of the one person who had ever loved him unconditionally, what Maxwell really blamed her for was not being more like his mother.

Richard Stott died in 2007, aged sixty-three, having edited five Fleet Street papers over the course of his career – two of them twice. As the Editor of the *Mirror* at the time of Maxwell's death, he was described in his *Times* obituary as 'the last man to wear that crown of thorns under Robert Maxwell's criminal activities'.

In his memoir, *Dogs and Lampposts*, published in 2002, Stott offered his own analysis of Maxwell's character: 'He was generous but never kind; far-sighted but, on occasions, blind, stupid, cunningly subtle yet numbingly unpleasant. Unhappy, lonely, terrified of boredom, constantly wining and dining the great and good of the world but never truly liking or trusting anyone. Nervous, uncertain and insecure, which he dealt with by being decisive to the extent of lunatic folly, secure in the belief of his own infallibility even when presented with incontrovertible evidence to the contrary, and charging through people and events like a demented rhino.'

One morning in May 1992, Lawrence Guest was looking through the *Financial Times* when he saw to his surprise that he had been replaced without warning as MGN's Finance Director. Afterwards he and his wife, Beverley, moved from Surrey to the South Coast. They went there partly because Guest was a keen sailor, but also because they wanted to get away from London – and his former life. A *Mirror* pensioner himself, he only received two thirds of the money he was due. When Guest died in 2016, aged eighty, he was described in his *Mirror* obituary as 'a gentleman amongst sharks'. A former colleague said of him, 'He was a popular man, well-liked. I suppose you could say that the only enemy he had was Robert Maxwell.'

Nick Davies died in 2016 aged seventy-six. After being sacked from the *Mirror*, he married Andrea Martin; together they settled in Surrey and had a son. As Davies once said of himself, his motto in life had always been 'Go for It'. This was advice he followed with particular gusto in the fourth and last of the books he wrote about Princess Diana, *The Killing of Princess Diana*.

The book's most eye-catching claim was that Diana had been murdered on the orders of MI5 with the assistance of the French secret service. Apparently Diana's unidentified assassins had first sabotaged the seatbelts of her car, then employed 'high-intensity strobe lights used by NATO forces' to blind her chauffeur. According to his publisher, Davies, 'who has close contacts within royal circles, doesn't write to be sensationalist, but pulls no punches'.

In July 2007, Conrad Black, once head of the third-largest English-language newspaper empire in the world, was sentenced to six and a half years in prison after being found guilty of fraud and obstruction of justice by a court in Chicago. Having served thirty-seven months of his sentence, he was released in July 2010. In 2018, Black published a biography of President Trump entitled *Donald J. Trump: A President Like No Other*. A year later, Trump granted him a full pardon.

For the last thirty years, Kevin Maxwell has worked on a number of business as well as philanthropic ventures with his brother Ian. Isabel Maxwell, a former dotcom entrepreneur and co-founder – with her twin sister, Christine – of the Internet reference guide Magellan, now works as a consultant for start-up companies and venture capitalists. Christine is a PhD Candidate in Holocaust Studies at the University of Texas in Dallas, and the author of several books, including *The Dictionary of Perfect Spelling*. Anne Maxwell worked as an actress before becoming a cognitive behavioural therapist. Philip, a private tutor, lives quietly in north London.

Of all the Maxwell children, the one hit hardest by his death was his favourite – his youngest daughter, Ghislaine. Shortly before Christmas 1991, the journalist Edward Klein visited her in her New York apartment. He found her dressed in a pair of jeans and a loose shirt, and not wearing any make-up.

'The floor was strewn with newspaper clippings about her father. Hundreds of letters of condolence lay on her desk, along with boxes of cards of acknowledgement waiting to be sent in reply. I did not recognize in Ghislaine Maxwell the young woman [she was about to turn thirty] her friends had described to me – the racy, glamorous, social flibbertigibbet.'

'He wasn't a crook,' Ghislaine told Klein. 'A thief to me is somebody who steals money. Do I think my father did that? No. I don't know what he did. Obviously something happened. Did he put it in his own pocket? Did he run off with the money? No. And that's my definition of a crook.'

As for what the future might hold, Ghislaine struck a defiant note: 'I can't just die quietly in a corner. I have to believe that something good will come out of this mess. It's sad for my mother. It's sad to have lost my dad. It's sad for my brothers. But I would say we'll be back. Watch this space.'

Just as she predicted, the world had not heard the last of Ghislaine Maxwell. Following her father's death, she began dating the millionaire financier Jeffrey Epstein. In 2008, after their affair had ended, Epstein was convicted of soliciting a minor for prostitution and sentenced to eighteen months in prison – he served just thirteen. In July 2019, he was rearrested, this time for the sex trafficking of minors. A month later he was found hanging in his prison cell at Manhattan's Metropolitan Correctional Center.

Twenty-three years earlier, there had been a notable absentee at the trial of Kevin and Ian Maxwell: their father. Now, once again, the main player had died in mysterious circumstances. With Epstein beyond the reach of the law, attention shifted to Ghislaine. It's alleged that she was involved in procuring underage girls for her former lover – allegations she has strongly denied. She also introduced Epstein to a number of her friends, including the Duke of York. Interviewed by the BBC *Newsnight* programme in November 2019, the Duke recalled how he had met him through his girlfriend (Ghislaine) back in 1999 – 'I'd known her since she was at university'.

In 2000 Epstein and Ghislaine had been guests at Windsor Castle and at the Queen's Norfolk retreat, Sandringham, for what the Duke memorably described as 'a straightforward shooting weekend'. He admitted visiting Ghislaine's house in Belgravia – a house where, in March 2001, Epstein's's principal accuser, Virginia Roberts, claimed she was pressurized into having sex with him when she was only seventeen. Ghislaine has categorically denied Robert's accusations, while the Duke has insisted that he has no recollection of ever having met Roberts. Widely reckoned to have been a PR disaster, the *Newsnight* interview led to the Duke retiring from public life.

On 2 July 2020, Ghislaine was arrested at a remote house in Bradford, New Hampshire and charged with the enticement of minors, sex trafficking and perjury. She has pleaded not guilty to all charges. At the time of writing, she is being held in solitary confinement at the Metropolitan Detention Center in Brooklyn. Her trial is due to start in July 2021.

42

A True Scotsman

Five years before his death, Maxwell had dinner in Edinburgh with the Editor of *The European*, Ian Watson. As they were eating their meal, the sun went down and the floodlights came on, silhouetting Edinburgh Castle against the night sky. Pointing at the view, Maxwell said, 'Look, Watty, there's a sight to warm the hearts of true Scotsmen like you and me!'

At first, Watson assumed he was joking. 'It took a few moments for me to realize Maxwell was being completely serious. I think that says a lot about him; it was as if he was a Scotsman in Scotland, an Englishman in England and a Czech in Czechoslovakia. But what did he actually think he was? Perhaps none of these things.'

Throughout his life, Maxwell took things from people that didn't belong to him: their accents, their behaviour, their manners, their lifestyle . . . anything he thought worth copying. Having learned English by imitating Winston Churchill's speeches – even though he couldn't understand a word Churchill was saying – Maxwell continued helping himself to whatever he needed at the time. He took the logo of Mirror Group Newspapers – a roaring lion – from the Hollywood studio MGM; the name of his headquarters, Maxwell House, from a brand of instant coffee; and the name of his parent company, MCC, from the Marylebone Cricket Club – one of the bastions of the Establishment he claimed to loathe so much.

In filching bits and pieces from other people's lives, it's as if Maxwell created a self that he could never quite believe in. Maybe his mania for having his photograph taken – and for putting those photographs in his own newspapers – was due simply to his colossal vanity. But maybe it was a way of reinforcing his identity, of proving, both to himself and the outside world, that he was who he appeared to be.

Once, Maxwell walked into Peter Jay's office while Jay was chatting with the Editor of the *Mirror*, at the time Mike Molloy. Maxwell wanted to know what they were talking about. Molloy told him they had been discussing President Reagan.

'Oh, I know Reagan,' Maxwell told them. 'We were in hospital together during the War.'

Later that day, an intrigued Molloy did some sleuthing of his own. 'I was puzzled by Maxwell saying he'd been in hospital with President Reagan, so I went to the library, where I confirmed my belief that Reagan had never left America during his war service. Still thinking about Maxwell's claim, I walked to my own office. Then I remembered a film I had seen in my childhood. It was called *The Hasty Heart*, and was set in a military hospital during World War Two. It starred Ronald Reagan and Richard Todd.'

In *The Hasty Heart* Reagan plays a wounded American soldier recuperating in a Burmese field hospital. One day there is a new arrival: an aloof, bad-tempered Scotsman called Lachie Mac-Lachlan (Todd), who turns out to be dying of kidney failure. At first, MacLachlan alienates all the other patients with his standoffish manner, but towards the end he confesses that he has been so deeply scarred by his childhood that he's never been able to get close to anyone.

Maxwell too was deeply scarred by his upbringing, and it was the one part of himself he couldn't change. Few people in the twentieth century travelled as far from their origins as he did, yet the older he grew, the more the past seemed to drag at his heels, almost mocking him for what he had achieved. 'However hard you've tried to become someone else,' it seemed to say, 'you can never escape what you were.' Like the hollow pillars in his office and the pretend books on his shelves, everything else was a sham.

As to who Maxwell really was, perhaps he never fully knew. Mike Molloy was also present one day when Maxwell's sister Sylvia came to visit him in the *Daily Mirror* offices. After trying to make her way as an actress, Sylvia worked for the Schools Council, which coordinated secondary school exams in England and Wales.

At the time Molloy was captioning some old wartime photographs, one of which showed Maxwell during the War as a soldier in the Czech army. When Sylvia arrived, Molloy was writing Maxwell's original name on the back of the photograph – Jan Ludvik Hoch. Seeing what he was doing, she said to her brother, 'Why do you always say your name was Jan Ludvik Hoch?'

'Because it is,' Maxwell replied.

'No, it's not,' said Sylvia. 'Your name is Ludvik. You were named after Uncle Ludvik, not Jan.'

Maxwell looked at her in astonishment.

'Was I?' he said.

According to some estimates, Maxwell spent as long as six hours in the water before he died. If this was the case, what did he do? Never a strong swimmer, did he strike out for the shore knowing there was no chance of his ever making it? Did he cry for help knowing that no one would hear him? Or did he just lie there, naked and alone in the middle of the ocean, with all hope gone and the lights of the *Lady Ghislaine* disappearing into the darkness?

In 2017, Rupert Murdoch's former wife Anna decided that she wanted to buy a yacht. Their son James, a keen sailor, offered to help. A few weeks later, he found just what she was looking for – a boat called the *Lady Mona K*, on the market for $14,500,000. His mother went to have a look and liked what she saw. It was only after buying the *Lady Mona K* that Anna learned the yacht's name had been changed several years earlier. It had previously been called the *Lady Ghislaine*.

A Note on Sources

General

Eleanor Berry, *Cap'n Bob and Me*, The Book Guild, 2003

——, *My Unique Relationship with Robert Maxwell: The Truth at Last!*, The Book Guild, 2019

Tom Bower, *Maxwell: The Final Verdict*, HarperCollins, 1995

——, *Maxwell: The Outsider*, Aurum Press, 1988

Nick Davies, *Death of a Tycoon*, Sidgwick & Jackson, 1992

Russell Davies, *Foreign Body: The Secret Life of Robert Maxwell*, Bloomsbury, 1995

Roy Greenslade, *Maxwell: The Rise and Fall of Robert Maxwell and His Empire*, Simon & Schuster, 1992

Joe Haines, *Maxwell*, Macdonald, 1988

Mike Maloney, *Flash! Splash! Crash! All at Sea with Cap'n Bob*, Mainstream, 1996

Elisabeth Maxwell, *A Mind of My Own: My Life with Robert Maxwell*, Sidgwick & Jackson, 1994

Mike Molloy, *The Happy Hack: A Memoir of Fleet Street in Its Heyday*, John Blake, 2016

Richard Stott, *Dogs and Lampposts*, Metro, 2002

Peter Thompson and Anthony Delano, *Maxwell: A Portrait of Power*, Bantam, 1988

Preface: The King of New York

Books

Kenneth M. Jennings, *Labor Relations at the New York Daily News: Peripheral Bargaining and the 1990 Strike*, Praeger, 1993

A Note on Sources

Press

New York Daily News: various articles
New York Magazine: John Taylor, 'Mad Max', February 1992
Playboy: interview with 'British Press Lord Robert Maxwell', October
    1991
Vanity Fair: Peter J. Boyer, 'Mighty Max, Robert Maxwell Storms Man-
    hattan', June 1991
Vanity Fair: Edward Klein, 'The Fall of the House of Maxwell', March
    1992

Interviews

Simon Grigg
Jim Hoge
Rupert Murdoch
Jim Willse
Charlie Wilson

1. The Salt Mine

Books

History of the Queen's Royal Regiment

Press

Playboy interview, October 1991

Radio

Desert Island Discs, 1987

2. Out of the Darkness

Books

History of the Queen's Royal Regiment

Interviews

Joe Haines
Ian Maxwell
Mike Molloy

3. An Adventurer of Great Style

Books

Ruth Andreas-Friedrich, *Battleground Berlin: Diaries 1945–1948*, Paragon House, 1990

George Clare, *Berlin Days*, Macmillan, 1989

John Loftus and Mark Aarong, *The Secret War against the Jews: How Western Espionage Betrayed the Jewish People*, St Martin's Griffin, 1994

Betty Maxwell: A Tribute from Your Family and Friends on the Occasion of This Special Birthday, privately printed, 1991

Victor Sebestyen, *1946: The Making of the Modern World*, Macmillan, 2014

Adam Sisman, *Hugh Trevor-Roper: The Biography*, Weidenfeld & Nicolson, 2010

Interviews

Peter Croxford

Television

Inside Story. Maxwell: The Downfall, BBC2, 1996

A Note on Sources

Archives

Czech Secret Service Archive – Státní bezpečnost (StB), Prague

4. Difficulties With Pork

Books

Richard Abel and Gordon Graham (eds.), *Immigrant Publishers: The Impact of Expatriate Publishers in Britain and America in the 20th Century*, Transaction, 2009

Captain Peter Baker, *My Testament*, John Calder, 1955

Edward de Bono, *Tactics: The Art and Science of Success*, William Collins, 1985

Sir George Franckenstein, *Facts and Features of My Life*, Cassell, 1939

Einar H. Fredriksson (ed.), *A Century of Science Publishing*, IOS Press, 2001

Jeffrey Robinson, *The Risk Takers: Five Years On*, Mandarin, 1990

Iain Stevenson, *Book Makers: British Publishing in the Twentieth Century*, The British Library, 2010

5. Mortality

Interviews

Christine Maxwell
Isabel Maxwell

6. Down on the Bottom

Interviews

Caroline Coleman
Christine Maxwell
Ian Maxwell

Isabel Maxwell
Brian Moss

7. The Man Who Gets Things Done

Books

Richard Crossman, *The Diaries of a Cabinet Minister*, Vols. One (*Minister of Housing 1964–66*) and Two (*Lord President of the Council and Leader of the House of Commons 1966–68*), Hamish Hamilton and Jonathan Cape, 1975–6

Harold Evans, *My Paper Chase: True Stories of Vanished Times*, Little, Brown, 2009

Hansard, 1966/67

Sir Gerald Nabarro, *Exploits of a Politician*, Arthur Barker, 1973

——, *NAB 1: Portrait of a Politician*, Robert Maxwell, 1969

Press

Assorted press cuttings

Interviews

Jonathan Davie
Sir Harold Evans
Ian Maxwell
Brian Moss

8. Roast Beef and Yorkshire Pudding

Books

Neil Chenoweth, *Rupert Murdoch: The Untold Story of the World's Greatest Media Wizard*, Crown Business, 2001

A Note on Sources

Simon Courtauld, *As I was Going to St Ives: A Life of Derek Jackson*, Michael
Russell, 2007

George Munster, *Rupert Murdoch: A Paper Prince*, Viking, 1985

Anna Murdoch, *Family Business*, William Collins, 1988

Simon Regan, *Rupert Murdoch: A Business Biography*, Angus and Robertson, 1976

William Shawcross, *Murdoch*, Chatto & Windus, 1992

Stafford Somerfield, *Banner Headlines*, Scan Books, 1979

Press

Assorted press cuttings

Interviews

Rupert Murdoch

Archives

Public Record Office

9. Robert Maxwell's Code of Conduct

Interviews

Sir Harold Evans
Isabel Maxwell

11. The Grasshopper Returns

Books

Brian Cox, 'The Pergamon Phenomenon 1951–1991: Robert Maxwell and Scientific Publishing', from *Learned Publishing*, vol. 15, no. 4 (2002), pp. 273–8

A Note on Sources

Press

New Yorker: 'Remembering Saul Steinberg', October 2014
Spectator: October 1969
The New York Times: August 1970
Plus assorted newspaper cuttings

Interviews

John Ashfield
Tim Bouquet
Ian Maxwell
Bob Miranda

12. Strife

Books

Wendy Leigh, *Unraveled by Him*, Simon & Schuster, 2015
——, *What Makes a Woman Good in Bed*, Frederick Muller, 1978

Interviews

Brian Basham
Roy Greenslade
Ian Maxwell

13. Written in the Stars

Books

Richard Crossman, *The Diaries of a Cabinet Minister*, Vol. Two. (*Lord President of the Council and Leader of the House of Commons 1966–68*), Hamish Hamilton and Jonathan Cape, 1976

A Note on Sources

Robert Edwards, *Goodbye Fleet Street*, Jonathan Cape, 1988
Harold Evans, *Good Times, Bad Times*, Weidenfeld & Nicolson, 1983

Interviews

Joe Haines
Ian Maxwell
Rupert Murdoch
Francis Wheen

14. Madness

Books

Bernard Donoughue, *Downing Street Diary: With Harold Wilson in No. 10*, Jonathan Cape, 2005
——, *The Heat of the Kitchen*, Politico's, 2003
Robert Edwards, *Goodbye Fleet Street*, Jonathan Cape, 1988
Bill Hagerty, *Read All about It! 100 Sensational Years of the Daily Mirror*, First Stone, 2003
Joe Haines, *Kick 'Em Back: Wilson, Maxwell and Me*, Grosvenor House, 2019
Roy Hattersley, *Who Goes Home? Scenes from a Political Life*, Little, Brown, 1995
Allister Mackie, *The Trade Unionist and the Tycoon*, Mainstream, 1992
Anne Robinson, *Memoirs of an Unfit Mother*, Little, Brown, 2001

Interviews

John Blake
Alastair Campbell
Andrew Golden
Bill Hagerty
Joe Haines

Mike Maloney
Andy McSmith
Peter Miller
Mike Molloy

15. *In the Lair of the Black Bear*

Interviews

Simon Grigg
Kate Hadley
Peter Jay
Magnus Linklater
Peter Mandelson
John Penrose
Eve Pollard
Anne Robinson
Yvonne Young

16. *An Enormous Spread*

Books

Nicholas Coleridge, *Paper Tigers: The Latest, Greatest Newspaper Tycoons and How They Won the World*, William Heinemann, 1993

Interviews

Gyles Brandreth
Martin Cheeseman
Nicholas Coleridge
Simon Grigg
Mike Maloney

18. Battle Rejoined

Interviews

Jeffrey Archer
Conrad Black
David Burnside
Peter Jay
Rupert Murdoch
Gerald Ronson

19. Homecomings

Books

Ronen Bergman, *Rise Up and Kill First: The Secret History of Israel's Targeted Assassinations*, John Murray, 2018
Gerald Ronson, *Leading from the Front: My Story*, Mainstream, 2009

Interviews

Julia Langdon
Gerald Ronson

20. The Party of the Decade

Books

Robert Maxwell & Pergamon Press: 40 Years' Service to Science, Technology and Education, Pergamon Press, 1988
Gerald Ronson, *Leading from the Front: My Story*, Mainstream, 2009

A Note on Sources

Interviews

Gyles Brandreth
Brian Cox
Peter Jay
Neil Kinnock
Julia Langdon
Peter Mandelson
Gerald Ronson

21. *Listening In*

Interviews

John Pole

23. *Crossing the Line*

Interviews

Janet Fielding
Roy Greenslade
Simon Grigg
Peter Jay
Mike Maloney
Deborah Maxwell
Ian Maxwell
Mike Molloy

24. Obsessed

Books

Leaders of the World. Leonid Ilyich Brezhnev: A Short Biography, Pergamon
    Press, 1977
Leaders of the World. Todor Zhivkov: Statesman and Builder of New Bulgaria,
    Pergamon Press, 1982

Interviews

Joe Haines
John Pole
Francis Wheen

25. Three Departures

Interviews

Simon Grigg
Peter Jay

27. Intangible Assets

Interviews

Neil Collins
Bernard Donoughue
Roy Greenslade
Tony Jackson
Maggie Urry

A Note on Sources

Archives

Public Record Office

28. *Légumes du Maurier*

Books

Betty Maxwell: A Tribute from Your Family and Friends on the Occasion of This Special Birthday, 1991, privately printed

Interviews

Jim Hoge
Ian Maxwell

29. *Selling the Crown Jewels*

Interviews

Richard Charkin
Anthony Cheetham
Beverley Guest
Tony Jackson
Christine Maxwell
Deborah Maxwell
Ian Maxwell
Anna Moon
Rupert Murdoch
Maggie Urry

30. *Don't You Worry About a Thing*

Interviews

Beverley Guest
Carolyn Hinsey
Jim Hoge
Ken Lennox
Christine Maxwell
Ian Maxwell
Isabel Maxwell
Taki Theodoracopulos
Jim Willse

31. *Hurricane Bob*

Books

Seymour Hersh, *The Samson Option*, Faber & Faber, 1991

Interviews

Janet Fielding
Beverley Guest
Joe Haines
Carolyn Hinsey
David Jordan
Simon Walters
Ian Watson

Television

Panorama. The Max Factor, BBC1, 1991

32. A Long Way Down

Interviews

Alastair Campbell
Dominic Carman
Joe Haines
Carolyn Hinsey
Neil Kinnock
John Pole

33. Lost

Interviews

Ian Maxwell
Rabbi Feivish Vogel

34. Found

Interviews

John Jackson
Ken Lennox

35. The First Autopsy

Books

Chester Stern, *Dr Iain West's Casebook*, Little, Brown, 1996

A Note on Sources

Interviews

John Jackson
Ken Lennox

36. A Hero of Our Time

Interviews

Conrad Black
Joe Haines
Max Hastings
Neil Kinnock

37. The Second Autopsy

Books

Chester Stern, *Dr Iain West's Casebook*, Little, Brown, 1996

Interviews

Ken Lennox

38. The Four Horsemen

Books

Sir Roger Thomas and Raymond Turner, *Mirror Group Newspapers plc: Investigation under Sections 432(2) and 442 of the Companies Act 1985*, a report for the Department of Trade and Industry, Stationery Office, 2001

A Note on Sources

Interviews

Joe Haines
Ian Maxwell
John Pole
Charlie Wilson

39. *Everything Must Go*

Books

Jeffrey Archer, *The Fourth Estate*, HarperCollins, 1996
Juval Aviv, *Max*, Century, 2006
Eleanor Beckman, *Never Alone with Rex Malone*, Merlin, 1986

Interviews

Jeffrey Archer
Conrad Black
Harry Dalmeny
Ian Maxwell

40. *The March of Time*

Books

Gordon Thomas and Martin Dillon, *The Assassination of Robert Maxwell, Israel's Superspy*, Robson Books, 2002

Interviews

Rupert Murdoch

41. *Curtain Call*

Press

Vanity Fair: Edward Klein, 'The Fall of the House of Maxwell', March 1992

Interviews

Beverley Guest

42. *A True Scotsman*

Interviews

Mike Molloy
Rupert Murdoch
Ian Watson

Acknowledgements

I'm extremely grateful to Ian Maxwell for taking a great deal of time to talk to me – even though what I've written does not in any way reflect his own views or sentiments, nor those of his sisters Christine and Isabel, to whom I'm also very grateful. Rupert Murdoch was kind enough to see me in New York City, Julia Samuel was characteristically perceptive about Maxwell's psychology, while I have benefited enormously from Joe Haines's recollections.

In addition, I'd like to thank the following people for their help: Jeffrey Archer, John Ashfield, Colin Barr, Brian Basham, Richard Belfield, Eleanor Berry, Conrad Black, John Blake, Tim Bouquet, John Brown, Gyles Brandreth, David Burnside, Alastair Campbell, Peter Capaldi, Dominic Carman, Deborah Chande, Richard Charkin, Martin Cheeseman, Anthony Cheetham, Caroline Coleman, Nicholas Coleridge, Elaine Collins, Neil Collins, Karen Colognese, Brian Cox, Peter Croxford, Harry Dalmeny, Jonathan Davie, Bernard Donoughue, Daisy Dunlop, Charles Elton, Harry Evans, Janet Fielding, Andrew Golden, Michael Gove, Anthony Grabiner, Roy Greenslade, Simon Grigg, Miriam Gross, Beverley Guest, Kate Hadley, Bill Hagerty, Max Hastings, Carolyn Hinsey, James Hoge, John Jackson, Tony Jackson, Gerald Jacobs, Peter Jay, David Jordan, Neil Kinnock, Julia Langdon, Ken Lennox, Magnus Linklater, Mike Maloney, Peter Mandelson, Flora McEvedy, Andy McSmith, Neil Mendoza, Peter Miller, Bob Miranda, Mike Molloy, Anna Moon, Brian Moss, Matthew Norman, Geoffrey Owen, John Penrose, Roland Phillips, John Pole, Eve Pollard, Anne Robinson, Gerald Ronson, Bill Snyder, Taki Theodoracopulos, Stuart Urban, Maggie Urry, Sarah Vine, Rabbi Feivish Vogel, Simon Walters, Ian Watson, Francis Wheen, Jim Willse, Charlie Wilson and Yvonne Young.

Acknowledgements

As always, my agent, Natasha Fairweather at Rogers, Coleridge and White, has provided support and wise counsel. At Penguin, I want to thank my editor, Venetia Butterfield, along with Isabel Wall and Amelia Fairney, and everyone else who worked on the book. My wife, Susanna, has listened to my woes, boosted my morale and given unfailingly good editorial advice. Over the three years I've spent researching and writing *Fall*, I'm grimly aware that I have been in even more of a preoccupied haze than usual. As a result, our two children, Milly and Joseph, probably know more about Robert Maxwell than any other twelve- or fourteen-year-olds on the planet.

Index

Rankin, Gus, 233–40, 244, 247, 254, 278
Reagan, Nancy, 199–200
Reagan, Ronald, 156, 199–200, 269, 287
Reed International, 103–7, 109
Rhodes, 175–6
Richardson, Sir Michael, 157, 209–10
Ridley, Nicholas, 196
Robert Maxwell's Code of Conduct for Direct Sellers, 75
Roberts, Virginia, 285
Rodriguez, Sergio, 237
Roemer, Benita de, 9
Romania, 216
Ronson, Gail, 200
Ronson, Gerald, 146, 147–50, 161, 200, 277
Rosenbaum, Dr Alfred, 226
Rosenbluth, Lou, 21–2
Rothschild, Jacob, 146
Rothschild's bank, 146, 239
Rusbridger, James, 254–5
Russia *see* Soviet Union

Samson (biblical figure), 275
Sasakawa, Ryōichi, 105–6, 107–8, 121, 122
Sassie, Victor, 16
Savage, Pat, 35–6
Schörner, Field-Marshal Ferdinand, 21
Schwarzkopf, Norman, 204
Second World War (1939–45), 5–18
Shah, Eddie, 142, 143
Shamir, Yitzhak, 148–9, 197, 261
Sharon, Ariel, 261
Simpkin, Marshall, 31–2, 33–4
Sinatra, Frank, Jnr, 225
Smith, Liz, xxvii–xxviii
Snowdon, Antony Armstrong-Jones, Lord, 113
Solotvino, 1–4, 17, 150–51, 215–16

Somerfield, Stafford, 66–7, 68, 70, 71–2
Soviet Union: RM spies on Russians, 22, 41; RM sells periodicals to Russians, 32; RM woos key scientists for Pergamon, 40; RM warns Thatcher that it may collapse, 196; RM helps to improve relations with Israel, 197; end of, 217
Spencer, Ivor, 129
Spilsbury, Sir Bernard, 255
Spot-the-Ball competitions, 193–4, 224
Springer, Ferdinand, 24–6, 27
Springer, Julius, 24
Springer-Verlag, 24–7, 30, 31, 41
Sputnik, 40
Standard Literature Company, 76
Steel, David, 67
Steinberg, Saul, 76–81, 88–9, 91
Stonehouse, John, 255
Stoney, Michael, 214–15, 218
Stott, Richard: becomes Editor of *Mirror*, 222; on people's behaviour round RM, 114; on Who Dares Wins prize presentation, 121; gives black-tie dinners for senior *Mirror* staff, 179; attends Gridiron Dinner, 202–4; interviews Davies about indiscretions and arms-dealing allegations, 222–3; on Guest, 225; helps with *New York Daily News* negotiations, xviii–xx; and collapse of RM empire, 263, 264; memoir about RM, 282–3; death, 282
Strand House *see* Maxwell House
Straubenzee, Sir William van, 58–9